WEAVING IDENTITIES

WEAVING IDENTITIES

*Construction
of Dress and Self
in a Highland
Guatemala Town*

by CAROL HENDRICKSON

University of Texas Press, Austin

Requests for permission to reproduce material from
this work should be sent to Permissions, University
of Texas Press, Box 7819, Austin, Texas 78713-7819.

∞ The paper used in this publication meets the
minimum requirements of American National
Standard for Information Sciences—Permanence
of Paper for Printed Library Materials,
ANSI Z39, 48-1984.

Library of Congress Cataloging-in-Publication Data

Hendrickson, Carol Elaine, 1949-
    Weaving identities : construction of dress
and self in a highland Guatemala town / by
Carol Hendrickson. -- 1st. ed.-
        p.   cm.
    Includes bibliographical references and index.
ISBN 0-292-73099-3 (alk. paper). --
ISBN 0-292-73100-0 (pbk. : alk paper)
    1. Cakchikel Indians—Costume.   2. Cakchikel
textile fabrics—Guatemala—Tecpán Guatemala.
3. Costume—Guatemala—Tecpán Guatemala—
Symbolic aspects.   4. Costume—Social aspects—
Guatemala—Tecpán Guatemala.   5. Tecpán
Guatemala (Guatemala)—Social life and customs.
I. Title.
F1465.2.C3H46 1995
391´.0089´974—dc20   95-7296

Earlier versions of Chapters 2 and 3 were published as "Dress
and Landscape in Guatemala: The Case of Tecpán, Guatemala," in *Textile Traditions of Mesoamerica and the Andes,* edited
by Margot Blum Schevill, Janet Catherine Berlo, and Edward
D. Dwyer (New York: Garland, 1991), and "Images of the
Indian in Guatemala: The Role of Indigenous Dress in Indian
and Ladino Constructions," in *Nation-States and Indians in
Latin America,* edited by Joel Scherzer (Austin: University of
Texas Press, 1991).

To Alice and Harold Hendrickson

CONTENTS

List of Tables and Figures   viii

List of Photographs   viii

Acknowledgments   xi

Note on Kaqchikel Orthography   xiii

1. Introduction   1

2. The Geography of Clothing   44

3. The Enduring Indian: Images of the Maya   76

4. Between Birth and Death:
    Traje and the Human Life Cycle   98

5. The Cultural Biography of *Traje*   144

6. Transforming the Traditional:
    The Creative in *Traje*   182

7. To Wear *Traje* Is to Say "We Are Maya"   193

Notes   201

Glossary   221

Bibliography   225

Index   235

TABLES

1. Kaqchikel consonants   xiii
2. Images of the Indian   95

FIGURES

1. Map of Tecpán and surrounding area in the central highlands of Guatemala   9
2. Map of the *municipio* of Tecpán   12
3. Map of the *cabecera* of Tecpán   16
4. Women's and men's *traje*   34
5. *Mafalda* cartoon strip   68
6. Backstrap loom   155
7. Parts of the *huipil*   157
8. Tecpán *huipil* with historical ties to *cofradías*   166

PHOTOGRAPHS

1. *Oratorio* in Xejabí, Tecpán, 24 January 1981.   2
2. Schoolgirls marching in Tecpán's Independence Day parade, 15 September 1983.   3
3. Soldiers stationed in Tecpán marching in the town's Independence Day parade, 15 September 1983.   4
4. Students from the Protestant school marching in Tecpán's Independence Day parade, 15 September 1983.   4
5. Municipal *huipiles* in a Tecpán market stall, 1990.   5
6. Tecpán's town center, viewed from the northwest, 1990.   8

7. The central plaza at Iximche' with its partially excavated temple sites, 1990.   10

8. Thursday market in Tecpán, 1990.   11

9. Outlying settlements to the southwest of Tecpán's town center, 1990.   13

10. Catholic church in Tecpán, 1990.   14

11. Main thoroughfare through the heart of Tecpán, 1990.   15

12. A room in the home of *cofradía* members where Santo Domingo and San Francisco are displayed, 1990.   17

13. Street in Tecpán near the plaza, 1992.   20

14. Agricultural land southwest of Tecpán, July 1990.   22

15. Harvesting broccoli for export, August 1990.   22

16. The author and her teacher weaving on backstrap looms, 1980.   27

17. Cotton *corte* cloth with tie-dyed *jaspe* designs on the warp and weft, 1990.   36

18. *Penecita* style of *corte* cloth, 1990.   37

19. Tecpán woman weaving on a backstrap loom, 1990.   45

20. *Penecita* cloth being taken off a foot loom in El Tejar, Department of Chimaltenango, 1990.   45

21. Tecpán market stall with woolen products from Momostenango, 1990.   47

22. Vendor selling *corte* cloth in the Tecpán market, 1990.   48

23. One *lienzo* for a Tecpán *ri'j po't*, 1990.   49

24. Detail of a *lienzo* for an *aj San Martín* style of Comalapa *huipil* made in Tecpán, 1990.   53

25. Tecpán children, 1990.   59

26. Type of jacket worn by men involved in revitalization activities, 1991.   62

27. *Traje* presentation sponsored by the Tecpán Indigenous Fair Committee, 28 September 1980.   65

28. An advertisement illustrated with an Indian woman in Quezaltenango *traje*, 1992.   83

29. Children with their grandparents,
    1990.   105
30. Patchwork *huipil* made from the square
    neckhole cutouts of ninety-six different
    huipiles, 1990.   106
31. Students from the secondary school march-
    ing in Tecpán's Independence Day parade,
    15 September 1980.   110
32. Woman with her wedding *huipil* and *corte*,
    1985.   122
33. Bride and groom, 1981.   124
34. Wedding procession in Tecpán following a
    marriage ceremony in the Catholic church,
    1990.   125
35. Shoppers at stalls selling shawls and *corte*
    cloth in Tecpán's Thursday market,
    1990.   131
36. Mother and daughter, 1981.   135
37. Women in *sobre huipiles* at the Tecpán *traje*
    presentation, 28 September 1980.   140
38. Audience at the Tecpán *traje* presentation,
    28 September 1980.   143
39. Preparing warp threads for a *huipil*,
    1990.   153
40. Setting up the backstrap loom, 1990.   154
41. *Huipil de Tecpán*, 1992.   163
42. *Xilon*-style cloth, 1983.   165
43. Woman wearing a *sobre huipil* inside out,
    1980.   179
44. One side of the tourist market surrounding
    Antigua's central plaza, 1990.   180
45. Indian fair princesses at the *traje* presentation,
    28 September 1980.   185
46. Maya students in *xilon* blouses marching
    in Tecpán's Independence Day parade,
    15 September 1983.   187

ACKNOWLEDGMENTS

I want to extend my gratitude to the numerous people who have helped me with this project, though I do so without naming names. While it is customary anthropological procedure to acknowledge the contributions of "informants" without disclosing their names, it has always struck me as somehow not quite right that writers then go on and provide lists of names and detailed thanks to many others. Good arguments certainly exist for differences in the situations of those named versus the anonymous and for the greater need to ensure the privacy of the latter; however, the practice has always left me with a distinct feeling of imbalance. My solution here is to have the rule of anonymity be the equalizing force (for all persons except for myself, which perhaps is a greater imbalance): I acknowledge my gratitude to categories of people rather than to individuals.

My greatest debt is to the people of Tecpán—friends, families, and acquaintances—who invited me into their homes, included me in their lives and conversations, offered me companionship during difficult and happy times, and coped with my endless questions and projects. My gratitude also extends to people in Guatemala City, Antigua, Jutiapa, and the towns surrounding Tecpán—Guatemalans and foreigners alike—who also shared their lives with me and, in doing so, helped me with this study. May our friendships continue well into the future.

Over the years, I have made use of a number of research institutions in Guatemala. In particular, the helpful administration and staff, fine library, and gracious surroundings of the Centro de Investigaciones Regionales de Mesoamérica (CIRMA) in Antigua offered me an excellent place to work when I was away from my home in Tecpán. What is more, for the past several summers CIRMA has hosted the Tijonik Oxlajuj Aj Kaqchikel language and culture program, and I now associate CIRMA with the fine training, lively interactions, and wonderful friendships I have gained from participation in that project. From my earliest days doing research in Guatemala I owe an immense debt to people at the Instituto Indigenista Nacional. They helped me secure a long-term visa, offered suggestions for contacts in the central highlands when I had to change field sites, and allowed me the use of their library.

In the United States I am indebted to faculty and fellow students in the Department of Anthropology at the University of Chicago. The intensity of my graduate education has put me in good stead now that I am on my own, and the sheer size of my cohort from my student days means that the good counsel and criticisms we provided each other continue in multiple ways. This study is also materially linked to the Field Museum of Natural History in Chicago. In 1990, funding from the museum allowed me to buy textiles from Tecpán and surrounding communities; these thirty-seven pieces now form a research collection at the museum (accession no. 3768). This book also owes a large debt to scholars writing on Guatemala, both in that country and abroad (including the two readers who put so much energy into reviewing this manuscript), and to my colleagues and students at Marlboro College.

Finally, I want to thank my family, consanguineal and affinal. They have supported me in many ways and will be glad to be free from having to ask, "Is it done yet?"

NOTE ON KAQCHIKEL ORTHOGRAPHY

The orthography used most often in this book is the unified alphabet promoted by the Guatemalan Academy of Maya Languages. This alphabet was approved by the national congress in 1987 and now serves for all twenty-one Maya languages found in Guatemala. The official alphabet replaces all previous systems of orthography, and its use accounts for spellings such as Kaqchikel (instead of Cakchiquel) and K'iche' (instead of Quiché).

Following the systems of Rodríquez Guaján, Yool Gómez, Calí Semeyá, and Chacach Apén (1988: 10) and Chacach Cutzal (1990: 155), there are twenty-two consonant phonemes in Kaqchikel (Table 1).

The unified alphabet has nine vowels for Kaqchikel—a, ä, e, i, ï, o, ö, u, and ü—which are being used in standardizing the written form of the language. The Tecpán dialect, however, can be described using only six vowels: a, ä, e, i, o, and u. The ä is lax and in general appears only in stressed, or final, syllables that end with a consonant.

In specific instances I use the older forms of spelling: in place names prescribed by the government (such as the Department of El Quiché) and

Table 1. Kaqchikel consonants

	Bilabial	Alveodental	Alveopalatal	Velar	Post-velar	Glottal
Occulsive	p	t		k	q	'
Glottalized occlusive	b'	t'		k'	q'	
Affricate		tz	ch			
Glottalized affricate		tz'	ch'			
Fricative		s	x		j	
Resonant						
Nasal	m	n				
Lateral		l				
Flap			r			
Semivowel	w		y			

in proper names that regularly appeared in the national print media in the 1980s and earlier (e.g., the Rabín Ajau and Tecún Umán). However, even with these names I sometimes switch to spellings in the official alphabet to reflect more recent usages (e.g., Princess Ixmucané in 1980 becomes Ixmukane a decade later). As for references to the sixteenth-century K'iche' Maya myth-history, I use the unified alphabet to write *Popul Wuj* and, in doing so, mark Maya ownership of this historic text.

My most difficult orthographic decision concerned the name of the ancient Kaqchikel capital. While it appears on government maps, in national newspapers, and all the literature for the 1980 period as Iximché, I have decided to use the revised spelling, Iximche', except where the word is part of a larger proper name with its own historical context of significance (e.g., Colonia Iximché, Princess Iximché, or the Declaration of Iximché). My reasons for this decision have to do with the multiple appearances of the proper name in this work—as archaeological site, park, meeting ground for protest—as well as more recent attempts by Maya within the revitalization movement to replace the name Tecpán with Iximche' as the label for the entire municipality. The changes in spelling should remind us of the shifting and political nature of Maya orthography as well as the object(ive)s for which these words stand.

WEAVING IDENTITIES

ONE

INTRODUCTION

Costume is a language. It is not more misleading than the
graphs drawn by demographers and price historians. In fact
[at the mid-millennium] the future belonged to societies
which were trifling enough, but also rich and inventive
enough to bother about changing colours, material and style
of costume, and also the division of the social classes and
the map of the world. Everything is connected.

CAPITALISM AND MATERIAL LIFE
(BRAUDEL 1973: 235–236)

24 January 1981; a village southwest of Tecpán. Though the night was cold
enough to leave hoarfrost on the cornstalks drying in the fields, the day
dawned sunny, with a promise of warmth. This made the early-morning
trip bearable as I rode the several kilometers out into the country on the
back of a Peace Corps volunteer's motorcycle. I was near the end of my
year doing fieldwork in Tecpán Guatemala (or Tecpán for short), and a
Maya family with whom I was close had invited me to attend the inauguration of a new Catholic *oratorio* (chapel) in Xejabí, the rural community
where some of their relatives lived. The old chapel had been destroyed by
the 1976 earthquake, and it had taken almost exactly five years for the
people, many working through the local cooperative, to raise enough
money from local and foreign sources to rebuild the structure (Photo 1).
For the occasion, Tecpán's new priest was invited to say mass. Unlike the
last priest in town, this one seemed to be well respected by the local
population—Maya and ladino alike. He had roots in the area and, though
ladino himself, thought enough of indigenous culture to have tackled the
Kaqchikel Maya language.

The service itself was packed; and, for those not fortunate enough to
find a space inside, a microphone hooked up to a car battery ensured that
the word was carried outdoors. Afterward, people gathered in front of the
chapel to socialize, and I took photographs of my friends, their family
members and neighbors, and the priest. As I was about to leave the chapel
yard, I noticed a frail, elderly Maya woman sitting to the side of the crowd.

1.   *Oratorio* in Xejabí, Tecpán, 24 January 1981. The photograph was taken on the
day that the newly constructed chapel was inaugurated.

She was wearing a frayed and faded *huipil* (the handwoven blouse worn
by Maya women) that I recognized immediately as a *xilon* blouse. Women
back in the town center with whom I was working had described this
style to me on a number of occasions and said that it was popular when
their grandmothers were young. Up to that point, however, I had never
seen one worn and neither had some of my younger friends.

15 September 1983; the streets in the center of Tecpán. Two and a half years
after leaving Tecpán, I returned for a visit. During the time I was gone, *la
situación* (the situation, as people euphemistically referred to the violence)
had intensified, altering life in Tecpán in numerous ways. The new priest
had been murdered less than four months after he helped inaugurate the
oratorio; his position was still vacant. The municipal hall, rebuilt after the
earthquake, had been blown up by "unknowns" in November 1981 and
had not been replaced. By the time of my visit, the army was well established in town, with a military stockade and scores of soldiers stationed
across from the post office.

The fifteenth of September is Independence Day in Guatemala. In
1983, in what was meant to be a public show of nationalistic zeal and local
unity, soldiers from the stockade and children from the schools in town
dressed up in their respective uniforms and marched through the streets

2.   Schoolgirls marching in Tecpán's Independence Day parade, 15 September 1983. Their *traje* and *vestido* were specially made for the event; the same cloth was used for the Indian girls' skirts and the ladino girls' jumpers.

to the rhythm of beating drums (Photos 2, 3, and 4). They passed through the plaza area, near the stockade and the empty lot where the municipal building used to stand, and ended up at the municipal soccer field with a round of speeches and gymnastic demonstrations. Maya schoolgirls from all but the Protestant school wore indigenous dress, with their *cortes* (Maya skirts) coordinated with the jumpers and skirts of the ladino girls in their classes. In many cases, their *huipiles* were new for the occasion, and, for some, they were woven in the latest local Maya fashion: a version of the *xilon*-style *huipil* that I had seen two and a half years before in Xejabí.

June–July 1990, 1991, 1992; the large Thursday market in Tecpán. After a five-year absence, I returned to Tecpán in the summer of 1990 and then again in 1991 and 1992. Each time I marveled at how large the Thursday market had grown and how vibrant it was, despite the hard economic times. Market stalls were crushed together, temporarily filling all the open spaces in the plaza, church square, and nearby streets, and pressed against the buildings that lined them. One of these buildings was the new municipal hall, constructed in the colonial style of its pre-earthquake predecessor; another was a new three-story hotel—the tallest structure in town—built where the military stockade once stood. By the early 1990s, the army troops had moved to the soccer field on the outskirts of town where

3.   Soldiers stationed in Tecpán marching in the town's Independence Day parade, 15 September 1983.

4.   Students from the Protestant school marching in Tecpán's Independence Day parade, 15 September 1983. Indigenous and ladino students in this school wear standard uniforms classified as *vestido*.

5.   Municipal *huipiles* in a Tecpán market stall, 1990. Top row, left to right: blouse with
doves and curls plus *arco*; *pequeño ri'j po't*; blouse with doves and curls plus *cruceta*
flowers; *pequeño ri'j po't*; blouse with *cruceta* flowers. Middle row: blouse woven *jun
ruwa kem* (with geometrics, center); blouse with doves and curls plus *cruceta* flowers
(right). Bottom row: *blusas* with floral designs on white cloth (left and center);
huipil from Chichicastenango (folded, to the right of the center *blusa*).

they had dug in, quite literally, to protect themselves from attacks: their
armed presence continued to be visible on the streets of Tecpán.

A survey of the market vendors selling *traje* showed a vast array of offerings (Photo 5). In the stalls specializing in *huipiles*, *xilon* blouses were but
one of many styles available, and not a very prominently featured style at
that. Joining them were other, more elaborate and expensive blouses, some
incorporating color combinations and materials that I had not seen on
earlier trips. The customers passing by also wore a range of *huipil* styles,
including some *xilon* blouses, faded and comfortable from months of wear
and repeated washings.

An Ethnography of Traje

The subject of this book is *traje*, or Maya dress, and its central and active role
in the lives of people in the town of Tecpán Guatemala.[1] More than mere

cloth, *traje* is a powerful and densely meaningful expression of social identity and a vital element of life in the highlands. I still believe in the basic truth of this statement, despite the fact that, in the twenty years since I first articulated my ideas on the subject, many things have changed—in Guatemala, in the discipline of anthropology, and in some of my own thinking.

Over the past two decades, the "eternal tyranny" (Simon 1987) of life in Guatemala has taken natural and human forms. The earthquake that devastated the central highlands in 1976 left between 20,000 and 25,000 people dead and whole towns destroyed. Many of these same communities had barely started to recover from nature's violence when waves of human violence overcame the highlands, leaving more than 100,000 persons dead or "missing" and over one million people displaced (Jonas 1991: 149). A whole generation has been educated in what people call the reality of life in Guatemala by seeing young soldiers toting large guns in the streets of their towns, hearing gunfire in the mountains at night, learning of family members and neighbors killed or abducted, and witnessing the horrors of violent death and destruction firsthand. While the Maya have not been the only people affected by the violence, they have suffered disproportionately and remain subordinate to the non-Maya in the Guatemalan state (see Smith 1990b).

On a more positive note, many people who were small children when I first met them have gone on in school, surpassing their parents' educational levels and graduating into jobs as teachers, social workers, agricultural specialists, church workers, and administrators. In fact, the battle for indigenous rights and for the articulation of issues pertinent to the indigenous community in Guatemala is now being fought with notable success by skilled and articulate Maya. These are women and men who are becoming increasingly savvy in the internal workings of the national and regional governments and who are reaping the benefits of expanded ties to groups (both Maya and non-Maya) throughout Guatemala and to an international community sympathetic with indigenous projects. A subset of these individuals also forms the core of what is being called the "Maya revitalization movement," a general label that refers to people interested in "the reconstruction of Mayan identity" and efforts "to resuscitate indigenous customs such as the calendar, traditional clothing, religious practices; to systematize the alphabets of the indigenous languages; and to take control of development projects and research in their communities" (Nelson 1991: 6). The "traditional clothing," or *traje*, of current interest to Maya activists has long been valued by members of Maya communities as well as tourists, collectors, retailers, and anthropologists and other researchers. The different valuations of indigenous dress and the ways in which *traje* has endured *and* changed over the years provide a rich material commentary on life in late-twentieth-century Guatemala; its active presence needs to be accommodated in an anthropological exploration of the highlands.

Exactly how *traje* is explained in an anthropological frame depends on the theoretical perspectives available as well as the training and disposition of the researcher. In the past twenty years my own thinking has been shaped and reshaped by my formal schooling, recent developments in the discipline, shifting events in Guatemala, and ongoing conversations with friends and colleagues in the United States and Central America. I first articulated my thoughts on *traje* based on observations made during a year of volunteer work in Guatemala prior to beginning my training in anthropology. I went on to produce a dissertation heavily influenced by symbolic and structuralist approaches and have since been persuaded of the need to problematize the material in terms of a multiplicity of voices, situated practices, and negotiated identities (to use the terms that are fashionable). When working with earlier drafts, I take on a reflexive mode and worry that I am dealing with an archaeological artifact—a would-be palimpsest but for the delete function of my computer. I also worry that my work will look dated unless I change each draft in all the right places, but then think I may be cheating because I reframe my arguments at home while the data from field trips long past remain "the same."

The angst subsides as I reconsider my motivations for this project (or succession of projects). Without thinking that anthropology is purposely developing in ways that will allow me better to articulate my concerns, I nonetheless feel fortunate to be working in the field at this point in history. I see anthropologists attempting to find new ways to give voices to those whose words and actions have been limited and showing their commitment to issues of power, resistance, identity, and change in ways that do not reduce these to mere theoretical matters. As far as the study of material objects is concerned, anthropology has recently expanded and embraced the subject outside of narrow frames such as market networks and production technologies. With cloth, attention is owed, in part, to the growing influence of feminist theories, which have helped increase the value and voice of a doubly damned subject: a "craft" and what is often seen as a product of "women's work."

For the most part, the ethnographic present described in this book is

6.   Tecpán's town center, viewed from the northwest, 1990. The photograph shows the large Catholic church and some of the buildings in the northern and central parts of town as well as the surrounding milpa.

1980–1981. While I also write about the years and events that have followed, I do so in relation to this earlier period and note any shifts in the time frame. By writing this ethnography of *traje*, I hope to make a modest contribution to ongoing conversations within anthropology and, more important, to an understanding of issues of importance to Maya and non-Maya alike.

The Ethnographic Setting

I decided to live in Tecpán after the highland town in which I had proposed to work became a center of guerrilla and army activities. In October 1979, when I made this switch, Tecpán was a relatively peaceful place, and I judged (or, rather, hoped) that it would remain so for the foreseeable future. Located eighty-eight kilometers west of Guatemala City at a point where high, fertile plateau lands give way to yet higher mountains, the town of Tecpán has easy access to the Pan American Highway and, for my purposes in the early 1980s, to a quick exit from the region (Figure 1).

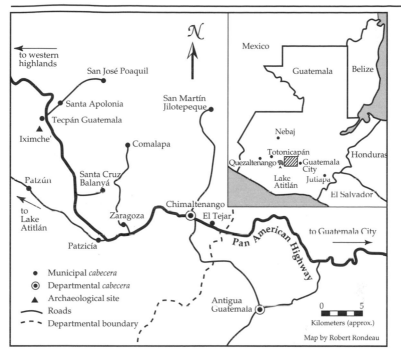

From maps by the Instituto Geográfico Nacional (1962, 1978) and Texaco/INGUAT (1980).

FIG. I. Map of Tecpán and surrounding area in the central highlands of Guatemala

Traveling from the capital to Tecpán along the Pan American Highway, one passes through fields of wheat, for which the municipality is renowned, as well as corn, potatoes, beans, and, more recently, such export crops as broccoli and sugar snap peas. Lying at seventy-five hundred feet, Tecpán is in a moderately cold zone that favors the presence of pine and oak in the forested mountainsides, but the weather is not so cold as to deter the growth of the occasional domesticated palm. Another noteworthy feature of the Tecpán landscape is the deep ravines that cut the mountains and adjacent plateau. So formidable an obstacle are these to individuals intent on crossing or controlling the area that they were used by the ancient Kaqchikel Maya as natural protective devices to safeguard their fortified capital of Iximche'.[2]

In late July 1524, the Spanish did, however, succeed in gaining access to the area, penetrating Iximche' and setting up the first capital of Spanish Central America. Santiago, as the site was renamed, served as headquarters of civil and ecclesiastical administration (Lutz 1994: 6). This status lasted only a matter of months, however, as the Kaqchikel people rebelled

7.   The central plaza at Iximche' with its partially excavated temple sites, 1990.

and the capital was moved to a politically more accommodating area.[3] Today the buildings of Iximche' are partially restored and complemented by a museum and picnic area, which are visited regularly by school-children, foreign tourists, and Guatemalan families on weekend outings (Photo 7).

Along with frequent service to the capital, bus routes link Tecpán directly to some of its nearest neighbors: San José Poaquil, Santa Apolonia, Patzicía, and Chimaltenango. Not only are these communities geographically close but their residents have strong economic, educational, and familial ties with Tecpanecos (the people of Tecpán). What is more, because Tecpán is an important market town, special buses for local buyers and sellers connect it with Santa Cruz Balanyá, Patzún, and Comalapa on Thursdays, the biggest market day of the week. This lively exchange of goods also attracts vendors from more distant places such as Sololá, Chichicastenango, Chimaltenango, Totonicapán, and Quezaltenango, and they join the hundreds of other people selling items in the central plaza, church park, and surrounding streets (Photo 8). However, despite the size

8. Thursday market in Tecpán, 1990. Vendors in the northwestern corner of the
    plaza are selling hats, ropes, brooms, housewares, and blankets from
    Momostenango.

of the market and its popularity among people in the area, it attracts few
tourists. What visitors do arrive usually pass quickly through on their way
to the Iximche' archaeological site. Consequently, there is almost no market for tourist items in town, a fact that relates to the nature of local *traje*
production.[4]

Administratively, Guatemala is divided into twenty-two *departamentos*
(departments). Departments, in turn, are divided into *municipios* (municipalities), which are often described—by local residents and foreign aca-
demics alike—as ethnically distinct and defined by differences in *costumbre*
(custom), *traje*, and speech. A *municipio* is further divided into a *cabecera*
(town center) and outlying *aldeas* (villages) as well as other small residential units.

Geographically and demographically Tecpán is considered large, at least
in comparison with its neighbors. It shares boundaries with eight other
municipalities in three different departments (Figure 2). In the 1981 census, the population of the *municipio* numbered 29,564, with 5,977 residents listed as living in the center of town (Dirección General de Estadística

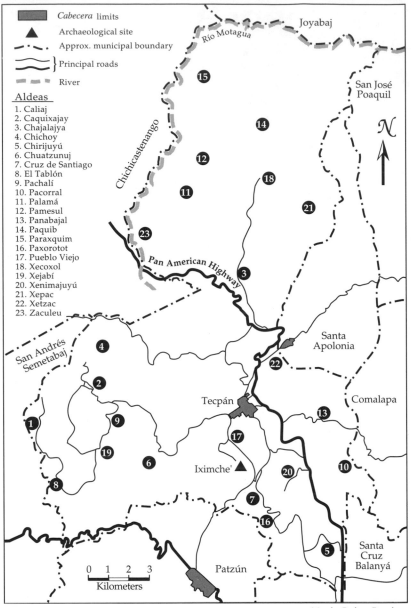

Map by Robert Rondeau

From maps by the Dirección de Estadística (1972), Instituto Geográfico Nacional (1962, 1978), and International Travel Map Productions (1991–2).

FIG. 2. Map of the *municipio* of Tecpán

9.   Outlying settlements to the southwest of Tecpán's town center, 1990. Cultivated
      fields alternate with densely wooded areas, and roads connect homes built on
      level plateau lands.

1984: 121). The remaining people live in the scattered rural villages, in
caseríos (small hamlets) or on *fincas* (large farms), and along the secondary
dirt roads that snake through the mountainous terrain. Population figures,
while never completely accurate, were particularly rough between 1976
and 1980 as a result of the earthquake, which killed some 510 people in
Tecpán's *cabecera*, according to one report (Diagnóstico de salud y nutrición
1979: 8). While that figure does not distinguish between deaths in the
"urban area" (as the census figures describe the *cabecera*) and deaths in the
country, I noted widespread agreement that the town suffered a disproportionately larger number of fatalities than the rural areas.[5]

Besides the loss of lives from the quake, Tecpanecos suffered almost
complete destruction of their property. I repeatedly heard how only two
buildings in town were left standing and salvageable after the earthquake.
The old, two-story, colonial-era *municipalidad* (municipal hall), remembered nostalgically by many, was in ruins and soon replaced by a plain,
one-story structure of cinder block and corrugated metal. The large Catholic church near the park, one of the oldest in Latin America, was severely
damaged but, owing to its historic significance, has benefited from years
of restoration efforts (Photo 10). In the meantime, a functional Catholic
church was built to the east of the old one and new structures for the

10. Catholic church in Tecpán, 1990, with signs of repair work following the 1976 earthquake. Part of the roof of the outdoor municipal stage can be seen at the lower right.

health clinic, post office, police station, and central businesses once again line the plaza and central park.[6]

While the streets of Tecpán adhere to the grid pattern common to colonial Latin American cities, its central plaza area is something of a variation on a theme (Photo 11; Figure 3). Instead of a single central plaza and park, with the Catholic church, municipal hall, and other public offices bordering the square, Tecpán's plaza and park are divided into separate but contiguous spaces. The municipal hall faces the plaza (as do the post office, health clinic, and police station along with a few shops); one block diagonally to the east, the Catholic church and additional shops face out onto the central park. Four *barrios* (neighborhoods)—Asunción, Poromá, Patacabaj, and San Antonio—divide the town center into quarters along lines running through the center.[7] To the four *barrios* has been added a new residential area known as Colonia Iximché and lying at the north corner of Barrio Poromá. The *colonia* (colony) was built with funds from the Salvation Army for Tecpán residents displaced by the earthquake. Far from simply giving money from afar, the funding body maintained an active presence in the *colonia* after the earthquake relief houses were built. Along with religious activities, the *colonia* had a community center that

11. Main thoroughfare through the heart of Tecpán, 1990. The municipal park is on the right (with trees), and the plaza starts at the corner beyond the buildings at the left. Men standing at the window of the Panasonic store are watching the World Cup soccer final.

offered day care, crafts classes for women, and other services. In 1980, a missionary family (a Hispanic couple from California) employed by the Salvation Army was also residing in the *colonia*.

The Salvation Army is but one of many local institutions with a religious mission. While the presence of the Catholic church has been central (literally, but also in many ways figuratively) since the days of the conquest, Tecpanecos estimate that the establishment of evangelical and other *cristiano* groups in town dates back to the 1940s.[8] Scattered throughout the town are permanent meeting places for the congregations of the Church of Christ, Assembly of God, Prince of Peace Church, Church of Jehovah's Witnesses, and Church of Christ of the Latter-Day Saints, to name but a few. In addition, adherents to smaller, less established groups meet to worship in homes or rented rooms and to make plans to increase membership as well as find permanent church facilities. In contrast to the variety of *cristianos* in town, Tecpán Catholics are more or less unified. Certain members of the congregation lean more toward involvement in the longstanding *cofradías* (religious brotherhoods) while others have taken up the work of Acción Católica, a fairly recent movement that Annis (1987: 91) labels as "modern Catholicism"; however, it is not uncommon for

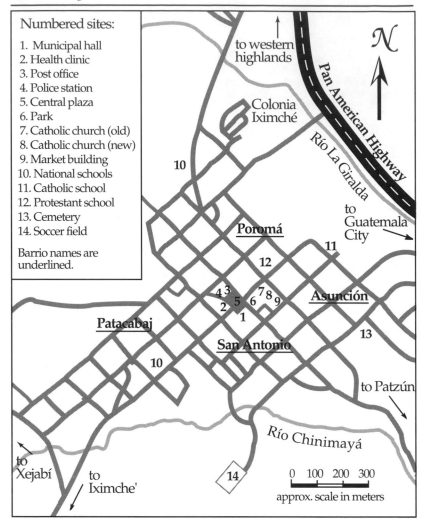

Numbered sites:

1. Municipal hall
2. Health clinic
3. Post office
4. Police station
5. Central plaza
6. Park
7. Catholic church (old)
8. Catholic church (new)
9. Market building
10. National schools
11. Catholic school
12. Protestant school
13. Cemetery
14. Soccer field

Barrio names are
underlined.

to western
highlands

Colonia
Iximché

Río La Giralda

Pan American Highway

to
Guatemala
City

Poromá

10

11

12

4 3
2   5   6   7 8
    1   9

Asunción

Patacabaj

San Antonio

13

10

to Patzún

Río Chinimayá

to
Xejabí   to
          Iximche'

14

0   100   200   300

approx. scale in meters

Map by Robert Rondeau

From maps by the Dirección General de Cartografía (1958), Dirección General de Estadística (1980), INGUAT (1991), and Instituto Geográfico Nacional (1978).

FIG. 3.   Map of the *cabecera* of Tecpán

12. A room in the home of *cofradía* members where Santo Domingo and San Francisco are displayed, 1990. Changes of clothing for the saints' figures—all sewn
from plain, dark, machine-made cloth—are kept in a large wooden wardrobe on
the other side of the room. The family in charge of fresh flowers for the week
poses in front. The man and boy wear *vestido*; the woman wears a *pequeño ri'j po't*
(with the arc design centered on the chest and the scissors design above and
below that) and an apron made with cotton *corte* cloth.

people to be involved with both groups. This contrasts with the situations in neighboring Comalapa and San José Poaquil, where there have been violent splits between *los tradicionales* (the traditional members who support the *cofradía* system) and adherents to Acción Católica. In both those towns, there are two different Catholic churches, each with its own congregation.

Politics, like religion, is a serious concern for many Tecpanecos. National and international news reaches virtually every home via radio, television for many, and newspaper for a few. Because most information on the civil war has been unofficially censored or minimally reported, people rely heavily on informal channels of communication: conversations with relatives, neighbors, or fellow workers in town or away from home; gossip passed around in offices or at the public sinks; and comments overheard in the market or on buses. These are also the channels used for learning about local news—political and otherwise—that would probably never make it into the national media under any circumstance: the decision to repair the fountain in the plaza, the theft of a neighbor's cow or television set, and the appearance of antigovernment graffiti spray-painted on the walls of buildings leading into town.

Members of key Tecpán families wield political power in the mayor's office and through associated bureaucratic positions. According to a number of indigenous Tecpanecos, up until the 1970s the mayor had always been ladino, with certain individuals known for having taken particular advantage of the office for personal gain; the siphoning off of earthquake relief funds and the private sale of archaeological artifacts from Iximche' were repeatedly described. Maya involved in municipal government are not automatically exempt from criticism by other local Indians; they too can be faulted for using the office for selfish ends, for acting "ladino." Finally, people living in *aldeas* have ties to and become involved in local government via elected representatives and work obligations. While the large Maya population in these rural areas (95 percent versus about two-thirds in the *cabecera*) does not necessarily guarantee indigenous representation, that is usually the case. Given this fact, along with the higher status of the "urban" positions relative to the "rural" ones, conflicts between elected officials from the *cabecera* and the *aldeas* often get redefined in ethnic terms.

While employees of the local government are generally "Tecpanecos" in the sense that they are full-time residents of the town, own a home and agricultural land or have family members who do, and can trace their family roots back generations, this is not necessarily the case for the professionals working in local offices of the national government. These professionals are men and women who have completed educational programs known as *carreras* (careers) that lead to specialized degrees in such areas as primary education, accounting, bilingual secretarial work, or agricultural education. The younger government workers especially are often unmarried, have close family ties in Guatemala City or other, more urban communities, and yearn for the day when a new position opens that will take them closer to home and out of what they consider a remote area. They would not label themselves "Tecpaneco." In 1980, I knew a number of postal workers, agriculture specialists, and teachers in this category. They had families—parents, wives, and children—living in other communities and commuted regularly (daily or on weekends, at the least) to their more permanent homes.

This pattern of employment had (and continues to have) to do with who is educated and, hence, eligible for government positions. However, nowadays, as more and more students from "rural" communities like Tecpán continue their schooling, they too are contenders for these salaried jobs. For them, it is ideal to live in the highlands, with or near their families, and, in the cases of Indian professionals, to work with a largely indigenous population and perhaps even use their Maya language skills. These are the hopes of many, at least. In most cases it takes months or years of waiting for more or less the right job (or any job, in some cases) in an acceptable location. The person waiting also understands that assignments are political and subject to the whims of individuals higher up the bureaucratic ladder.

Among the self-employed in Tecpán, a large number of businesses are operated in spaces that adjoin the homes of their owners. General stores, pharmacies, bakeries, clothing boutiques, shoe shops, restaurants, and stores selling items of *traje* open directly onto the sidewalks and beckon people in, while the rear or upstairs areas of these properties serve the private, domestic functions of the owners' families and are off-limits to customers. Some of these establishments are quite large and hire people to work fixed hours serving shoppers or preparing items for sale; other, smaller places are single-family operations. A common arrangement among this latter type is for the women in the house—often several generations—to engage in their normal domestic duties except when the occasional customer appears. This system also allows a mother of small children to work in a salaried job outside the home while leaving the children with her mother or mother-in-law and a hired *muchacha* (girl, but more specifically a young woman hired to work in the home or shop).

13. Street in Tecpán near the plaza, 1992. Shops line the sidewalks, and painted signs on walls announce products sold inside. Here the national bird, the quetzal, is shown above a brand label for *mish* thread and pictures of various threads and velvet ribbon (*terciopelo*). A shop sign partly visible at the left reads "Commercial Texas," a play on the word "Tecpán."

Businesses without retail outlets may be tucked away in the back or sides of properties. In Tecpán, items produced under this system include sweaters knitted on manually operated knitting machines, mercerized and dyed thread, *corte* cloth woven on treadle looms, and cinder blocks. Maya women with their backstrap looms who produce pieces for sale also have to be included in this category. Relatively speaking, their efforts do not pay well.[9] However, the work is flexible, fits in with other domestic duties, and provides an additional source of income for the family. And the future prospects of the business seem solid, given the enthusiastic use of *traje* in Tecpán (cf. Ehlers 1990).

The market is a major commercial operation in Tecpán, with the largest market on Thursdays, a medium-size one on Sundays, and a few vendors all other days. The year I lived in town, there was no permanent market building (the old one had collapsed in the earthquake), so the whole enterprise was basically created and torn down from week to week. Since that time, the permanent market building has been rebuilt to the east of the Catholic church, just off the central park, but it almost does not count. It is what Goldin (1987) calls the "compartmentalized enclosed market," in contrast to the "quasi festive plaza" of the open-air market. The concrete walls are dark and inflexible, the presence of soldiers hanging around uninviting, and its size pathetically small compared with the enormity of the Thursday market. The people with whom I shop rarely go into the building and, instead, frequent vendors elsewhere in the market.

The transformation of the Tecpán plaza from Wednesday to Friday is fantastic to witness. On Wednesday morning the plaza is virtually empty, by late afternoon scores of people are constructing stalls of poles and tarps or displaying fruits and vegetables on squares of cloth, and by early Thursday morning everything is in place.[10] While the market as a whole has its rhythm, particular categories of vendors come and go by their own clocks: the men who sell grinding stones appear only on Wednesday afternoons over by the health clinic, and people from Chichicastenango who have the sticks used for backstrap looms sit under the evergreen trees on the west corner of the park and usually sell out well before noon on Thursday. Unless the day is rainy, most vendors stay until mid- to late afternoon. As buyers begin to thin out, goods that have not sold are packed up and loaded onto buses or trucks or otherwise carted home. By Friday morning the last bits of trash are swept off the streets and traffic can easily pass through town once again.

Though the Thursday market might look chaotic to an outsider, it is, in fact, quite organized. To a certain extent, things are arranged by type: most of the *traje* sellers are grouped together, as are vendors of pottery or furniture or livestock. While there are exceptions to this rule, the one thing that can generally be relied on is the location of individual vendors over time. With few exceptions, I can visit the market in Tecpán after being away for several years and almost immediately locate a stall and vendor I remember from a decade ago.

The abundance and variety of fresh produce in the market reflects the importance of agriculture in Guatemala. In Tecpán the majority of families own or rent tillable land within an hour's walk from their homes and either farm this themselves or, in the case of the wealthier families, hire day laborers to do the work. Typically land is sown at the start of the rainy season in April or May to yield all or part of the domestic supply of corn by January. The dried ears of corn are harvested, stored in cribs at home, and prepared as needed for the family's supply of tortillas and other corn-based dishes. In the same fields, Tecpanecos often sow black beans and squash, which grow up and around the corn. Finally, depending on interests, energy, and the availability of additional land, fruit trees, grasses for work animals, garden vegetables, or a cash crop may also be planted. While the cultivation of major cash crops calls for a great deal of planning (e.g., arranging a contract for the sale of broccoli to exporters), excess

14.   Agricultural land southwest of Tecpán, July 1990.

15.   Harvesting broccoli for export, August 1990.

produce from smaller efforts—a dozen or so squashes, an armful of gladi-olas, some avocados or peaches—can be sold in the Thursday market.

For most Tecpanecos, work in the milpa during the yearly agricultural cycle meshes with home life and the rhythm of daily chores, church and the cycles of religious celebrations, and the patterns of local commerce, including the weekly markets and the Monday-to-Friday workweek for students and salaried employees. To these I add my own irregular cycles of visits—relatively brief appearances and longer absences—that influence my relationship with the town and its people, the sorts of events I witness, and the types of information I can record and discuss here.

Fieldwork in Tecpán

Were I clairvoyant, I would have paid more attention in 1974 when I quickly passed through Tecpán on the back of a Peace Corps friend's motorcycle. I would have taken in the church, municipal building, and houses in what is now remembered as their pre-earthquake glory and made mental note of the current use of dress by local inhabitants. My future, however, did not flash before my eyes, and I left with few memo-ries aside from the general one of having been there.

I was in Guatemala at that time working as a volunteer home econom-ics teacher through a 4-H international program (4-S in Guatemala). I had recently finished college with a degree in mathematics and a late-blooming interest in the visual arts, and had volunteered to work abroad while I made up my mind whether to pursue a career in painting and printmaking. I left home with a lot of questions about what was going on in the art world in the United States. An academic understanding of vari-ous art movements and some practical experience selling my work had not dispelled a feeling that there was more to the subject. How, for ex-ample, did the energies and thoughts of the publicly proclaimed, preemi-nent creators of the visual in our culture fit in with the lives and ideas of everyone else? And what would our world look like if the appreciation, production, and ownership of art had a broader social and economic base?

In 1973–1974, I worked in Jutiapa, a large ladino town near the El Salvador border. It was during that year that I made my first visits to the highlands and, in June of 1974, enjoyed a month-long stay in the largely Maya town of Comalapa. Because of ties to the community through my Peace Corps friend, I was able to attend a local wedding, participate in a range of activities connected with the celebration of the town's patron saint, and spend most weekdays learning backstrap weaving with a family of women. Though these initial experiences in the highlands were limited, I was struck by the central role of weaving and handwoven clothing in Comalapa life. This came in sharp contrast to my experiences with local clothing production and use in Jutiapa, where there had been little or no community associated with the activity. It also contrasted with my earlier efforts in studio art. While I understood both fine arts in the United States and *traje* in Guatemala to be the preeminent visual expressions of a certain segment of each society, the latter seemed to have a wider, more all-encompassing audience and an immediacy of relevance that marked it as being very different from what was produced in my own society. Were these reasonable points of comparison, or was I seeing Guatemala through several layers of Western stereotypes of "non-Western" art? In an effort to move beyond these first impressions I applied to graduate schools in anthropology with a proposal to do research on *traje* and, four years after entering the University of Chicago, was ready to return to Guatemala and start my fieldwork.

Both Paul Rabinow (1977: 1) and Loring Danforth (1989: 300) write about vivid memories of key events that took place immediately before they left for the field: Robert Kennedy was assassinated two days before Rabinow left Chicago, and Nixon resigned five days before Danforth left for Greece. In both instances the upsetting national events became symbols for the disgust and alienation they felt toward their own cultural identity, and fieldwork was seen as a means by which each could become "a different person" (Danforth 1989: 300; see also Todorov 1988: 4). That, however, was not my experience. I left the States having just completed an internship in applied anthropological work on issues that I saw as having important human rights implications. After years as a graduate student, I had thrived in a work environment where I felt valued and able to make a concrete contribution. In contrast (and despite the celebration of the Sandinista victory in Nicaragua), reports of civil strife in Central America made me question why I was going to Guatemala—why I needed to challenge myself by doing work in what I knew could become a dangerous situation.

As it turned out, the memorable and upsetting events that marked the start of my fieldwork all took place in Guatemala. I arrived on October 22, 1979, and nine days later learned that two tourists had been killed in the area where I had hoped to work. I took that as a clear sign that I could not live in Nebaj, in the increasingly embattled northern El Quiché region, and chose to work in Tecpán instead. After a quick trip back to the States and a mad scramble to locate ethnographic materials on a different town, a different region of the highlands, and a different Maya language, I returned to Guatemala. On January 31, three days after my return, thirty-nine Maya and Maya supporters were massacred by the Guatemalan army at the Spanish Embassy in Guatemala City. I contemplated my own future in light of those events: I wondered how long I would be able to live in Tecpán, whether I would be forced to leave the country, and if, under those circumstances, I would have enough data to write a dissertation.

From February 1980 to February 1981 I worked in Tecpán and returned for brief stays during the summers of 1983, 1985, 1990, 1991, and 1992. I chose Tecpán because, at that time, it was located in a relatively peaceful area, its weaving tradition was strong, and it had a local branch of the Ministry of Agriculture with an active home economics teacher, which meant I could volunteer to work with women's 4-S groups as I had in Jutiapa. Another factor that I had not explicitly considered but that greatly benefited my work was the progressive spirit of Tecpán—"*el municipio vanguardista*" (the avant-garde municipality), as one local writer put it (Ajozal Xuyá 1977b: 13). Tecpanecos have a knowledge of and participate in national and international trends, events, and policies to a notable degree. This characteristic distinguishes them from residents of other highland towns—at least, as they are portrayed in older ethnographies—who live in closed corporate communities seemingly without significant involvement in activities outside their own municipal boundaries. Moreover, there is a push for education and professional jobs among Tecpanecos (Maya and ladino alike) that is noteworthy; the display of material wealth is substantial (especially considering the destruction by the 1976 earthquake) among people engaged in such capital-intensive work as building comfortable homes, running trucking businesses, and operating modest-size stores and cooperatives; and outside advances in science and technology—categories generally treated as neutral in a society where so much is categorized as "ladino" or "Indian"—are sought out and embraced under select but widely occurring circumstances. At the same time, the strength of cultural expression by the indigenous segment of the community is evident.

Once settled in the Tecpán area, I began work with the local home economics teacher. I presented myself as a student doing her *práctica* (field practicum), a standard requirement at Guatemalan schools and universities. Tecpán, in fact, is a frequent field site for Guatemalan students completing professional degrees in home economics, health care, and nutrition. Although I explained that my field of study was anthropology, my interest in weaving and my activities with the 4-S teacher more often than not labeled me a student of home economics.

Some of my earliest contacts with townspeople were with members of 4-S clubs (principally one in the town center and another in a nearby *aldea*) and girls in the home economics classes at the local Protestant school where my co-worker also taught. The two groups presented an interesting contrast as the women and girls in the clubs tended to be from somewhat poorer homes, were largely uneducated beyond the primary-school level, and ranged from fifteen to twenty years of age. With one or two exceptions, all were Maya. In the school group, the girls ranged from ten to fifteen years of age, were approximately 80 percent ladino, and came from somewhat wealthier families who placed emphasis on school learning and discipline and who could afford the monthly tuition fee.

From this start, my connections grew to include other families and members of different organizations. Though I strove to work with a wide range of people, I spent much more time with women, especially Maya women—which, given my topic, made sense. Maya women in Tecpán wear *traje* much more than men and are much more likely to be involved in its production. They are also generally more involved in making clothes for children, dressing children, washing clothes, repairing them, and storing them. This is not to say that *traje*—or clothing, more broadly put—is a "women's topic." While there is a strong gender dimension to the subject, any study that focuses exclusively on women ignores the important ways in which men are—and are not—involved with *traje* and why. In this study I have tried to emphasize the importance of women's roles in the production and use of *traje* in Tecpán while also discussing men's more limited concerns.

As my contacts in Tecpán widened, I also started weaving (Photo 16). I found that this activity gave me an opportunity to be with women and to engage with them in conversations on clothing, cloth, and production processes.[11] And as a result of my ability to knit, sew on a treadle sewing machine, read English and hence English-language repair manuals for the same treadle sewing machines, fashion children's parade costumes from crepe paper, make *piñatas*, and construct serviceable ovens from five-gallon lard tins, I found myself with invitations from homes in all parts of town and sufficient opportunities to ask research-oriented questions. In addition, I accompanied people on shopping trips for thread, cloth, and clothing; shopped for clothing and sewing materials for others (which necessitated their telling me in detail what they expected me to buy); acted as a photographer for special occasions (and, hence, of special outfits); and discussed photographs of *traje* as well as *vestido* (clothes) or *ropa corriente* (common clothes), as the clothing worn by ladinos and "grin-

16.   The author and her teacher weaving on backstrap looms, 1980.

gos" is labeled, from a number of sources (e.g., books on indigenous dress, fashion or craft magazines, and snapshots of local people).

At other times I had occasion to function in more "elite" roles. During the year, I helped evaluate school and fairtime competitions having to do with cake decorating, flower arranging, traditional Maya dress, and what was labeled folk dances and costumes. In each of these instances it seemed that my eligibility to serve as a judge was based on my status as a university-educated, home economics teacher from the United States rather than any concrete knowledge of the topic at hand.

I also developed a small survey and hired a local student to administer it. Its purpose was not to assemble broad-based statistics on the town, for by and large I have relied on existing materials for this type of quantitative data. Rather, I used the survey to check some of my own findings against those collected by a local Kaqchikel speaker. The results, which I discuss later, generally supported what I had already learned.

While the focus of this work is on contemporary Tecpán, I also researched the historical record of the town and early written references to municipal dress. Archival material in Tecpán itself was minimal since everything from before 1976 was lost when the municipal building, which reportedly housed a small library, collapsed in the earthquake. To date, the materials I have found in the General Archive of Central America in Guatemala City do not contribute greatly to this project, since they pertain largely to topics such as land claims, milling rights, and archaeological sites. Mention of dress is found in travel accounts from the late colonial period onward and, more recently, in the field reports of government employees, university students, and textile specialists. Though very early material on Tecpán is limited (see, for example, Cortés y Larraz 1958 [1769–1770]: 172–173; Stephens 1969 [1841]: 147), a field report written in the 1940s by Rosalio Saquic (1948) for the Instituto Indigenista Nacional provides an account of local clothing use in an era still within memory of many Tecpanecos.

Nearly all my field research has been done in Spanish. As soon as I started work in Tecpán, I began lessons in Kaqchikel Maya, but I did not pursue these for more than a month as it became apparent that I could manage well in Spanish and that I should get on with my research as quickly as possible in light of the political situation in Guatemala. The vast majority of the indigenous population living in the center of Tecpán is bilingual, with Spanish the preferred language among many. To communicate with some of the older, monolingual Kaqchikel speakers and to understand the occasional event *en lengua* (in language—i.e., in the Kaqchikel language), I asked friends to translate for me. During trips to Guatemala in 1990 and 1991, I started studying Kaqchikel again, this time in Antigua as part of the Tijonik Oxlajuj Aj language and culture program organized by Tulane University and the University of Texas at Austin. Our teachers were from throughout the Kaqchikel region and saw themselves as part of the larger Maya language revival movement in Guatemala. This recent study of the language has allowed me to check some of the basic terms associated with clothing collected a decade earlier and to move forward slowly with research in both Spanish and Kaqchikel.

With hindsight, I can see that I went to the field with a set of unspoken, perhaps even unrealized, assumptions about the nature of data collection and "good" anthropological data. While I knew that I wanted to go beyond simple word lists and explanations of techniques associated with *traje*, I found myself hoping to find a "text"—a story, myth, or history about clothing—that I could record, transcribe, translate, and then describe (thickly, of course). This general formula appeared in many pieces of anthropology writing that I admired from my graduate course work, and I longed to try my hand. I was also surprised by my interest in finding something that could count as a "ritual," or rather a ritual as a metaphor for culture. I now see this latter interest as an expanded version of my search for a "text," but it had its own appeal. On one occasion—as I sat watching a Mother's Day skit—I saw my dissertation flash before my eyes:

Was this the "ritual" I was looking for? In the end, however, pages of field notes written enthusiastically after the event were reduced to a sentence or two in this book. I slowly came to realize that, on the subject of *traje* at least, information does not exist in an institutionalized, codified form and does not present itself as neat, prepackaged "facts." Rather, it is embedded in "'attitudes,' . . . individual comments or opinions or judgments about what so-and-so did [or wore] or should have done [or worn], about what ought to be, [and] about what does or does not 'make sense'" (Urciuoli 1983: 2; see also Urciuoli forthcoming), as well as nonverbal actions and activities that complement, contradict, clarify, confuse, or otherwise take place along with the verbal messages. What this means is that such time-honored field methods as the survey and the formal interview are likely to fail or misinform unless the person is extremely familiar with the ethnographic context (see Briggs 1989). Indeed, many of the most important observations derive from being in a place over a long period of time and becoming increasingly familiar with and able to comment on the content and interconnectedness of various forms of knowledge in a community.

Part of the problem with placing so much importance on "things that go without saying" (Comaroff and Comaroff 1991: 23, paraphrasing Bourdieu 1977: 167) is that the very information that is most desired by the anthropologist—what is presupposed by the local population—is hardest for an outsider to grasp and disentangle from its social context, especially an outsider intent on turning everything into written words, photographs, maps, and diagrams. In addition, the process of converting field notes to formal anthropological writing turns up numerous holes in the data—the very things one forgets to ask about or look for because they go without saying. In my own work, I was lucky enough to be able to return to Guatemala several times before I finished the dissertation and, again, before writing this book. Each time I went with lists of questions for people and mental notes of different activities I hoped to witness. My intent was always to fill in the holes, an often difficult proposition for someone who has stepped outside of the sweep of life as I had.

When I began writing the thesis on which this book is based, my efforts were helped immeasurably by a talk that Paul Friedrich gave to graduate students at the University of Chicago. In the course of about one hour he outlined what later appeared as "Experience and Methods" in *The Princes of Naranjo* (1986). I was especially struck by his discussion of "the personal experience of writing up the results of fieldwork" and, in particular, his "principles of composition" (ibid.: xv, 226). Inspired by Friedrich's ideas and other recent attempts at innovations in ethnographic writing, I have tried to weave a text that is complex but not obscuring and that gives multiple voices (Friedrich's partial holography [ibid.: 228]) to the issues of concern to both Tecpanecos and anthropologists.

Classifying Ethnicity in Guatemala

Up to this point I have used terms to refer to different ethnic groups without much comment. The labels, however, do much more than divide the more than nine million inhabitants of Guatemala into two groups of roughly equal size. In Tecpán, as is more or less true throughout the highlands, people refer to themselves, their families, or neighbors as belonging to one group or the other. The terms appear regularly in casual, everyday speech—in describing a stranger, gossiping about a neighbor, or commenting on a new vendor in the market—and largely go unnoticed. The terms, however, have the potential to inflame emotions, as when a member of one group makes a coarse generalization about the other group at, say, a political rally or a bar.

Of the two principal categories, the group designated with the Spanish terms *indígena* (indigenous), *natural* (native), or *Maya* or with the Kaqchikel terms *qawinaqi'* (our people) or *Mayab'* is the least general one.[12] Unless an institution or object is labeled "Indian" or qualified by a term that serves the equivalent function, it can generally be assumed that it has little or nothing to do with the indigenous population per se. Thus, the name of the Comité Indígena Pro-fiestas Franciscanas (Indigenous Franciscan Fair Committee) specifically labels it as a Tecpán Indian fair group whereas the companion organization run by ladinos is more simply named the Comité Pro-fiestas Franciscanas (Franciscan Fair Committee). One of the effects of the labels is to make the former group look like an offshoot of the latter, and in this case, from a historical perspective at least, it is. But in addition, the difference in specificity of the titles hints at an asymmetry in relations as well as the differential power of the committees and committee members. The people involved in the former group are not members of simply the Fair Committee but rather the *Indigenous* Fair Committee.

In Tecpán and throughout Guatemala, "ladino" and "Indian" are considered labels of one's *raza* (race) or *grupo étnico* (ethnic group). As they are most commonly used, the terms point to a division of people according to (1) certain overt markers (dress and language are regularly mentioned); (2) actions that have ethnic significance, with *costumbre* used to refer to Maya customs; (3) one's blood, heritage, or historical roots (as in ties to Maya ancestors or European stock); and (4) a history of relations between the conquering and conquered that still holds true today. However, how different people define themselves, even how the same person presents himself or herself under different circumstances, is not set. Hence, different Maya women have told me that they would feel positively naked if they had to wear *vestido*; they would be scorned by their family and friends and feel great alienation.[13] At the same time, the husbands of these very same women do not wear *traje*, and most never have. In fact, the vast majority of the men in the Kaqchikel region do not wear indigenous dress, although males who are working to revitalize Maya culture are actively exploring ways to express their ethnicity through *traje* (see Otzoy 1992a).

Ethnicity also provides a rationale for action, at least in the case of the Maya population. An indigenous person might consciously and explicitly speak out, act a particular way, or criticize another human being in accordance with his or her perceived ideal of what it is to be Indian and how this ideal should find expression in the world. Maya people and the Maya way of life are seen to be threatened by nonindigenous forces that are powerful, nearly omnipresent, and often opposed to indigenous values. At the local level, ladinos are representatives of these forces, as are the national government and the United States within certain "higher-level" contexts.

Judged by its breadth of use and its power to explain the widest range of social phenomena, ethnicity must be considered one of the fundamental classifiers of the person in Guatemala. Other systems of labeling the person exist, but, in the eyes of many Indians at least, a number of the more sociopolitically oriented labels need to be understood in terms of basic ethnic distinctions. Thus, Maya will charge ladinos with prejudicial actions based on ethnic considerations (the low level of government farm credit to Indians is one example), while non-Maya, talking about the same situation, will disclaim indigenous charges and contend that the division is based on contextually appropriate and racially unbiased criteria such as wealth, the size of land holdings, or the number of votes. Maya, commenting on the latter claims, will agree that criteria other than ethnicity can be used to divide the population. However, as they see it, it is *because* they are Indian that they are confined to the lower socioeconomic rungs and therefore can always be separated out by classificatory schemes that divide according to elements of power.

While pan-Maya awareness is growing in Guatemala and has meaning in many contexts, the boundaries of the community implied by the terms for "Indian" are often much smaller than the nation or the highlands.[14] As

I mentioned earlier, the municipality is recognized locally as a key unit for Maya identity, with municipal styles of *traje* important visual signs of local ethnic unity. In 1937 Sol Tax first articulated this idea in an anthropological context when he claimed that municipalities were the basic units for defining Indian communities and Indian identity in Guatemala. Municipalities also became the basic unit for anthropologists doing fieldwork in the highlands (recent examples of the resulting ethnographies include Warren 1978, Brintnall 1979, Hawkins 1984, Annis 1987, Ehlers 1990, and Watanabe 1992). My work in Tecpán is no exception to this tradition. However, in contrast to earlier works in which highland residents often come across as blinkered and oblivious to events beyond their cornfields, recent writings take a more broadly integrated approach: local ideas and interactions are described in multiple forms and linked to social phenomena inside and outside of the community.

"Ladino," as I noted, is the usual complement to "*indígena*," but this term, too, has its complicating factors.[15] Pansini (1977: 138–177) further distinguishes "European Guatemalans"—those with strong, direct ties to families and life abroad—and "*Guatemaltecos*"—a label that goes beyond referring to the person's nationality and indicates group status akin to the *criollos* of Guatemala's past (that is, native-born descendants of foreigners with upper-class socioeconomic ties). Non-Indians in both these categories generally do not refer to themselves as "ladino," in part, he suggests, because the class status that this term implies is lower than what they consider to be their own. In fact, along with the markedness factor, the status element might be another reason why I heard non-Indians of Tecpán use an ethnic label to refer to themselves much less often than indigenous residents. While no non-Indians in Tecpán have European connections in any immediate sense, a number of the children from ladino homes attend school in the capital and, hence, are likely to come in contact with more "European" or "*Guatemalteco*" types. A feeling for the hierarchical system into which all non-Indians fall (vis-à-vis other non-Indians, not to mention in comparison with Maya) can only be highlighted by choosing one label over the other.

Finally, there are people who are, as one Maya woman put it, "in the middle." In a 1979 statistical survey of Tecpán completed by a team of students from Guatemala's national university (Diagnóstico de salud y nutrición 1979), male and female heads of households from one-seventh of the town's homes were asked to define themselves using one of the following categories: "ladino," "*natural*," "*otro*" (other), or "*no aplica*" (does not apply). Of the 180 homes surveyed, 109 people (male and female) or

30 percent of the sample population classified themselves as "ladino," 230 people or 64 percent classified themselves as "*natural*," no one selected "*otro*," and 21 people (all men) or 6 percent selected "*no aplica*."[16] When I asked one of the survey team members what kind of people tended to choose the last of these categories, he commented that they were largely "*naturales*" but generally those who as youths had forsaken the use of Kaqchikel and other public markers of Indian ethnicity, gone to the capital, married non-Indians, and then returned to live in Tecpán. While these individuals take what are seen as steps away from being Indian, at least for a while or on certain occasions (some also reclaim their Indian status), neither are they accepted as members of the ladino community. Others' perceptions of them plus their own self-definition may put them "in between."

In my own experience each quandary, hesitation, or shift in ethnic classification is surrounded by a complex of stories and judgments. As examples from Tecpán will show, evaluations of character, actions, relationships, ambition, social status, moral worth, as well as dress and other physical dimensions can come into play in an assessment of one's own or someone else's relative ethnicity. I say "relative" because it is not so much a matter of an Indian *becoming* a ladino as a person trying to blur the lines or to act like one in certain contexts and for particular reasons. What is more, the categories applied to people are not stagnant. The defining factors associated with the ethnic terms shift over time, with people offering explanatory criteria selectively and changing their stories (not to mention their clothes) according to the situation. A group of people discussing the same person, object, or event might vary considerably in their ethnic assessment.

The Basic Vocabulary of Traje Indígena

Maya clothing is referred to as *traje, traje* or *vestido típico* (typical *traje* or dress), *traje* or *vestido tradicional* (traditional *traje* or dress), *traje indígena*, or *traje Maya*.[17] As a preface to the ethnography of clothing that follows, I list the Kaqchikel and Spanish terms for the different parts of Maya women's and men's *traje* and give a simple description of each. This vocabulary list allows me to present *traje* as a whole—a complete outfit—since, with some exceptions, a person wearing only select pieces of *traje* is not considered to be wearing *traje* in an unqualified sense.

What exactly constitutes *traje* differs from person to person and town to town. The terms listed below are ones given in an illustrated Kaqchikel-

Spanish dictionary produced by PRONEBI (the National Bilingual Education Program) and used in some of the primary schools in Tecpán (PRONEBI 1989: 26–27). In some cases I have noted variations particular to that community, since the standardized vocabulary of the dictionary cannot accommodate all dialect forms. The entries in the dictionary are listed under *ri tzyäq / la ropa* (the clothes) and are accompanied by illustrations (Figure 4).[18]

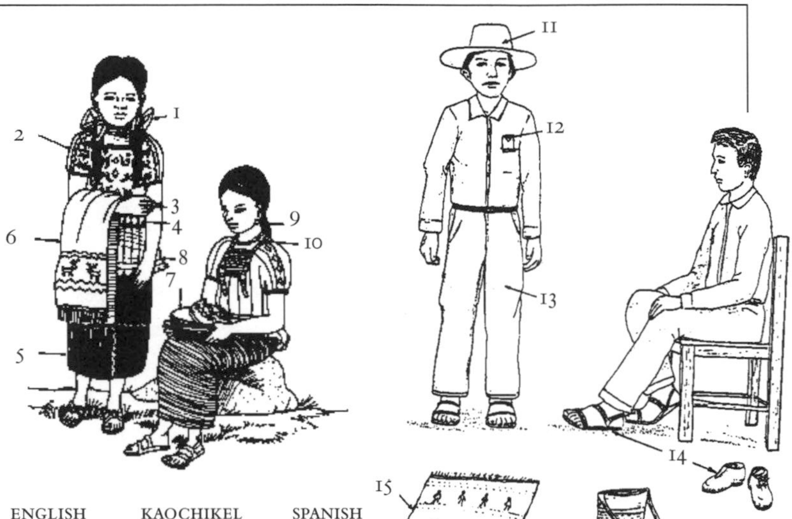

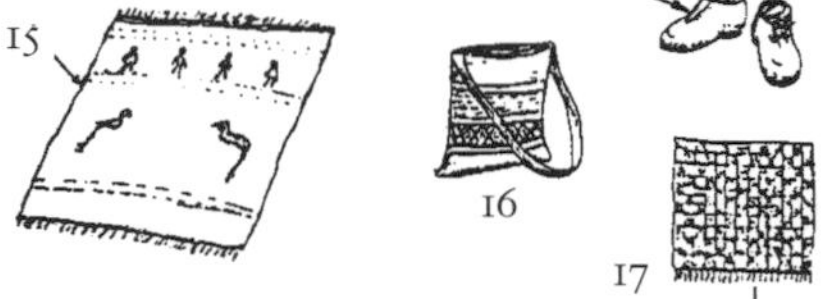

	ENGLISH	KAQCHIKEL	SPANISH
1.	hair ribbon	*pach'ub'äl wi'aj*	*listón*
2.	blouse	*po't*	*huipil*
3.	ring	*ichi'q'ab'aj*	*anillo*
4.	belt	*ximb'äl*	*faja*
5.	skirt	*uq*	*corte*
6.	shawl	*peraj*	*perraje, rebozo*
7.	cloth	*su't*	*pañuelo, servilleta*
8.	apron	*lantar*	*delantal*
9.	earring	*ichixkinaj*	*arete*
10.	necklace	*ichinaj*	*collar*
11.	hat	*pawi'aj*	*sombrero*
12.	shirt	*kamixa'*	*camisa*
13.	pants	*wexaj*	*pantalón*
14.	shoe, sandal	*xajab'*	*zapato, caite*
15.	poncho	*k'ul*	*poncho, chamarra*
16.	bag	*peqe's*	*morral, bolsa*
17.	—	*xerka*	*rodillera*

FIG. 4. Women's and men's *traje* (drawings from *Ri nabéy qasolb'äl tzij: Kaqchikel-Castellano;* courtesy Programa Nacional de Educación Bilingüe)

The basic pieces of Maya women's *traje* are as follows:

1. *pach'ub'äl wi'aj / listón* (ribbon). A five-foot-long strip made of brocaded satin cloth in a pastel hue and braided into the hair.
2. *po't / huipil* (blouse). Made of fabric handwoven on a backstrap or treadle loom, with embroidery, velvet, or other cloth ribbons sewn around the neck and armholes, depending on current styles in a town. Rectangular in shape and formed by folding the woven cloth in two, *huipiles* have slots in the side seams for armholes and a hole in the top for the head. They are also the single most distinctive piece of women's attire, often elaborately and expensively created and signaling a particular municipal origin.
3. *ichi'q'ab'aj / anillo* (ring). At one time locally made from silver or gold, now more commonly produced outside the highlands and of unknown materials. *Nupq'a'* is another Kaqchikel word for this item.
4. *ximb'äl / faja* (belt). Generally two to three yards long and woven on a backstrap or treadle loom. It is worn wrapped around the waist, the end tucked in to secure the belt. Design motifs or color combinations often indicate a particular municipal or regional origin. Tecpán Indian men also use woven belts for their *traje*, securing the *rodillera* (wool "apron") at their waist with a belt that may be over five yards long. In some contexts, *ximb'äl* refers exclusively to a man's woven belt while *pas* refers to a woman's.
5. *uq / corte* (skirt). In Tecpán this article generally consists of six *varas* of cloth wrapped around the body.[19] Two types of *uq* cloth are common in the central highlands—one made of acrylic threads with bands of cotton threads *jaspeado* (tie-dyed) to form intricate designs on the weft, and the other made entirely of cotton, with *jaspe* (ikat or tie-dyed designs) on the warp and weft threads (Photo 17). Both are made on treadle looms in standard eight-*vara* lengths. While these two types of *uq* are seen as "Maya," they do not link the wearer with a particular municipality.

An older, more "traditional" style of *corte*, called a *morga*, is made from dark, indigo-dyed threads. This thick cotton cloth has patterns of white lines that form stripes and rectangular patterns distinctive of particular central highland municipalities. The Tecpán style is referred to as *penecita* (Photo 18).

6. *peraj / perraje, rebozo* (shawl). A long rectangular shape often woven so that bands of solid color alternate with bands of *jaspe* designs. *Q'ub'äl,* another Kaqchikel word meaning "shawl," is the preferred term for some

17.   Cotton *corte* cloth with tie-dyed *jaspe* designs on the warp and weft, 1990.

indigenous speakers who are involved with the revitalization activities and who want to avoid using Maya terms derived from the Spanish.

7. *su't / pañuelo, servilleta* (general-purpose cloth, covering cloth). Handwoven, often in a style that is town-specific, these may range in size from a foot square to three or four feet square. They are used to cover or wrap a number of items, including tortillas and other foods in the kitchen, television sets and other electrical appliances, and the contents of baskets carried to market. *Servilletas* are also part of what people call *el mero traje* (the real *traje*) of Tecpán. Folded and placed on the head, women wear

these to Catholic mass or on occasions when reference is made to the most traditional or authentic *traje* from Tecpán.

8. *lantar / delantal* (apron). Made of pleated *uq* fabric, usually adorned with rickrack or other decorative touches, and with a deep, zippered pocket for guarding money.

9. *ichixkinaj / arete* (earring). Like rings, earrings are made in the area from silver and gold, though many women prefer to wear "imported" styles. The term used in Tecpán is *chixkin*.

10. *ichinaj / collar* (necklace). Traditionally made from glass beads and, at times, old coins. These, more often than rings and earrings, have been replaced by pieces not marked as "Indian."

Not listed but always mentioned in Tecpán as an element of women's *traje* is the *ri'j po't / sobre huipil, huipil de gala* (overblouse).[20] Larger than the regular *po't*, which is also called the *rupam po't* (inside *huipil*), the *sobre huipil* is worn loose, something like a poncho, over the blouse and skirt. Though armholes exist, the wearer's arms generally hang down inside the garment and extend out under the bottom selvage.

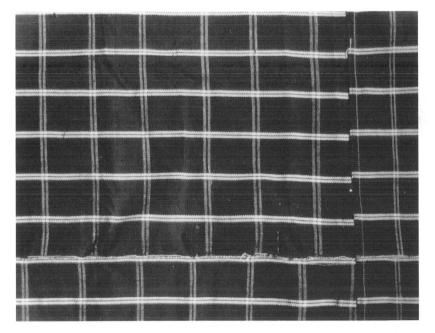

18. *Penecita* style of *corte* cloth, 1990. This older type of skirt cloth is specific to Tecpán.

Men's *traje* in the Kaqchikel region includes the following:

11. *pawi'aj* / *sombrero* (hat). Generally made from plaited straw.

12. *kamixa'* / *camisa* (shirt). Made of white or light blue cotton. The Kaqchikel term is derived from the Spanish.

13. *wexaj* / *pantalón* (pants). White, straight-cut through the leg, and rather loose. In almost all cases now, these are made from industrially manufactured cloth. In 1990 the major choice in the Tecpán market was between the cheaper, all-cotton pants made from Guatemalan fabric and the more expensive pairs made from a synthetic fabric produced in El Salvador.

14. *xajab'* / *zapato, caite* (shoe, sandal). The same terms are used for women's footwear. The Kaqchikel term *b'ukut* refers more specifically to enclosed shoes and boots, such as those shown on the right in the figure.

15. *k'ul* / *poncho, chamarra* (poncho). No longer worn as part of a man's *traje* in Tecpán. The only article I have seen that I would assign to this category is a piece in a private collection. Woven of dark blue wool with a white zigzag just above the bottom, fringed edge, it was said to have been used for *cofradía* functions years ago.

16. *peqe's* / *morral, bolsa* (bag). Knitted, crocheted, or woven and used to carry a range of things such as a lunch or school books. Girls and women also use these for school books and items related to their jobs, though *morrales* would probably never be listed as part of women's *traje* in Tecpán.

17. *xerka* / *rodillera*. A rectangle of black-and-white wool, woven in a checkered pattern, and measuring approximately four feet by one and three-quarters feet. A *rodillera* is worn folded in half so that the white fringed edge hangs down. It is secured at the front of the man's waist, over the front of his white pants, by a woven belt.

Not listed but, in my experience, always named as part of men's *traje* in Tecpán is the *chaket* / *saco de hombre* (men's jacket). Made from a dark blue or black wool, it has a notched collar, patch pockets, and a single row of buttons down the front. The *ximb'äl* / *faja* (woven belt) used by men is identical to one style used by women: it is warp-faced, with blue, pink, green, and white the predominant colors.

While this list provides basic vocabulary, it can only hint at the complexity of social meanings. The *mero traje*—real *traje*—of a municipality is assumed to be a unique form of dress that has been handed down from preconquest times to the present. Yet what counts as municipal *traje*—or even *traje*, more broadly put—is much more context-dependent. Questions having to do with the wearer, the occasion, and the other clothing options available all come into play.

Interpretive Frame

The academic framework for this book is drawn from two broad sources. One body of literature is largely nonanthropological in orientation and is written by a wide range of people, including art historians, professional weavers, and museum specialists; the other reflects my anthropology training. The former focuses on Guatemala in general and *traje* more specifically; the latter deals with cultures around the world and with subject matter ranging from language to ritual to revolution. The first has provided much background detail and technical insight; the second has provided more of the theoretical inspiration. Both are ancestors of this work.

While virtually every anthropologist writing on the Guatemalan highlands acknowledges the distinctive role of dress as a marker of ethnic identity (usually in the opening pages of the book and then rarely again), nonanthropologists produce the bulk of the published material on *traje*. Much of the research has adhered to models of data collection in the folklore or folklife tradition that focus sharply on the reality of the physical object and its visible, describable characteristics. These studies privilege the sorts of data that are most accessible to outside investigators, namely, lexical items that refer to and label the world "out there." *Traje* production, for example, can be described with an extensive technical vocabulary that is articulated fairly readily and translated into roughly parallel terms in Spanish or English (see, for example, Anderson 1978, Bjerregaard 1977, Maxwell Museum of Anthropology 1976; Sperlich and Sperlich 1980). Similarly, the formula that equates one municipality to one style of *traje* (or somewhat more complex variations on this) is at the root of another large portion of this literature, with photographs, drawings, or paintings complementing text (e.g., Atwater 1965; Bunch and Bunch 1977; Conte 1984; Delgado 1963; Dieterich, Erickson, and Younger 1979; O'Neale 1945; Pettersen 1976; Wood and Osborne, 1966). As something of a blend of these two approaches, works also focus on design motifs associated with different towns and provide detailed design outlines or thread counts (see, especially, Mendez Cifuentes 1967 and Morales Hidalgo 1990, but also parts of Atwater 1965; Delgado 1963; O'Neale 1945).

Other trends in writing about highland *traje* move more into the realm of ethnohistorical or ethnographic accounts of data. For example, a number of texts emphasize the history of the subject and examine the general chronology of weaving in an area or trace historical changes in the *traje* of particular municipalities (e.g., Anawalt 1981; Pancake 1977; Rowe 1981; Schevill 1985).[21] Following the lead of *Penny Capitalism* (Tax 1971 [1953]) and other studies that emphasize the economic dimension of highland life (e.g., Nash 1958; Wagley 1941) are works concentrating on the economic aspects of *traje* production and marketing (Hagan 1970; Pancake and Annis 1982; Rosales Arenales de Klose 1978). Two recent, long-term ethnographic studies on textile entrepreneurship and economic change—Annis (1987) and Ehlers (1990)—relate weaving production to religion and gender, respectively. To my mind, these last two plus a series of municipality-based studies published through the Ixchel Museum of Indian Dress (e.g., Asturias de Barrios 1985; Asturias de Barrios, Mejía de Rodas, and Miralbés de Polanco 1989; Mayén de Castellanos 1986; Mejía de Rodas and Miralbés de Polanco 1987; and Miralbés de Polanco, Sáenz de Tejada, and Mejía de Rodas 1990) provide some of the most insightful ethnographies on *traje*, weaving, and related subjects. They are built on in-depth research in one community and bring current theoretical issues to bear on the topics. This combination has the effect of enabling the subjects to "speak" with greater vitality.[22]

Theoretically, this book reflects my evolving interests in issues being debated within anthropology and related disciplines in the United States and Guatemala. If one were to think of this project as a geological site, the oldest layers—the symbolic and structuralist concerns—are now somewhat obscured, but they remain fundamental nonetheless. Motivating this work since its earliest days are the ideas that the material world must be understood as a cultural system, that objects reflect a wealth of cultural categories, and that meaningful patterns relate all "objects" within a cultural universe. I was formally introduced to these concepts in a first-year graduate course given by Marshall Sahlins as he was sending *Culture and Practical Reason* (1976) to press. In the course and in the book, as well as in Petr Bogatyrev's work on folk costume (1971 [1937]), I also found analyses of the structural-functional dimensions of two different clothing systems. From these rather sparse and formal treatments, I went on to read the more field-based (but nonetheless structurally informed) work of Marie Jeanne Adams (1969, 1971) on Sumba, Indonesia, and Terence Turner (1979) on the Kayapo of the Brazilian Amazon.

In those early days I was also inspired by work in the ethnography of speaking, as this was introduced to me in classes with Michael Silverstein. I was attracted to works that focused intensely on the contextual interpretations of a single linguistic "object" or set of "objects" (whether myths, songs, sermons, jokes, promises, or intimate conversations). From these studies I drew parallels to the material world, not in the sense of seeing textiles as "texts" in any literal sense, but rather considering them to be culturally bounded entities that must be understood as contextually situated and multiply meaningful within a society.

Since my original fieldwork, the writing of the dissertation, and now the rethinking and writing of this book, my work has remained within the historical trajectory of symbolic anthropology. However, along the way I have tried to update and refine my thinking on and sensitivity toward issues arising within Guatemala *and* anthropology—for example, issues having to do with gender, ethnicity, identity, and conflict as well as questions of agency, intention, and boundary. Written in such terms, my concerns may seem bloodless—just words. However, what has motivated me to keep writing about *traje* is a desire to put to work theoretical perspectives that are alive within the social sciences in the service of understanding a topic that is very much alive in the highlands.

The general organization of this book was inspired by the works of Fernand Braudel, which I began reading after I returned from the field. At that point I had a year's worth of data that I had collected in Guatemala as well as an assortment of interpretive passages written in an attempt to prime the dissertation-writing process, but little idea of exactly how all the pieces were going to fit together. Back in a university setting, I took particular interest in looking at books to see how other authors crafted a whole from a series of parts, to see how the parts were ordered and the pieces made to add up.

Braudel's ability to combine details of the daily and the mundane along with the extraordinary of any epoch appealed to me. In my own work, I had been frustrated by my inability to represent the apparent discontinuity between the ordinary—the everyday recurrence of dressing, washing, and making clothes, for example—and the timely and politically loaded use of dress in public spectacles. In *The Mediterranean World in the Age of Philip II* (1976), Braudel achieves this integration of materials within an interpretive framework of three categories of time that I have appropriated and manipulated. While I will not try to pass these off as "Maya," it does seem appropriate to me to use time as the frame through which I organize and translate my field experiences in Mesoamerica into text for an English-language audience.

The first measure of time, which Braudel sees as tied to the geography of a place, is characterized by persistent, unchanging, virtually timeless patterns—*la longue durée*, as he labels it (1980 [1958]). This idea is also reflected in a culture's notion of "human nature"—that part of a person or group that goes beyond individual lives or particular historical moments and reflects some essentially timeless core. Chapter 2 examines the enduring relationship between *traje* and municipal identity and contrasts this with non-Indian dress and the geographic elements associated with it. Chapter 3 emphasizes the wearers of *traje* and the role of dress in the construction of images of the Maya that claim to reflect some essential, unchanging truth.

The second category, labeled "social time" or "social history" by Braudel, is characterized by regular patterns that repeat within human memory. I prefer to think of this as conventional or stereotypical change. Time in this sense occupies a unique, intermediate place in the scheme of Braudel's histories and my ethnographies. On the one hand, the stereotypically repeating patterns can be considered constants of sorts: changes occur in the short run, but the pattern taken as a whole holds a constant shape over time. On the other hand, emphasizing the change in "stereotypical change," ephemeral and transformative aspects of phenomena emerge, though these fall within the frame of repeated appearances.[23]

While the social histories discussed in this book are labeled "life cycles," perhaps a better term would be "life span." Unlike the economic and political cycles examined by Braudel, the life cycles of highland Guatemalans and *traje* pieces are linear developments with specific starting points and end points (the former even more so than the latter). In a certain sense they are like Geertz's cockfight gatherings, namely, "a particulate process that reoccurs rather than a continuous one that endures" (1973: 424). However, the discreteness of these life spans or cycles does not erase the similarities among the instances nor does it preclude comparisons between different people or *traje* articles. Tecpanecos, for example, are more than willing to draw parallels or cite differences between, say, the quality of *cortes* produced today versus those of thirty years ago or the types of *huipiles* worn by their teenage daughters in the annual Independence Day parade versus those of neighbors' children.

The differential emphasis on the wearer and the worn that distinguishes Chapters 2 and 3 carries over to the life cycle in Chapters 4 and 5. Chapter 4 focuses on the process of socialization and the role of *traje* in defining and creating different stages of a person's life. Chapter 5 examines the stages of the "life" of indigenous dress, beginning with thread bought in the market and following the production and use of articles of clothing over time.

Braudel calls his third measure of time "traditional history," the history of events and individuals, who are passionately engaged in their own worlds but essentially blinded to the larger contours of social life (1976, 1:21). Filled with reports of the actions and people considered important in their day, this history is, for Braudel, "the most exciting of all, the richest in human interest, and also the most dangerous" (ibid.). The excitement lies in the possibility of locating the germ of long-term structural change within the particulars of daily life; the danger lies in the possibility of prematurely labeling something as "new" when, over the long run, it will turn out to be just "more of the same."

Chapter 6 is my attempt to locate possible points of "real change" in the contemporary production and use of *traje*. However, instead of focusing on the great men and momentous political and economic events that affect a vast region—Braudel's traditional history—the events that interest me are more local in scale, more female-centered, and seemingly insignificant. Here I examine several instances of the creative in Maya clothing from the early 1980s and discuss how these relate to changes in other parts of society. As if to bear witness to the truth of Braudel's warnings, the spirit of this chapter, much more than the others, has changed in the years since the data were first collected. What I and a segment of the Tecpán population saw as "new" in *traje* more than a decade ago now seems only mildly innovative, if not downright routine, in terms of current classifactory schemes.

When his book on the Mediterranean was first published, Braudel received a note from a colleague asking why he had not written his three histories in the reverse order. In answer, Braudel referred to "the metaphor of the hourglass, eternally reversible" (1976, 2:903). And so it is with the central, ethnographic chapters of this work, balanced as they are between discussions of change versus stasis, meaningful whether read in forward or reverse order.

Chapter 7, on the other hand, stands apart and relates to the preceding chapters as a whole. Here I consider the ideological identification of *traje* with the people who label it "our dress" (in a sense similar to the term "our mother tongue").[24] I examine how *traje* can be taken as an active, enduring cultural object—one that summarizes and symbolically maps some cultural core of the people with whom it is related—at the same time that it is actively manipulated by different individuals for changing audiences. In this instance the power of *traje*, seen as a quintessential Maya expression, reflects the totality, uniqueness, and vitality of "our culture."

TWO

THE GEOGRAPHY
OF CLOTHING

*And the earth was formed first, the mountain-plain. The
channels of water were separated; their branches wound
their ways among the mountains. The waters were divided
when the great mountains appeared.*

POPOL WUJ (TEDLOCK 1985: 74–75)

By a particular spacio-centric logic, it might seem that a disproportionate
number of the world's fiber manufacturers aim to supply Tecpanecos with
threads and fabric. Materials arrive in the marketplace and shops from
factories and workshops in the immediate Tecpán region, more distant
highland towns, Guatemala City, and such far-flung places as Colombia,
Mexico, the United States, England, France, Spain, and China. Some of
these even include place-names in the terms used to refer to the objects:
"Cantel cloth," "German dye," and "American velvet" (as distinguished
from "German velvet").[1] New types of fibers and fabrics are constantly
appearing on the scene and adding to the map of textile products.

Of the three types of natural fibers used in Tecpán, two are produced
within the country while the third is foreign in origin. The former are
representatives of the two major ecological zones about which every Guatemalan schoolchild learns: wool is a high-altitude, cool-weather "crop"
while cotton is a coastal, hot-weather one. Silk, on the other hand, requires a special producer—the silkworm—and cultivation techniques only
found outside of Guatemala. Increasingly scarce and expensive, it is used
little in Tecpán nowadays.

As for the two local raw materials, the production of wool is more
limited to small-scale indigenous "businesses." Traveling through the high-
altitude areas to the west of Tecpán, one regularly sees Maya women and
children, couples, or young men along the roadside tending their flocks of
black and white sheep. The fleece from these animals is sheared and then
processed in small workshops where men, in general, are employed to
weave on large wooden-frame treadle or foot looms.[2] This weaving is
considered *a maquina* (by machine) and contrasts with weaving *a mano* (by
hand) on backstrap looms (Photos 19 and 20).

19.   Tecpán woman weaving on a backstrap loom, 1990.

20.   *Penecita* cloth being taken off a foot loom in El Tejar, Department of Chimaltenango, 1990.

On the whole, wool pieces woven on the treadle loom are sold and used widely—at times even exclusively—far from the community where they are made. In contrast, *traje* pieces made on backstrap looms are much more often town-specific and likely to have restricted markets for indigenous consumption. Thus, for example, the municipality of Momostenango produces large quantities of woolen goods on treadle looms and is invariably mentioned as the source of wool products sold throughout the highlands. This pattern certainly holds true in Tecpán, where a couple of shops and itinerant vendors in the Thursday market offer piles of woolen products of two main sorts: *ponchos*, or bed blankets, with their geometric or animal designs, something used by ladinos and Maya alike, and *rodilleras*, the wool "aprons" worn by older Maya men in Tecpán and neighboring towns in the Department of Chimaltenango (Photo 21).

Cotton, unlike wool, is a crop of major economic importance to Guatemala; in 1980 it was second only to coffee in export value (Banco de Guatemala 1980). It is grown on *latifundios* (large estates) on the flat, low-lying coastal plain that runs parallel to the Pacific shoreline. In sharp contrast to production patterns for wool, most of the cotton in Guatemala is grown by a handful of elite families with long-established records of wealth in agribusiness (Barry 1990: 70). It is ironic, then, that cotton, a crop native to the Americas, should be controlled by the nonindigenous population and sold in the international market while sheep, animals introduced by the Spanish after the conquest, are now largely the object of local, indigenous production and use.

Because of the enormous volume but seasonal nature of cotton production, the *latifundistas* (estate owners) import laborers from poor highland communities. In many cases whole families go to work the fields for several weeks at a time in order to erase past debts and supplement meager incomes (see Menchú 1984). On these coastal plantations people must contend with heat, substandard living conditions, crops sprayed with pesticides such as DDT (the use of which is banned in the United States at the same time that it is exported abroad [Cultural Survival 1981: 6]), and wages that, in 1980, had only recently been set (though not necessarily paid) at Q3.20 per day.[3] The Tecpanecos with whom I worked were not involved in this cycle of labor, and I know of only one man who, in his youth, contracted to work on the coast (cf. Smith 1990a: 206). At that time, however, he did not live in the town center but rather in one of Tecpán's distant (and poorer) villages.[4] Townspeople, however, are aware of the general situation in the lowlands, as was evidenced by a short-lived graffiti slogan spray-painted on a school wall that proclaimed support for

21. Tecpán market stall with woolen products from Momostenango, 1990. Hanging and piled on the left are large woolen blankets and the smaller *rodillera* (with white fringe); blankets not marked as "Maya" are piled on the right.

the efforts of plantation workers to get the new, higher minimum wage (i.e., Q3.20 per day).

Because the yearly process of debt and debt labor—subsistence farming on small unproductive highland plots followed by periods of wage labor on huge lowland plantations—does not relate directly to life in Tecpán, I do not elaborate on the topic. But suffice it to say that the majority of the Guatemalan fibers that end up in the cotton *huipiles* and *cortes* sold and worn in the municipality have a history that is substantially different from their woolen counterparts.

Between its beginning as a crop in the lowlands and its arrival in Tecpán as a finished product of some sort, Guatemalan cotton can travel any number of roads. Large, private, Guatemalan-owned factories, such as the Cantel complex described in Manning Nash's *Machine Age Maya* (1958), produce thread and a variety of fabrics. Other, smaller factories and workshops, including a couple located in Tecpán, buy the basic processed thread and add to its value in a number of ways. It is here that this central ingredient in clothing production takes on a number of qualities that are important later on in the weaving process. For example, the threads can be mercerized, colored with aniline dyes or bleached, and plied. They can be processed further by specialists who tie and dye them so that later, in the weaving, *jaspe* (ikat) patterns of black and white (or another color) appear on the warp or weft face of the fabric or on both. Though by no means confined to a single municipality, the tying and dying of *jaspe* threads and their incorporation into *corte* fabric is perhaps most active in Salcajá, a town located near Quezaltenango in the western highlands. It is from this town that vendors regularly claim that their merchandise has its origin.

Falling outside these patterns of production and distribution is the natural

22.   Vendor selling *corte* cloth in the Tecpán market, 1990. All of the pieces visible here are made of cotton and have intricate *jaspe* designs.

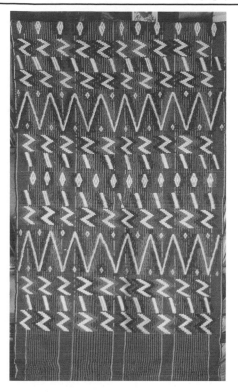

23. One *lienzo* for a Tecpán *ri'j po't*, 1990. The two predominant background colors are red (forming the five vertical bands) and brown (striped with yellow and filling the space between the red bands); the latter is woven with *k'aqo'j*.

brown cotton called *k'aqo'j*. Grown in extremely small quantities in the lowlands, it is laboriously handspun into thread and then used as the basis of Tecpán's most prestigious form of *huipil*: the *ri'j po't / sobre huipil*.[5] Both of these factors—the scarcity of the raw material and the time-consuming process of hand spinning—are blamed for making cloth from the brown cotton costly and hard to find. In 1980 only a small percentage of Tecpán backstrap weavers used *k'aqo'j* to make the *sobre huipiles*. This is still the situation, though increasingly women are making *ri'j po't* from synthetic thread that more or less mimics the color (but not the feel) of *k'aqo'j*. I discuss this alternate construction of ceremonial blouses in Chapter 4, where I link this change to shifts in attitudes toward religion over the last several years and the development of the Maya revitalization movement in the 1990s.

Thus *ri'j po't* are something like the mink coats of Tecpán, with garments made with *k'aqo'j* and silk designs selling for between Q125 and Q200—in a country where, according to U.S. Agency for International Development statistics, three-quarters of the population receives a per capita income of less than Q300 per year (Washington Office on Latin America 1983: 3). The elevated cost of a *ri'j po't* goes along with its elevated status. Taken to be the most special and honored piece of Tecpán *traje*, it is worn for ritual occasions associated with Maya tradition or the Catholic church, with its wearers, largely older women but increasingly younger Tecpanecas, seen as the female perpetuators of Maya *costumbre*.

Synthetics constitute yet another important class of materials used in making *traje*, though one whose production is far removed from the highland consumer and the local agricultural base. Shoppers in the Tecpán market, for example, can find synthetic threads for *huipiles*, *cortes*, belts, and shawls; synthetic fabric for men's shirts and pants; and metallic threads woven into skirt cloth, belts, and lace trim. These products come in a wide range of types and qualities, from the cheapest threads and cloth available for weaving, knitting, and sewing to among the most costly. Threads in the latter category, along with expensive types of cotton, are increasingly being substituted for silk in the design motifs on *sobre huipiles*; the synthetics also substitute for *k'aqo'j*. Thus, while foreigners may grumble about the loss of tradition in the shift to artificial fibers, that is not a sentiment generally expressed by Tecpanecos. Instead *lana* (wool, but also acrylic thread) is subject to the same considerations as any other material used for clothing; these include price, the warmth of the cloth, the quality of the color, and the fastness of the dye.

The map of the world is reflected in the provenance of *traje* materials used in Tecpán. Threads, certain types of cloth, and adornments (such as lace, rickrack, and ribbons) frequently come from abroad. Among the most popular brands of embroidery threads are Paleta from Spain, DMC from France, Iris from Mexico, Clark's and J. & P. Coats (both sold under the Anchor trade name) from Great Britain, and Ancla from Colombia.[6] While people may make claims about the higher quality of non-Guatemalan goods, the prestige of an item's point of origin is not the only reason for buying it. Rather, other properties—such as shine, color, and sturdiness—give a particular product the competitive edge, and one producer nation is generally taken to be as good as the next as long as the desired standards of the product are met.

Thus, after being raised, grown, or chemically produced in the lowlands, highlands, or industrial settings, in Guatemala or abroad, fibers are processed and packaged and then flown, driven, or bodily carried to Tecpán.

There, at least once a week in the large Thursday market, virtually every-thing one needs to produce the current Tecpán *traje* is available. In fact, the quantity of materials is so vast within a particular range that every-thing seems geared toward the creation of a particular clothing style, espe-cially in towns where the materials themselves are unique to the location (as opposed to Tecpán, where the unique qualities of the local *traje* are revealed only in the weaving). Thus, as far as municipal dress goes, com-munities are inward-looking, with people generally having to venture no further than their market squares for all the necessary ingredients. In this way Tecpán acts as a giant magnet attracting specific materials to satisfy local demands for *traje*.

The Municipal Identity of Traje

Writers have stated—and Tecpanecos would generally agree—that "each [highland] community has a distinctive *traje* which is distinguished from those of its neighbors by color, style, design patterns and manner of wear-ing it" (*La Nación* 1977: 16, my translation). Thus Tecpanecos describe the clothing of Indians from neighboring highland municipalities by specifi-cally noting what are considered to be the maximally differentiating visual factors: the red cloth and embroidered necklines of blouses from Patzún or the black, woolen, pedal-pusher-length pants worn by men in Chichicastenango's *cofradías*. What this structure of differences means in practice is that highland residents can often readily identify the municipal origin of particular *traje* pieces and equate the wearer with what is being worn. For example, Tecpanecos in the marketplace, or in any other situa-tion where a large number of strangers are present, hesitate little in iden-tifying the town origin of a particular woman's *traje* (or part thereof) and, in most cases, the probable town allegiance of the wearer.

This simple equation of *traje* style with municipality is a bit deceiving, however. In a town like Tecpán, there are a number of different styles of *huipiles*, *cortes*, belts, and other articles worn at any one point in history, and each of these items has its own history of changes and contexts of use. What is more, not all the items that make up the *traje* of a particular town are equally marked as being "from that town." In Tecpán and other com-munities in the area, the *huipil* is maximally marked as being from a par-ticular *municipio* and the "leading indicator" of the municipal identity of the entire outfit.

I have discussed women's *traje* here because men's *traje* in the Tecpán area is not as easily identified with a single muncipality. As I noted earlier,

Maya men in this part of the highlands have a regional style of dress that does not distinguish a Comalapa man from a Tecpán resident. The lines for Maya women's clothes are sometimes blurred, too. For example, weavers occasionally borrow ideas from other towns and create pieces that have strong visual affinities to the *traje* of these other places. An example that illustrates this point is a *huipil* I bought for the Field Museum of Natural History in 1990 (catalog number 236823). Because of what I took to be its strong associations with a conventional style of Tecpán blouse, I assumed that the weaving was a creative interpretation of the basic *huipil de Tecpán*. Only later, after a number of conversations with Tecpán women, did I understand the situation. The blouse is a *huipil de Comalapa* made in the *aj San Martín* style and woven in an eastern *aldea* of Tecpán. That is, it is a type of *huipil* "from Comalapa" whose identifiable style derives from the town of San Martín Jilotepeque and which, in this case, was made in the municipality of Tecpán (Photo 24).

Despite instances such as the *aj San Martín* blouse and the trend among women to wear *traje* from a number of different municipalities, Tecpanecos repeatedly expressed the importance of maintaining clear disctinctions between municipal styles of dress as well as preserving the use of municipal *traje* within their own town. Before considering why this is so, I want to look at some cases in which the power of dress to signal municipal identity is of utmost importance. Along the way I will also explore the idea of women "being from" or "associated with" particular towns as it applies to *traje*. A good place to start is the national-level Indian queen competitions. For these events, representatives of the various highland towns appear dressed in their most beautiful municipal *traje*. However, unlike nonindigenous competitors who wear evening gowns in similar pageants, contestants in *traje* do not have to wear satin ribbons pinned across their chests, each announcing a place of origin. For the competitors dressed in *traje*, the Maya clothing worn by the young woman specifies the municipality being represented as well as the hometown of the contestant. Further identification is redundant for those who have the cultural knowledge to see clothes and equate towns.

Another example of town-*traje* ties is found in the "traditional *traje*" contests, such as the one held in 1980 for the girls of Tecpán's secondary school. For that occasion, each contestant—Maya or ladina—was supposed to represent a specific highland town. While Tecpán *traje* was represented by four of the eighteen participants, the others wore indigenous dress from a wide variety of municipalities (e.g., Santa Apolonia, Patzún, Cobán, Cantel, and San Pedro Necta). Among the girls in Tecpán *traje*

24. A detail of a *lienzo* for an *aj San Martín* style of Comalapa *huipil* made in Tecpán, 1990. In the finished *huipil* the narrow band of *cruceta* flowers will fall across the shoulders and the wide band across the chest.

(whose selection of available clothes had to be greatest), the participants wore very old pieces or newer ones that preserved the "look" of the ritual dress. Music, Maya language, and props were also used to evoke the spirit of the municipality and to complement the image of the particular town elicited by dress.

A final instance of the important link between town and dress is seen on the fifteenth of September, Guatemala's Independence Day, when town festivities are organized that primarily emphasize allegiance to the nation, but also encourage a sense of municipal pride. Students from all the local schools participate in the day's events, the majority of them in new school uniforms or, in the case of many Maya girls, new pieces of *traje*. For this occasion, the indigenous girls usually seize the opportunity to wear, not just any local *po't*, but one of the latest interpretations of traditional fashion. As I mentioned earlier, in 1983, the "newest" fashion took the form of the *xilon*-style *po't*, a type of handwoven blouse that had been used in Tecpán several decades ago but had fallen into disuse.

In each of these three instances, *traje* functions to tell the viewer that the wearer is (or is meant to be) from a particular town. This message comes across even though the young women in Tecpán *traje* wear what would seem, on the surface, to be very different clothes. Described only in terms of *huipiles*, the Tecpán entry in the national queen's contest in the early 1980s appeared in a brand new and especially beautiful blouse of the most common style, which was seen everyday in the streets of the town. In the school competition the contestants wore their grandmother's or great-grandmother's *sobre huipiles*, which were old and supple from years of use. Finally, many of the schoolgirls in the 1983 Independence Day parade, like the Tecpán candidate in the queen contest, wore newly woven *huipiles* in popular contemporary styles, only in this case some of them wore a "new" style: the *xilon* blouses.

But surely a *xilon*-style *po't* would do as well as a handspun brown cotton *ri'j po't* for announcing the wearer's municipal affiliation if both are recognized as being "from Tecpán" and if signaling municipal affiliation is all that is intended. The point, of course, is that municipal affiliation is never all that is intended. In a national Indian queen competition, *traje* not only needs to be easily identifiable in terms of town affiliation for a broader audience, but should also function to establish other important dimensions of the contestant—for example, that she is pretty, youthful, and *bien preparada* (well prepared, with the added sense of being "on the ball"). This function is especially important in the national Indian queen contest run by INGUAT, the Guatemalan government's Institute of Tourism. The audience for this competition is national and international in reach, and often ignorant of fine distinctions between different sorts of municipal *traje*. In addition, the contest is modeled on Western beauty pageants, with the expectation that the candidates and queen will participate in the commercial endeavors of the sponsors—that is, "selling" Guatemala on behalf of INGUAT. The event therefore raises a whole range of questions about the government's use of Indians and, hence, is quite controversial among Maya. I explore this controversy in the next chapter.

In contrast to the queen contest, the traditional *traje* competition emphasizes the historical dimensions of dress and Maya *costumbre*. For such an occasion, *sobre huipiles*, *morgas* (the older style of skirt), and *caites* (Maya sandals)—all associated with older people and old styles of dress—are perfect for accenting ties with one's Maya ancestors or, in the case of ladinas, showing a knowledge of and interest in the indigenous heritage of the nation. Particularly fine examples of these items further emphasize the worth of Maya traditions as well as the wealth of the wearer.

Finally, in the case of the Independence Day parade, an Indian school-girl and her family are keenly aware that she is marching in front of a local audience, one that has a ready knowledge of the history of municipal *traje*. Here a young woman's attempt to accent her personal beauty, poise, and sophistication may take the form of appearing in the latest *traje* fashion. What is more, in the 1983 case of the updated version of the older *xilon*-style *po't*, the strength of the historical roots of the piece was not lost on the crowd. It was a time of intense violence in the highlands, a time when many outspoken Maya were being killed or forced into silence, and the appearance of the new-yet-old *huipil* was a visual expression of the vitality of the indigenous people and their culture.

Other Reasons for Selecting Traje

While the use of *traje* to signal municipal identity is a central function of Maya clothing, it is not always the most important one. Municipal *traje* is neither a necessary uniform nor a mode of dress uniformly worn at all times and by all local *traje* wearers. In order to play upon other possible meanings of dress, people purposely select articles of *traje* that originate in or are associated with other highland towns, and they do so for very specific, culturally motivated reasons.

Accounting for the geographic range of *traje* pieces found in a given municipality is like taking an ethnographic snapshot of the many factors that unite and divide Maya and the different ways in which people determine their community identity. Transitions in life—marriages, in particular—account for a large number of the situations in which habits of dress and the municipal identity of a person are challenged. Marriage between individuals from different towns, for example, is a common occurrence. In such cases, it is the woman who normally goes to live with her husband and, often, with his family (especially during the first years of marriage). However, despite the move across town lines, the woman generally retains the regular use of *traje* from her birthplace, though she might also use the occasion of her marriage to begin wearing *huipiles* from her husband's town. Women I knew in Tecpán wore *huipiles* from Chichicastenango, Patzún, or another community more or less regularly and claimed they did so because of their natal ties. Likewise, when I asked others why particular women living in Tecpán wore non-Tecpán *traje*, the answer that respondents gave most quickly and with the greatest confidence was that the woman was from (i.e., born in) another *municipio*.

The situation for daughters born to one of these couples is also telling.

The girl is often dressed in *traje* from the father's municipality (especially when the family lives in that town). Some fathers have definite opinions about what clothes their children should wear and believe that their daughters should bear the mark of their paternity and their community in the form of *traje*. In other instances, the father cares little what a child wears, while the mother might have strong feelings and dress her daughter accordingly. However, all of this seems a bit too simplistic and formulaic in the face of the situation I lived and felt in Tecpán. Birthplace and marriage (as well as other factors I have yet to discuss) do affect what people wear and how they think of themselves in terms of place. But, along with these singular events and their easy explanations, there is a greater sense of belonging—to a community, to a family, to a particular group—that comes not in a day but develops only through time, repeated activities, and constant associations. Individual events bear meaning because of this larger sense of belonging, which, in turn, grows more meaningful with each passing event.

When municipal identity is not of utmost concern, there are other reasons for choosing *traje*: economic factors (cost), weather (the heat or cold), a general pride in being Maya, and what I will call the "*al gusto*" rationale. When I asked why a particular person wore the dress of another town, the response was often "*Es al gusto de uno*" (It is a matter of one's personal taste). While not meaning to shun the subject of individual taste, I will concentrate on elements of choice that can be described by broader, socially defined parameters—namely, economic factors, climatic considerations, and what I see as a growing awareness of access to the larger world based on greater educational opportunities, better transportation, improved communications, and a shifting, expanding sense of what it means to be Maya.

Economic Factors
Cost figures prominently in most decisions to acquire a new article of *traje*. In 1980, the prices of Tecpán *huipiles* and *cortes* averaged Q30.00 apiece, while most Tecpán Indian families had an income ranging from Q2.00 to Q8.00 per day. Through the decade, the general ratio of prices to income stayed about the same or worsened, especially by the start of the 1990s. Given this situation, it is little wonder that people seek less costly routes to acceptable indigenous dress. Conceivable solutions are many; actual solutions are fewer in number, owing to the limitations of what is acceptable within any particular municipal context. In Tecpán, for instance, cheaper *huipiles* in a local style are still woven on the backstrap

loom but have fewer, less complex, and more crudely woven figures. In neighboring Comalapa, cheaper handwoven blouses are also available; however, the cheapest Comalapa *huipiles* are made on treadle looms.

People also look to town-external solutions for cheaper but satisfactory clothing. Totonicapán and Quezaltenango, for example, are two major suppliers of the more reasonably priced *huipiles* sold in Tecpán.[7] Produced on treadle looms, these pieces are faster to weave and often made of good-quality but modestly priced cotton thread, factors that are reflected in their selling price of Q11.00 to Q20.00.

Of course, price alone is never a reason to buy a particular item, and Tecpán families weigh several timely considerations in the balance when a purchase is made. For example, some women simply do not care about weaving or handwoven clothes and may be more likely to choose the treadle-loomed varieties of *huipiles*. They may prefer to spend their time and money on their homes and housekeeping (one woman equated weavers with poor housekeepers), other craft projects (needlework, crochet, knitting), or special events (work with *cofradías* or preparation for family celebrations). Maya identity is expressed in a multitude of ways, and even the strong tie between an Indian woman and handwoven municipal dress can be violated without calling into dispute her commitment to her heritage.

Another instance where the less costly *traje* pieces are used concerns mothers, particularly women who do not have professional jobs and who have marriage-age daughters. These women may buy the cheaper *huipiles* and *cortes* and keep wearing these clothes until they are threadbare in order to save money for the purchase of more expensive items for their children. They see this as important because young women in their mid- to late teens and early twenties are at an age when they want to attract a suitable *novio* (boyfriend, fiancé) and establish themselves as poised, *bien preparada*, and fastidious adults. Good grooming plus impeccable outfits bode well for a young woman's future prospects, whether these be through matrimony or a salaried position. Whatever the case, the mother who makes the sacrifice generally does not need to worry about either in her own life.

Climatic Considerations

Differences in temperatures and other climatic factors are taken into consideration when it comes to dress. Climate in Guatemala is determined largely by altitude, not latitude, and Tecpán lies in a moderately cold zone. December and January nighttime temperatures can drop to the freezing point even though the daytime highs regularly approach seventy degrees.

March and April are the hottest months, just before the arrival of the wet season, with its cooling afternoon rains and cloud cover. Yet, even in the heat of a March day, the thermometer is only temporarily driven into the eighties. For this hotter weather, women claim that light cotton *blusas* (blouses), such as those associated with Cobán and San Cristóbal Totonicapán, are ideal.

Made of factory-loomed cloth and decorated with hand- or machine-embroidered designs around the neck and armholes, *blusas* are familiar to every woman in Tecpán (see Photos 2 and 5). While some claim that the inspiration for the blouses arises from those typical of the aforementioned towns, many consider them to have evolved into a generic highland style now produced for use within the family or for sale in markets and shops. Because of their light weight, *blusas* are worn both indoors (for heavy housework) and outdoors (under a hot sun). Because they are cheap and easier to wash than the thick, brocaded *huipiles*, *blusas* are also common attire for messy toddlers and active, growing girls.

While it seems that "common sense" dictates the use of *blusas* for hotter weather, climate is only one consideration. Each time a person wears *traje*, several levels of meaning are called into expression and accommodated simultaneously. However, simultaneous accommodation is not always possible. Sometimes priorities must be set and choices made. For example, as part of my work with 4-S clubs, I accompanied a group of young women on a field trip to an area of Guatemala that is lower in altitude and, hence, warmer than Tecpán. Most of the Indian women had prepared for this change in climate by bringing lighter-weight *huipiles* woven on treadle looms and *blusas*. However, one woman brought only heavy Tecpán pieces. Asked why she did this, she replied that her husband wanted her to wear municipal *traje* so that everyone would know she was from Tecpán. A sense of pride in community, more than the heat, governed the husband's thoughts. The young woman, going along with her husband's recommendation, showed that respect for her husband (and an equal pride in community) was cause enough for her to wear hot, heavy *huipiles* when other women on the trip claimed that lighter blouses would have been more comfortable.

An Expanding Awareness of the World
The use of *traje* from other towns signals a growing awareness of and access to other highland Maya communities. While familiarity with different locations generally decreases with distance, Tecpanecos readily ad-

mit that greater educational opportunities, better transportation, and improved communications mean that young people today are much more worldly than in years past. As far as *traje* is concerned, these developments mean that now individuals are able to obtain items of *traje* from more distant towns, ones not usually represented in the local market.

Because these "foreign" pieces are not necessarily the ones commonly sold in the Tecpán market, they are either chanced upon, made by modifying existing materials, or specifically sought out in other towns. Whatever the case, their use may reflect the wearer's education, work experience, travel, family connections (often related to wealth), and *preparación* (preparation; specifically, the knowledge and competence that often comes with schooling). The following examples illustrate these points.

Felipa is the marriage-age daughter of a family that runs a trucking

25. Tecpán children, 1990. The girl is dressed in *traje* from Quezaltenango. *Huipiles* from Quezaltenango are readily available in the local market, but *cortes* are not. Her brother is dressed in *vestido.*

business as well as a small shop in their house.[8] Well educated, she has completed twelve years of school, the last three in Guatemala City. Now working in Tecpán, she (as well as other members of her family) maintains an active interest in local and regional Maya events. When Felipa's male family members are away from home on business, they sometimes buy her clothes. Wearing articles of *traje* from distant municipalities, she signals her appreciation for and awareness of *costumbres* from throughout the highlands.

Teresa, too, is the marriage-age daughter of an Indian family and has the same teaching degree as her friend Felipa. Her uncle has a good job in the capital and, as a consequence of his work, has been able to travel throughout Guatemala. When he goes to different highland towns, he sometimes buys his niece local *huipiles*. She is generally pleased to receive these items, which signal special access to sources of *traje* rare in the Tecpán area. However, even without her uncle's help, Teresa can tap into distant *traje* sources. Through her school connections, she has become friends with a number of young Maya women from around the highlands. Since graduating and getting a job, Teresa has been able to save a portion of her earnings and, through her school friends, has commissioned articles of *traje* from the friends' hometowns. As she obtains new items, they become part of her work wardrobe and, given her position as teacher and role model for the young women with whom she comes in contact (ladinas and Indians alike), her dress is an expression of her own competence and pride in ethnicity.

Another example illustrates the influence of foreign *traje* styles on young Tecpán Indian women who go to the capital and take jobs as domestics in wealthy urban households. When they return home, it is often with alterations in their *traje*.[9] One change mentioned by two middle-age women was an increase in skirt length—something that can be done relatively easily by decreasing the amount of cloth doubled over at the waist. While I assumed that this change was an indigenous response to a current ladina fad in "*maxi faldas*" (maxi skirts), I was promptly corrected when I offered this opinion. Both women saw the length of a woman's skirt as yet another indicator of municipal affiliation and, in this case, took the change to be influenced by skirt styles in San Cristóbal Totonicapán. While I am not so sure that the popularity of maxi skirts was unconnected, the two women and I did agree that the actions of the young women were those of individuals on their own for the first time and eager to express their worldly ways.

A final example focuses on the men's *traje* worn for a unique public

event. Each year during the week of October 4, Tecpán stages a fair celebrating St. Francis of Assisi, the patron saint of the town. Starting in the
late 1970s, a committee of indigenous Tecpanecos was formed to plan a
series of fair activities focusing on a different aspect of Maya culture each
year. In 1980 *traje* was highlighted. To inaugurate the week of events,
members of the Indigenous Fair Committee organized a presentation of
highland dress, held Sunday morning on the outdoor municipal stage. For
the occasion, eight local girls modeled as many different municipal *trajes*.
Commenting on their appearances were two male emcees from the Instituto
Indígenista Nacional (National Indian Institute, or IIN), both of whom
had families from the Tecpán area, though they themselves lived and worked
in the capital. For the presentation, one man wore a cowboy hat, gray
pants, and a long-sleeved shirt made from cloth generally marked as
"Indian." The other man wore rustic sandals with tire soles, a white woolen
poncho, knee-length pants, a plaited straw hat, and sunglasses. None of
the people with whom I talked could identify the municipal origin of the
second man's *traje*, though everyone agreed that it was Maya and some
thought it was from a specific municipality. The shirt of the first man was
also marked as "Maya" though not as municipal *traje* per se (if anything, it
seemed to me to be associated with shirts sold to foreigners).[10] These
outfits stood in sharp contrast to the ones worn by the Maya girls, with
their abundance of place-specific references. Instead, the clothing of the
two men exhibited a generalized reference to Maya *costumbre* in Guatemala, but it was not geographically specific.

Thinking about this example now, more than a decade after the fact, I
see parallels between the clothes worn by the two emcees and the jackets
worn by Maya men who are involved in the revitalization movement and
who are trying to develop a role for clothing in men's expression of ethnicity
(Photo 26). For this latter group of men, the principal article of clothing
to serve as an ethnic marker during the early 1990s was a bomber jacket,
most commonly one made of footloom-woven cloth in a dark indigo
blue (akin to the cloth of women's *morgas* but also like the dark, blue-
black wool of men's *traje* jackets as well as dark, jean-jacket denim). Down
either side of the front zipper and accenting the sleeves, the back of the
collar, and the pockets are strips and patches of cloth with designs woven
on a backstrap loom. In the cases I noted, these designs are the dove, curl,
and other figures from Tecpán women's *huipiles*. Despite this link to Tecpán
(with its many participants in revitalization activities), the jacket is used by
men from throughout the highlands, seemingly without reference to that
or any other municipality. In 1990, this style of jacket was worn exclu-

sively by the men associated with the revitalization movement (including
a few foreign linguists active in Maya language projects). However, since
that time I have seen it on sale in Maya-run shops in Antigua and Tecpán.
By 1992 other versions of the jacket, some made with the even less place-
specific, double-*jaspe* cloth (the type used for women's *cortes*), were being
worn by men involved in revitalization activities.

But why is the scope of geographic references for men's and women's
traje so different? Why is women's clothing so community-specific and
men's so general, at least in the central highlands? Irma Otzoy (1992a: 112,
my translation), writing about Maya clothing and identity, states that "if
Maya men were the first to establish (by force or voluntarily) interethnic
communication in Guatemala, Maya women were those who insured the
maintenance of one of the principal cultural emblems [i.e., *traje*]." Maya
men, then, may be seen to have lost their use of *traje* during the course of
a history of hostile cultural interactions. And now, in the efforts to recon-
struct a male identity through *traje*, women's dress is one of the remaining
sources of rich visual inspiration (hence the references to women's clothes

26. Type of jacket worn by men involved in revitalization activities, 1991.

in the revitalization jackets). Furthermore, if at times men's prominent roles in intercultural communication have reduced them to simply "Maya," this might also help explain the general nature of men's *traje* in contrast to women's much more community-specific dress.

Municipalities and municipal boundaries are important in defining what it is to be Maya, and there are numerous ways in which men contribute to the definition and maintenance of a local sense of place; it just happens that *traje* is not one particularly elaborate means for doing this, at least not in Tecpán. On the other hand, women's *traje* is not only used to signal local, municipal divisions; at times it can also stand for all of Maya culture.

Traje *as an Expression of All Maya Culture*

Tecpanecos are not alone in their selective and purposeful use of *traje* from outside the municipality. However, this borrowing of *traje* pieces across town lines is often asymmetrical and sometimes almost entirely unidirectional. For example, women from nearby Santa Apolonia regularly wear *traje* from Tecpán, San José Poaquil, and other local municipalities; yet I know of no Tecpán resident who wears Santa Apolonia dress, even among Santa Apolonia women who have married and moved to Tecpán. This asymmetry hints at a valuation of *traje*—a ranking of one as "better" or "worse"—for particular instances of use. In the Santa Apolonia case, Tecpán women claim that the local *po't* is out of favor because its plain white background and minimal number of designs make it less attractive than the colorful and intricately woven ones from other towns. Attractiveness or beauty in this context is measured in terms of contemporary fashions in *traje* (such as the general propensity for elaborate weaving and a rich array of color), which are favored when a woman wants clothing that reflects well of her. The judgment on *traje* also reflects a more general evaluation of the town. Asymmetries of all sorts exist throughout Maya culture and society—from dialect status to relative merit of *costumbre*—and residents of Santa Apolonia experience their own local version of the cultural power structure. Dwelling as they do in the shadow of Tecpán, they are constantly aware of their large and bustling neighbor with its noteworthy history, huge market, extensive schools, and wealthy citizenry.[11] The status of *traje* also figures in this expression.

But this hierarchical ranking of municipal *traje* does not apply to every situation: other systems of valuation hold sway in other contexts. In the traditional *traje* contest mentioned earlier in this chapter, Santa Apolonia was one of the towns presented, along with such widely acknowledged weaving centers as Chichicastenango, Nebaj, and Tecpán. The schoolchildren who elected to represent the community—two girls, one dressed as a woman and the other as a man—described the *traje* and spoke of its uses. The audience received them enthusiastically, and the judges ranked their presentation—the clothes they wore, their manner of wearing them, the props they used, and their narration—as one of the best. There was clearly no stigma attached to Santa Apolonia dress.

On other occasions, with judges absent, Maya culture is celebrated with displays of municipal *traje*. In these instances, each outfit, with its ties to a different town and different *costumbre*, is meant to be taken as an equally valuable expression of Maya culture in Guatemala. The 1980 *traje* presentation inaugurating the fair was such an event. On stage in the acoustical shell in the central park, the eight local girls in various municipal *traje* stood alongside the two male emcees, the Princesses Ixmucané and Iximché, their two attendants, and a marimba band (Photo 27). The eight outfits on the models represented eight Maya communities—including Cobán to the northeast, Santiago Atitlán to the southwest, and Santa Cruz del Quiché to the north—while the outfits of the two princesses and their attendants were marked as "Tecpán." The young women said nothing while the emcees, speaking in Kaqchikel, discussed local *traje*, Maya weaving traditions, and pride in heritage through dress. As the men explained, the purpose of this presentation, plus the week-long public exhibition of indigenous dress that accompanied it (with pieces borrowed from the Instituto Indígenista Nacional), was to impress upon the audience the complexity and variety of indigenous cultural expression as a whole. In this context, each style of *traje* from a different highland town was presented as equivalent to the next as a rich and valid representation of place and a way of life. Each outfit reflected its roots in the Maya past, each told of the active presence of indigenous people, and each stood for the contrast between Maya and ladino constructions of social reality in Guatemala.

Traje used as everyday clothing can also represent Guatemalan Indians as a whole. Since the early 1980s, the growth in activities organized by Maya for Maya (*all* Maya) has been marked visually by the increasing use of *traje* to signal pan-Maya identity. Women who see themselves linked to revitalization efforts, as well as those not directly involved but in general agreement about the need to express pride in ethnic identity, have begun to wear *huipiles* from different municipalities to reflect their expanded sense of cultural affiliation. The use also tells of the women's growing

27. *Traje* presentation sponsored by the Tecpán Indigenous Fair Committee, 28 September 1980. Shown on stage are a member of the marimba band (far left); the two Maya fair princesses (seated, center), each flanked by an attendant in Tecpán *traje*; and eight local girls dressed in *traje* from around the highlands.

network of contacts in highland communities. Judith Maxwell (1992: 10–11), who writes about *traje* in the context of language revitalization, gives the example of a woman from San Antonio Aguas Calientes, whom she first met in 1975 when the women wore only local *traje*. In 1989, when the two met again, the woman explained that while she was not "like this" fourteen years ago, now she wears *huipiles* from different highland towns. Maxwell goes on to conclude from this conversation and others like it that "several levels of identification began to be explicitly used and referenced in discourse [and, I would add, via nonverbal channels such as dress]: activist speakers identified themselves first as Maya; second, by language group; third, by home community; and fourth, by nation" (ibid.: 11). This is not to say that every Maya woman who begins wearing *traje* from other towns is reconfiguring her identity this way. Rather, in certain contexts and for some women, *traje* serves to signal pan-highland Maya solidarity in a conscious, visible way.

This use of women's *traje* has its counterpart in men's clothing. As noted in the previous section, by the early 1990s the dark blue jacket with the handwoven accents had become associated with men in the revitalization movement and was worn regularly when activists gathered for cultural events. If these men, especially in their activist roles, consider themselves first and foremost Maya rather than members of a certain town, then the jacket, with its lack of municipal specificity, is an appropriate symbol. This also goes a step further in answering the question of why Maya women's clothing is so town-specific whereas men's, at least in the case of the jacket, is so general. The short answer here is "history." The history and creation of the jacket is very much tied to contemporary concerns about ethnic revitalization within Guatemala, while women's *traje*, with its centuries-old associations with municipalities, retains its important link to local communities even when it is worn as an emblem of pan-Maya identity.

Widely Acclaimed in the United States and Abroad: Non-Maya Dress in Guatemala

Despite the variety and complexity of ties between *traje* and the geography that surrounds it, the most publicly, elaborately, and consciously expressed equations are those between dress and municipality and between dress and pan-Maya identity (meaning Guatemalan pan-Maya identity). Relationships between groups are implied by both. *Traje* used in the former mode describes a world divided up into "self-ascribed ethnic enclaves" (Watanabe 1992: 10, referring to work by Carol Smith), which are seen as relationally defined within a Maya context. The latter equation, on the other hand, describes a situation in which all Maya within the national borders of Guatemala are united by dress. In this instance, *traje*/Maya is defined in part by its opposition (theoretical or actual) to *vestido*/ladino within the nation-state.

In this section I want to begin examining the much-neglected subject of "common clothes" in Guatemala. I limit my discussion to an aspect of *vestido* that contrasts with *traje*—namely the foreign element in clothing merchandise and fashion (inspiration). While I do not discuss the historical background of styles and goods, important structural relationships that were set in place centuries ago are still present today. Central among these is a hierarchical ranking of objects (and the people associated with them), which becomes public in terms of status, rank, and privilege.

In the spirit of this chapter I examine the hierarchical ranking of *vestido* as it is expressed in terms of specific geographic locations and associations. My first step will be to present, somewhat uncritically, a whole array of materials that link common clothes to particular areas of the world and that refer to or imply an ordering and value. I do this, in part, to give some sense of the quantity and types of messages that are present in Guatemala and to argue that, on the surface, a large number of these repeat more or less the same "cultural text" (Basso 1979: 16; Geertz 1973: 448). While these messages or "texts" are open to multiple and very critical readings, criticism has not made them disappear. Because the hierarchical ordering of *vestido* in Guatemala is "true enough"—that is, it makes enough sense to enough people enough of the time—it has a certain social reality. In the final section I return to the topic of *traje* and examine how indigenous clothing, seen as an emblem of a Maya universe, contrasts with *vestido*, seen as an emblem of a world (economic/cultural) system. Here the two systems of dress, understood in socially meaningful but limited terms, stand in stark and rigid opposition. For Tecpanecos, things are seldom that polarized: objects have multiple meanings, all of which are subject to some sort of challenge or play within specific cultural contexts.

While the geographical reference points explicitly associated with *traje* are confined to Guatemala, those signaled by *vestido* are regularly and, often, enthusiastically attributed to Europe and the United States. *Vestido* is seen as having foreign sources of inspiration that affect styles in dress and changes in fashion. Expressed in the extreme, once the foreign wellsprings of fashion are identified, all other places can be arranged hierarchically, with more status accruing to clothes that come from places "higher up" on this scale and less status to items from "lower down."

Going along with this ordered ranking of sites are relational considerations: a particular place may take on the role of the mecca of fashion relative to other, less privileged spots. Comparisons are made between locations in terms of how *civilizado* (civilized) or *abandonado/retirado* (abandoned/distant) each is considered to be. Typically, these labels refer to relations between more or less urban (or rural) locations with their access to (or lack of) modern conveniences, material goods, and ideas. Thus, for example, a ladina from a village in Jutiapa told of an invitation to visit the home of a social worker whose family lives in Antigua, Guatemala's fashionable colonial capital. She never went, she said, because she was embarrassed by the fact that she only had homemade clothes that she herself had sewn. Nevertheless, in making these clothes she incorporates ideas from fashion magazines and dress-shop windows in Jutiapa, and she considers herself and her teenage daughter to be quite fashionably attired when compared with other village members whose clothing is not so inspired.

PHILIP:	Bye, girls.
GIRLS:	Bye, Philip.
MAFALDA:	That Philip is really great, isn't he?
SUSANITA:	Is he widely acclaimed in Europe and the United States?
MAFALDA:	What? What's that got to do with anything?
SUSANITA:	Just that nothing is great if it isn't widely acclaimed in Europe and the United States.

FIG. 5.   *Mafalda* cartoon strip (© Joaquín Salvador Lavado, QUINO; MAFALDA 2, Editorial Patria)

The ultimate inspiration for *vestido* is suggested by two items that are not directly related to clothing. The first is a cartoon by the Argentine artist Quino, whose work appears in one of Guatemala's national newspapers. In this particular strip his central character, Mafalda, interacts with her status-conscious little friend Susanita (Figure 5).

The second is an advertisement for pizza that appeared in one of the national newspapers:

> It was born in New York; It triumphed in California
> AND NOW IN GUATEMALA
>
> EL GRÁFICO 28 FEBRUARY 1980[12]

The Mafalda cartoon is funny in part because something that the reader recognizes as being serious or true outside the context of the strip has been distorted and made ridiculous by the circumstances inside the rectangle. I see this situation as similar to the joking events that Basso (1979: 16–17) analyzes in terms of "present relationships" (the joke situations) and "absent relationships" (serious "cultural texts" whose meanings are not dependent on particular contexts): the former are modeled on but distort the normal understanding of the latter. In the case of the Mafalda cartoon, the "cultural text" is the grandiose but serious claim that something can be "widely accepted in Europe and the United States." The humorous twist occurs when Susanita earnestly applies the idea to small, mild-mannered Philip, her neighborhood chum. We, the readers, laugh because we have been caught off guard; we recognize that at times some people *do* see the United States and Europe as the ultimate source of all worthiness and acceptability, but here the idea has been taken to a ludicrous extreme.

In the pizza advertisement a similar claim for acceptability is made, and in this case there are no clues within the ad itself that suggest that the message should taken other than seriously. Here, the life history of the product is summarized in terms of the order of its appearance in the Americas, with the implication being that, while Guatemala is not New York or California, it is in direct line with the two. Proximity or accessibility to the desired source places an item in a high (if not the highest) ranking.

And so it is with clothing. Media in Guatemala—television, radio, newspapers, and magazines—carry a wide variety of messages having to do with dress and places abroad. Associations with Europe and the United States ("América") are regularly singled out and emphasized as being a particularly positive aspect of an article of *vestido*. Thus, for example, we find the following newspaper advertisements (all are my translations):

FIORUCCI: everything in clothes with the stamp of Europe
EL GRÁFICO 23 DECEMBER 1980

AMERICAN SWEATER WITH BUTTONS
EL GRÁFICO 25 MARCH 1980

Skinflicks: AMERICAN DESIGN BATHING SUITS
EL GRÁFICO 25 MARCH 1980

For this time of year, exclusive designs in sports clothes,
imported directly from Europe and the United States
PRENSA LIBRE 1 MARCH 1980

"Ellas" Boutique: European and American clothing from
the best firms
EL GRÁFICO 31 JANUARY 1981

Particular geographic locations—countries or cities—are often singled out for specific mention: Italy or France; London, Miami, or San Francisco.

And in lengthy, detailed articles, Paris, Milan, and New York are regularly featured as the centers of haute couture and the perennial sources of the best of the new fashion. Outfits are described, specific designers are interviewed, and the showings of new collections are reported as the seasons turn. Even though the Guatemalan seasons turn differently from those in Europe and the United States, this is one way Guatemala participates in the international fashion scene and thereby signals its sophistication in such worldly matters.

Among Tecpanecos, however, I never got the slightest impression that Europe mattered: status commodities come from the United States, as reflected in this children's game played in Tecpán:

A: Where are you coming from?
B: From New York.
A: What did you bring?
B: Something really nice.
A: What letter does it start with?
B: With ____. [names the first letter of the object; *A* then tries to guess the object][13]

There seem to be several reasons for this particular view as it pertains to clothing. First, the United States figures in (and often dominates) much more than just fashion news. In the realm of politics, the United States has a persistent presence in activities that regularly command media attention. Throughout 1980, U.S.-dominated news events included the U.S. hostage situation in Iran, the U.S. boycott of the Moscow Olympics, and the Carter-Reagan presidential race. Many Tecpanecos not only knew about these current events, they also held the opinion that some U.S. issues (foreign aid, for example) concerned Guatemala directly and in a potentially adverse manner. Somewhat ironically, this view was particularly prevalent among younger people and those with more education—that is, just those most likely to associate the United States (and associate it positively) with the latest in fashions.

Apart from indirect and impersonal ties, several families have personal connections with the United States. A handful of Tecpán families have relatives living in the States; others have family members who have traveled there (as students, for professional reasons, and, in the case of one indigenous man, as a government representative); and nearly everyone can lay claim to knowing someone who knows someone who has visited there at least once. Part of the reason for this frequency of travel is that the United States lies relatively close to Guatemala, as airline advertisements stress. Travel abroad is within the budget of very few but is not unheard of in Tecpán. In fact, at the start of my field stay a young teacher from Chimaltenango who worked in Tecpán had just returned from a trip to Miami. Her first account of activities abroad consisted solely of naming different articles of clothing that she and a friend had bought on sale in discount stores at one-quarter of the price being asked in the more fashionable Guatemala City boutiques, where only recently the items had become available.

Proximity, however, cannot be the only criterion for the appeal of the place or else Mexico and all the other countries of Central America would be equally (or more) enticing. Rather, the United States is seen as both categorically different from and better than the nations of Latin America. It is something of a fabled place where quality products of high technology and fashion are born (as illustrated in the children's game); it is the fountainhead of progress and abundance, the shape of things to come in Guatemala.

Thus, a visit to the United States may be considered a journey not only through space but through time as well. Traveling there, a person can almost literally leap forward months, if not years, to buy the products of Guatemala's future. Many people are aware that when an item is popular in the United States, only mention of it reaches Guatemala; and when the product finally arrives in local markets, its fashionableness in the United States has probably already worn thin (see also Friedlander 1975: 71). But this fact is not always regrettable. For the fortunate few who can travel to the United States, passé items are cheap and readily available, and, by merely carrying them home, the Guatemalan purchaser can transform them into scarce luxury goods. However, most people cannot take advantage of this time lag to tap into cheap sources of desirable objects. Instead, they are left with knowledge of this situation, one that signals, once again, that Guatemala is in a subordinate position and, in effect, *abandonado* in the larger world.

When the rare Tecpaneco has the chance to travel abroad, he or she generally does so as the purchasing representative for whole families and networks of friends. Requests are many and orders quite detailed in terms of brand names, styles, and prices. For many, requests are restricted to the small consumer pieces (such as clothing and electrical appliances) that are within the price range of most people at some point in their lives; others want and can afford big-ticket items. Whatever the product, strong opinions are common and reasons for buying one brand rather than another quite detailed.[14]

While foreign markets are preferred, access is rare; so Tecpanecos generally look to Guatemala City as the best place inside the country to buy manufactured items such as *vestido*. Within the shops and stores of the capital, quality local goods and foreign products are readily available, though sometimes for a sizable price. Given the choice between similar products—one local in origin and the other from the United States (or Europe)—Guatemalans tend to favor the latter. Capitalizing on such preferences, local manufacturers make use of plays on foreign brand names, either to imply a close association between the two products or to fool the unsuspecting buyer. A hand cream called "Oil of Ulay" and a chocolate bar in a distinctive brown wrapper labeled "Milky Best" are but two examples of this. Lifting an exact product name, logo and all, is just an extreme version of this ploy, as I discovered when I uncovered a case of shoes fraudulently labeled with a popular U.S. trademark.

U.S. manufacturers, likewise, turn cultural preferences into financial gain when they dump items that do not sell well at home onto the markets of poorer nations. America's leftovers—in the shape of John Travolta handbags and Pink Panther T-shirts—are commonly sold on the streets of Guatemala City or in marketplaces throughout the country. That these are not wanted in the United States but are considered good enough for Guatemala is seen locally as further evidence of the Central American nation's position in the western hierarchical scheme.

After Guatemala City, Tecpanecos think of Chimaltenango, the department capital, as the next best location for certain goods and services. Chimaltenango, for example, is often regarded as better than Tecpán but not as good as Guatemala City for some services and supplies (e.g., schools, banks, government services, and medical facilities; medicines, fertilizers, and photographic supplies). However, as far as clothing goes, it holds relatively little status. Only some raw materials (e.g., cloth and knitting supplies) and selected finished items (e.g., shoes and shirts) are said to be found in slightly greater variety, with more attractive styles, and at cheaper prices than in Tecpán. Tecpanecos, however, generally do not think of making specific trips to Chimaltenango to shop for clothes and so, on this count, the city is pretty much ignored.

There are three principal options for *vestido* in Tecpán: *ropa ya hecho* (ready-made clothes with factory labels), tailor-made clothes, and homemade pieces. The ready-made items are available in several of the small stores in town as well as from market vendors on Thursdays and Sundays. In addition, Tecpán has a number of small clothing factories that produce knitted sweaters, for which the town is known, and men's shirts. The outlet shops connected to these factories offer a wide selection of colors and styles within a narrow range of clothing articles and contrast with the market stalls and permanent shops, which offer a wide range of clothes but little variety in styles.

If the prices, styles, colors, or fabrics of the ready-made clothing are not satisfactory, a person can take some fabric and a picture or a description of a garment to an experienced tailor. Although most of the work of these craftspeople is the routine construction of pants, jackets, skirts, and shirts, some are also capable of reproducing a radically different style. By commissioning skilled tailors to produce items in the mold of the latest styles, Tecpanecos signal their awareness of developments in the capital and abroad, if not their ability to locate or pay for the "real" item.[15]

People who make their own clothing might also try to copy popular fashion items and succeed quite nicely. However, homemade clothing, which can look particularly "rough hewn" for a number of reasons, can also have very negative connotations, which grow out of its association with the lower class and with rural areas of Guatemala that are isolated from retail sources. Thus homemade dress may conjure up images of cheaper materials sewn on treadle sewing machines, the result being an item that totally lacks tailoring and finishing touches. While a particular sewer's efforts might escape this characterization, in general homemade clothing is the least desirable of all *vestido*.

Traje and Vestido

Both Indians and ladinos in Tecpán are critics of people who believe too fervently that "higher up is better" in the scale I just described. They comment negatively on individuals who chase after name-brand items and create financial difficulties for their families because of their desires. They also find it humorous when an item that is currently fashionable in Guatemala City, but (to them) totally inappropriate for Tecpán, becomes popular in town because of its associations with Guatemala City's "highlife" (an English loan word used in Guatemala). I recall, for example, the appearance of high-heeled platform shoes on Tecpán's bumpy dirt streets. Advertisements for clothes, or anything else, are often regarded cynically as trumped-up claims made only in the interest of greater profits. A person will mention an article of clothes he or she bought in the capital on the strength of a sign, label, or logo claiming or implying the U.S. origin of the piece. Too often the point of the story is the rapid demise of the item—faded after two washings, shrunken beyond use, or broken in six months. One common conclusion is that the product was only an imitation of some better and more costly article that really does exist. Tecpanecos thus feel themselves preyed upon because they value these higher-status items but either are unable to distinguish real from fake or are too poor to afford "the real thing" even if available.

When ladinos (and here I am thinking principally of educated ladinos living in Tecpán, who tend to be more verbal on this subject) analyze this sort of situation, it is common for them to bemoan the place of Guatemala within the world economic system. For example, a teacher described to me the presence of tax-free enterprise zones near the capital where shirts with U.S. brand names are assembled. Upon completion, these shirts are immediately sent to the United States without giving Guatemalans, even the ones who made them, a chance to buy the fruits of their labor. To her, this situation was representative of a more general one in which Guatemala and Guatemalans rank in the lower class in a worldwide economic-cum-geographical hierarchy. *Vestido*, then, reflects in miniature the structure of the larger system.

For Maya who speak in similar terms, the analysis does not stop here. They, too, feel that Guatemala lacks global status because of its poor economic standing. However, within Guatemala they see a further ranking, with Indians consistently subordinate to ladinos because of ethnic or cultural prejudices. In terms of clothes, Indians play into this larger system of subordination when they abandon *traje* and take up *vestido*. One of a series of inspirational messages adorning calendars published by a group of culturally active Maya summarizes this sentiment: "When we renounce our Maya *traje*, we are renouncing our own being" ("*Al renunciar a nuestros trajes mayas, estamos renunciando a ser nosotros mismos*"; Editorial Maya Wuj 1991, my translation).[16] Abandoning *traje* means that a Maya is thrown into the ranking system of *vestido*, where people who are Guatemalan Indians are doubly damned on national and ethnic grounds, for economic and cultural reasons.

However, all sorts of Maya, from the most isolated rural dweller to the activist working for the revitalization movement in Guatemala City, wear at least some articles of clothing considered *vestido* and often do so for very positive reasons. These can range from women's sweaters and men's jackets, to underwear, to certain types of men's and women's shoes, to whole wardrobes for men. I would also suggest that hybrids of *vestido* and *traje* be considered here—the jacket used by men in the Maya revitalization movement seems a good example. While markedly "Indian," there are many aspects of these items that appeal to Maya for the same reasons that they appeal to ladinos. And while there are risks for Indians who wear common clothes (for example, if they are judged to be imitating styles poorly or trying too hard to be "ladino"), there are also definite rewards for those living in a highly ladinoized world.

In recent years, a growing number of Maya have been actively voicing the idea that *traje* should be worn proudly, with a clear awareness of its power to represent both local highland communities and Guatemalan Maya as a whole. The 1980 Tecpán *traje* presentation was just such a public event. Warnings not to abandon *traje* and not to teach non-Maya how to weave were mixed with encouragements to wear *traje* and keep weaving traditions alive. A more recent articulation of some of these sentiments appears in additional inspirational messages published by Editorial Maya Wuj (1991, my translation):

> Each town has its own *traje* . . . Will we let Maya *traje* disappear from the face of the earth? [*Cada pueblo tiene sus trajes propios . . . ¿Dejaremos nosotros que los trajes mayas desaparezcan de la faz de la tierra?*]

> To wear Maya *traje* is to accept the challenge to fight for a multilingual and multicultural Guatemala. [*Vestir traje Maya es aceptar el reto de luchar por una Guatemala multilingüe y multicultural.*]

> Maya girls and boys have the right to be Guatemalan citizens without disowning their Maya *traje* and culture. [*Las niñas y los niños mayas tienen derecho a ser ciudadanos guatemaltecos, sin que se les niegue su traje y su cultura Mayas.*]

> To promote the use of Maya *traje* is to maintain and revitalize our Maya cultural identity. [*Fomentar el uso de los trajes mayas es mantener y revitalizar nuestra identidad cultural Maya.*]

These words convey succinctly important themes about *traje*, heritage, and a Maya sense of place.

THREE

THE ENDURING INDIAN
Images of the Maya

A tapestry woven in colors . . . surrounds you each minute of your happy vacation in Guatemala. Nature has blessed this peaceful republic with green hills, dense flowery forests, deep blue seas, mountain lakes, and sun-filled tropical skies. The Indian cultures and traditions offer flashy costumes, exotic plumages, woven articles, and the colorfulness and excitement of the native dances and spectacles. The Spanish colonial architecture presents a marked contrast with the ingenious buildings of the ancient Maya Indians [Indios Mayas], and all blend happily and subtly so as to create a vacation land, superior in atmosphere and delightful in entertainment.

GUATEMALA EN CENTRO AMERICA
(INGUAT 1980A, MY TRANSLATION)

[And for the criollos *(the locally born descendants of the Europeans)] the Indian is there as something that exists together with the land and exists in order to work it . . . . In the homeland of the* criollo *the Indian is and ought to be the complement of the land.*

LA PATRIA DEL CRIOLLO
(MARTÍNEZ PELÁEZ 1979: 255–256, MY TRANSLATION)

In Guatemala, images of the Indian are constructed, marketed, praised, manipulated, and denounced at the local, national, and international levels. Among those engaging in such activities are, on the one hand, the national government itself (through institutional actions), individuals representing the government, and members of society whose personal proclivities generally align them with what can be taken to be a government stand and then, on the other, those who see themselves falling outside of or in opposition to the above categories. While "ladino" certainly does not always translate into the former, dominant group and "Indian" into the latter, subordinate group, these terms nonetheless reflect the general polarization of the material associated with *traje*. Refinement will come as I examine not only the range of images—the variety of concrete instances of "the Indian" made public—but also the nature of the representations, the composition of the groups that produce them, the work that the images do (or are supposed to do) for those employing them, and the comments these elicit from those who define themselves as *indígena* under all circumstances.

As with material in the last chapter, the classifications of the Indian that I examine here point to models of the construction of Guatemalan society and the relation between the two principal ethnic groups. Within this set of images, society is seen as composed of interrelated peoples, on the one hand, or autonomous units, on the other. Likewise, it is characterized by the unity created by a common history and heritage or a disunity bred from conflict and centuries of domination. Furthermore, indigenous attributes are seen as natural, even biologically based, on the one hand, or imposed from the outside by nonindigenous sources, on the other.

Finally, each image of the Indian is seen to have a judgmental or evaluative aspect. Thus, for example, Tecpán youths moving out into the larger social world speak of coming to know the "reality" of life in Guatemala. This coming-to-know speaks of their growing awareness of the political dimensions of highland life and of the full range of classificatory schemes that shape and label Indian existence. This is a knowledge of when, where, and how the "given" of any social situation is likely to be construed as conforming to one particular image or another. What is more, it goes along with an ability to work around or through these stereotypes (i.e., representations recognized as incomplete or somehow untrue) in an effort to control and shape not only one's personal life as a Maya but the larger construction of the image of the Indian in Guatemala.[1]

The Image and Its Object

In *The Colors of Rhetoric*, Wendy Steiner examines the relationship between the verbal and visual arts, and between each of these and the reality it depicts. In this context she characterizes Charles Peirce's three types of icons—the image as "a sign which *substantially* replicates its object," the diagram as "a sign whose *relations* replicate those of its objects," and the metaphor as "a sign that represents what Peirce terms the 'representative character' of another sign through a *parallelism*" (Steiner 1982: 20)—and adds that Peirce, by labeling these "hypoicons," notes the conventional nature of all three. Thus, the image, far from distinguishing itself from the diagram and metaphor by representing its object in every possible way, instead represents it to a point that satisfies the dictates of a particular time and people. Gombrich (1972: 90), speaking on a similar theme, notes that images (visual images, portrayals, pictures, and so on) represent their objects to whatever degree of accuracy is required for the particular purpose at hand.

While I do not mean to adhere too closely to a technical, Peircean notion of the image for the materials I examine, the implications of such a characterization are valuable nonetheless. An image and what it represents contain within its standing-for relationship a judgment that, for somebody, under some circumstance, and for some particular purpose, the "degree of accuracy" of the representation is adequate or correct. In fact, if the image is accepted as so perfectly representing its object, the line between the two can become largely invisible and the image can be taken (or offered up) as actually *being* the thing. On the other hand, if the criteria for representation are not agreed upon, what is an acceptable image for one group can be a horrible distortion for another, and conflict may arise around this point.

The images of which Gombrich and Steiner speak are conventional visual ones (e.g., paintings, woodcuts) as well as, in Steiner's work, the verbal images of literature. In the case of *traje*, I will be concerned with a wider assortment of representations—photographs, descriptions in tourist brochures, performances for public holidays, appearances in beauty pageants, and the like—with the Indian as the common theme. Nonetheless, each of these images has a conventional form, something bracketed or framed off as a separate entity geared for public consumption. What is more, each is put to work as an act of definition or persuasion—defining what it is to be Indian in Guatemala or persuading a particular group that the image being conveyed is an adequate representation of the Maya people. In cases in which the Guatemalan government or its allies are attempting to maintain cultural hegemony, the notion of an "adequate representation" of the Indian will take on the added dimension of a "natural representation"—one that presents itself as complete and true, for both ladinos and Indians alike. The flip side, of course, is that people, indigenous people in particular, can fail to be persuaded or to agree with the wholeness and truth of one expression and can move to present their own (see also Hebdige 1983; Scott 1985). Such is, in fact, the case in Guatemala, where a struggle involving images of the Indian is being waged on a number of fronts, not with guns and bullets but with tourist brochures, festival presentations, and beauty queens.

Non-Indian Perspectives

Non-Indians from the national level on down embrace Indians as "us" in expressions of Guatemalan national identity. Despite the claim of one Guatemalan author (Guzmán Böckler 1975: 101) that, among ladinos, there is no such thing as "*nosotros los Guatemaltecos*" (we Guatemalans), non-Indian citizens routinely embrace the spirit of the Indian as their own and, in fact, proclaim themselves of the same historical essence (if not always of the same blood). This embrace is often visually marked by the use of *traje*, which beautifully sums up their pride in national-cum-ethnic heritage.

On the international level, the use of indigenous (material) culture as *the* image of Guatemalan national identity is seen yearly in the Miss Universe contest. Each year, INGUAT sponsors a local pageant and the (ladino) woman who is elected Miss Guatemala represents her country in the world competition, decked out in Guatemala's "national costume"—*traje*. In 1975, Miss Guatemala won the national costume division of the contest and was heralded internationally as having the most beautiful outfit in the world: she was wearing a ceremonial *traje* from Nebaj, a town renowned by ladinos and Indians alike for its striking *sobre huipiles*. Subsequent to this, INGUAT distributed masses of posters and postcards showing the young contestant—white-skinned, heavily made up, and posing like a Paris model—radiant in indigenous dress. The point of all the publicity was clear: the honor was something for all Guatemalans to be proud of. Guatemala had been selected above all other countries of the world and recognized for its unique cultural wealth. Its rich Maya heritage, as symbolized by the clothing, defined Guatemala's identity and presented the nation in a positive light.

Strictly national audiences likewise embrace Maya culture. For example, February 20 is the day set aside to honor Tecún Umán, the K'iche' Maya warrior defeated by the conquering Spaniards. Proclamations emanating from the capital herald him as ancestor of all—"the symbol of American man" created "without distinguishing between Indian or ladino" (*El Gráfico* 1980c: 6, my translation). While Tecún Umán appears in Tecpán as the subject of school plays and a key character in the Dance of the Conquest, it is really only in the capital that February 20 is celebrated at length.

It was also in Guatemala City in 1959 that three prominent professionals founded the Committee for the Exaltation of the National Hero of Guatemala.[2] Their purpose was to extol the memory of Tecún Umán, and they claimed that "to deny him [his existence] is to deny our own national essence" (*El Gráfico* 1980d: 5, my translation).[3] Tecún Umán, therefore, is properly praised each year by public servants, military regiments, and schoolchildren, and laudatory articles appear in the national newspapers:

> Tecún Umán, the warrior prince, is not only a national hero, but the symbol of Guatemalan nationality: he is the image of the honorable warrior who dies in the defense of his territory. But also he is the symbol of American nationality: of the American man—that is to say, of the man who populated this continent before the arrival of Columbus . . . of the mixture [*mestizaje*] produced by the encounter and the fusion of two different ethnic groups: the indigenous Guatemalan and the Spaniard. In him we venerate our indigenous ancestor—part of our essence; in him we venerate the heroic defender of the land of his ancestors and his children; in him we venerate the dignity of a people who succumbed to . . . the better troops of a more technically and scientifically developed continent, but not without presenting heroic resistance, paying the price with his life.
>
> (EL GRÁFICO 1980C: 6, MY TRANSLATION)

Although this account of the subjugation of the Indian population carries themes of the subordination of indigenous culture, the irony of the subsequent praise of Tecún Umán is not acknowledged by the author. Rather, the point stressed is that Tecún Umán, as primordial Guatemalan being, may have been "just" an Indian, but through death, the conquest of his people, and resurrection as national hero, he is transformed. By dominating the autochthonous leader, the Spanish, in fact, liberate him from representing just one of the opposing sides and elevate him so that he stands for a whole new society, the unity of which is suggested to be the principal product of the conflict.[4]

It is not just at the national level or for foreign audiences that ladinos wrap themselves in *traje* and embrace or "become" the Indian as an expression of what it is to be Guatemalan. This symbolic use of the indigenous person and traditional dress is also employed in the highlands, in contexts where Indians themselves are present in much greater numbers. For example, at a ceremony for the regional office of the Ministry of Agriculture in Chimaltenango, stage walls and the table for featured dignitaries were covered with Indian shawls and *corte* cloth. In this environment, ladino speakers discussing government-supported local projects appealed to an ethnically mixed audience to cooperate "as Chimaltecos" (here meaning residents of the entire department) and "as Guatemalans."

Mention of allegiances to bounded geographical units and the visual presence of artifacts that were meant to be taken as unique to Guatemala, in general, and to the Chimaltenango area, in particular, helped stress the unity of those addressed and served to contradict (or camouflage) the growing evidence of sociopolitical tensions and conflicts in that area of the highlands. In addition, because all the pieces had strong associations with women and because women, in turn, are symbolically associated with the domestic sphere, both the Indian population and Guatemalans-as-Indians were portrayed as essentially apolitical, creating an atmosphere that removed the audience from the sociopolitical reality of the highlands at that time.

As suggested by the previous examples, the "ritual" use of *traje* (especially women in *traje*) by ladinos can be a powerful means for tactically constructing a space where common interests are expressed. At the local highland level the presence of indigenous dress can be even more laden with meaning owing to the large number of common experiences and shared pragmatic assumptions of participants and members of the audience. A particularly telling example of this function of *traje* concerns another queen contest, this one a pageant preceding the celebration of the Tecpán fair in 1983. It was a little more than two years after the town first began experiencing the waves of killings and disappearances that had touched other municipalities to the north and west of Tecpán throughout 1980 and 1981. The separate Indigenous Fair Committee that had organized the *traje* exhibit for the 1980 fair no longer existed, and in its place was a unified body of ladinos and Indians who planned activities together and who were meant to represent the interests of all Tecpanecos. The fair committee had operated in this form up until the mid-1970s. At that time, some of the Maya leaders began to feel that inequalities between the two ethnic groups were being perpetuated by the committee, which, as if a microcosm of all society, was dominated by its ladino members. For example, every year there is both an Indian and a ladino queen of the fair. However, in the early 1970s the Indian fair queen, known officially as Princesa Iximché, Reina Indígena (Princess Iximché, Indigenous Queen), was given Q50.00 to spend on her festival *traje* while the ladino queen, known as Reina de las Fiestas Franciscanas (Queen of the Franciscan Fiestas), was given Q100.00 for what the Maya population considered intrinsically less expensive clothes. As a consequence of this and other perceived injustices, the indigenous segment split off into a separate organization with its own budget, planning committee, and events. What were once rivalries within a single group turned into rivalries between groups as each organization vied to hire the best marimba band for fair dances or attract the largest audience at programs.[5]

The two committees existed separately into 1981. However, in the weeks and months following the murder of the town priest in May of that year, a number of the Tecpán Indian leaders were killed and others were forced to leave suddenly. The effect was a decline in the leadership of Indian organizations (fewer people were willing to assume power or even participate), and organizations such as the Ixmucané Youth Circle and the Indigenous Professional Association ceased to exist.[6] The Indigenous Fair Committee simply reverted to the earlier structure by joining with the ladino group.

In September 1983, the newly reconstituted group presented its first major activity—La Primera Fiesta Folklórica de Tecpán (Tecpán's First Folkloric Festival). The event was sponsored by Maybelline—"Cosmético Oficial/Concurso Miss Universo" (Official Cosmetic/Miss Universe Contest), as a banner over the stage proclaimed. Because the event was largely a queen competition, twelve young candidates were the focus of the show: six young ladino women, one of whom would become Reina de las Fiestas Franciscanas, and six young indigenous women, one of whom would be crowned Princesa Iximché (the indigenous fair queen) and another Princesa Ixmucané, Reina del Agricultor (Queen of the Farmers).[7] For their first appearance of the evening, all twelve candidates—Indians and non-Indians alike—dressed in *traje*, the former all in the oldest, most traditional Tecpán outfits, with *sobre huipiles* and the *penecita* skirts, and the latter in contemporary *traje* from Tecpán or, in one case, Chichicastenango. In retrospect, this differential use of Maya dress seems understandable, not only from a practical point of view—the older pieces are not always part of an indigenous family's possessions, let alone those of a ladino family— but also in terms of messages each group wished to communicate. While the Indian women showed a respect for their heritage and a knowledge of local customs, the ladino women, in effect, were admitting that their relation to Maya tradition was more superficial. It was enough for them simply to appear in any contemporary outfit to acknowledge the current attempts at solidarity between the two ethnic groups. This sentiment, in fact, emerged as the emcee stressed in rather dramatic rhetorical terms that the goal of the unified celebration was to celebrate "*nuestra Guatemalidad*" (our Guatemala-ity or Guatemala-ness) and, what most hoped for but some doubted possible, a restoration of peace and good relations in the town.[8]

However, Maya dress does not have to be worn by ladinos (as in the Miss Universe contest) or by ladinos and Indians in tandem (as in the Tecpán presentation) in order to be seen as representing all Guatemalans. In the travel literature produced by INGUAT as well as private enterprises, attractive photographs of Indians introduce potential visitors to the warm and friendly people of Guatemala—"pleasant people," "smiling people," as the brochures point out—who welcome foreign tourists to their country and Guatemalan tourists to the exotic reaches of their own land. These Indians join with images of volcanoes, mountain lakes, ancient ruins, colonial architecture, and weavings; and all these symbols of national identity are shown as exhibiting a passive beauty that the beholder may contemplate much like an object of art. All, it is suggested, remain untouched as a visitor passes through their midst.

Photographs that emphasize this friendly manner typically feature close-ups of faces—often of children, a revealing reflection of the producers' attitude toward the larger population (cf. Dumont 1988: 270)—or medium-range shots of people ready to serve. Waiters, waitresses, hotel clerks, vendors with mounds of handcrafted items, marimba players, and artisans (some in *traje*, others not) beam out from the page and beckon the visitor.

28. An advertisement illustrated with an Indian woman in Quezaltenango *traje*, 1992. This image, painted on a bar in San Felipe, Retalhuleu, is being used to advertise liquor; a slogan to the left of the door reads, "Our liquor, our tradition."

Indians in this context are smiling and alert, though, in my experience, they would not assume these poses were the photographs for their own private use. But then these photographs are not within their subjects' control. They belong to the entrepreneurs behind the camera, serve business and government interests, are designed to appeal to the vacation-seeking foreigner or national, and fit a formula for tourist brochure images that is used internationally. The intent, then, is to have the photographs function publicly as statements that convince outsiders that Indians as "all Guatemalans" are excitingly different and, at the same time, extremely approachable (cf. Albers and James 1983). Simultaneously they function to counter news reports of violence in the country and to convince the would-be visitor of the peace of the people and the land.

Maya textiles also play an important role in the tourist experience. Tourist brochures, a form of national advertisement, are filled with their intense colors, intricate designs, and handwoven textures. The viewer sees these images, and a common response is "desire," not only for the cloth itself but also for a "look" (Goldman 1992: 24) that I call "primitive glamour."[9] In Guatemala these abstract desires can be fulfilled in the marketplace, where weavings, silverwork, pottery, wooden carvings, tinware, and more may be purchased and photographs taken, then carried home as material reminders of a trip. Textiles are particularly appealing purchases. Fashioned into clothing and layered onto the body, they transform their Indian subject into a particularly colorful and exotic sight; yet, at the same time, they can be detached from the person and transported home as souvenirs. Worn by non-Indians in nonhighland contexts, items of *traje* (especially used clothing, with its patina of use by "real Indians") become costumes that carry with them and bestow upon their wearer some of the aura of the highland experience.[10]

There is, however, another aspect of the indigenous Guatemalan portrayed in the tourist literature that begins to move the reader away from the image of the Indian as symbol for all that is Guatemalan—both Indian and non-Indian—to an image of the Indian as a unique being, essentially different from the nonindigenous half of the population. This feeling is perhaps most elaborately, publicly, and positively expressed in tourist literature. In these pieces, the Indians who are not in service roles are shown engaged in what are meant to be seen as culturally specific activities: worshiping at stone altars or in dark, candle-filled churches; weaving on backstrap looms; and carrying water jugs, large baskets, or other unwieldy objects on their heads. Unlike the aforementioned photographs, in which locals are shown interacting either with tourists in the scene or, by means of eye contact, with the viewer of the photograph, this second type of image is meant to be viewed from afar, like some awesome scenery that is admired but little comprehended.[11]

Perhaps more than in the photography, the texts of tourist literature describe the Indian as being distinct and categorically different from the visitor. Examples will help illustrate how the Indian is portrayed:

[The tropical growth in Guatemala] is an almost human vegetation. Human because it explodes and lives with rapid vigorous movements and with expressions which are similar to the . . . animal world. For all of it is mystery, it is suggestive and provokes myths and legends. In a world like this man becomes an interrogator and believes god-like answers and myths similar to the nature which surrounds him.

In this environment the Mayan culture was born. It is not a serene culture as is the Greek which is a product of clear islands and transparent seas but rather baroque in its widest sense, which means to say: confused, full of mystery and dark and terrible legends.

(INGUAT 1980B)

The place [Chichicastenango] is full of people, incense, prayers, and many fragrances. Voices praying to the Christian God in the Quiche Language, asking for the same things that they implored their heathen gods many years ago. An enormous amount of textiles and local articles, shirts, ponchos (woolen blankets), fabrics, hats, wooden carvings, and pottery. Typical cobbled streets, old churches tarnished by the patina of old age and above all, the purest presence of the Guatemalan indian, who without his taking into consideration the presence of strangers, reveals a little of his enigmatic nature.

(PHOTO-STUDIO CANCHE SERRA 1980: 7)

The same themes—even the same words, at times—are repeated in other passages and stress the bonds between the Maya and their mysterious past, the Indian's unchanging quality, the ties between *los naturales* and *la naturaleza* (nature), and the gap between Indians and nonindigenous people.[12]

While some aspects of Indian nature emphasized in the tourist material relate to features recognized by the Maya themselves, essential differences exist between the two. For example, ties with the past are stressed in both the tourist literature and by the Maya. Yet, while the former emphasizes the unchanging nature of this relationship, the indigenous people stress a continuity with the past that is based on a thoughtful, creative reproduction of traditional themes and that fits into a broader, coherent, and culturally rational vision of the social world. By contrast, the image projected by the tourist material is one of mysteriousness akin to irrationality—a spirit closer to nature than other human beings (compare, for example, the pairing of Indians with "almost human vegetation"); a lack of awareness of other, nonindigenous forms of being; and adherence to the past that is automatic instead of conscious and purposeful. Indians are not seen as having a vision of society that is equally valid to (although different from) that of non-Indians; rather they are seen as different, puzzling, and essentially limited beings.

In Tecpán, public expressions of negative sentiments about Indians are rather rare (much more so than I had anticipated).[13] When they do occur, it is almost always in private conversations between persons who already know the other's sentiments, in more public situations where at least one party (often the outspoken one) is foreign to the area, or in episodes involving alcohol.[14] The infrequency of more open or direct statements should not seem entirely surprising in a community where Indians and ladinos live and work side by side, where a certain level of integration of ladinos and Indians exists in all aspects of life, where there is genuine friendship between individuals (students, in particular, mention this), and where the general community sentiment is that ethnic relations are better in Tecpán than in many surrounding towns.

However, not all Tecpán ladinos who speak well of Indians do so from a sense of friendship. As one woman put it, many are "speaking with masks on." People with political power, in particular, are criticized for saying one thing publicly but then acting on very different principles— for example, praising the Indian contribution to local life and then being implicated in the death of a local Maya leader. Given this discrepancy between what one says in public and what one does, it was all the more surprising and memorable when, in the late 1970s, Tecpán's ladino mayor publicly proclaimed that Indians are the "*escalas*" (ladders) for ladinos trying to better themselves. And if the comment itself were not enough, its context was the Indigenous Fair Committee's queen contest. That is, the speaker made the claim in his official capacity as mayor in front of an almost exclusively indigenous audience—one expecting to hear the usual government-sponsored rhetoric in praise of Maya culture. The violation of the normal etiquette for public appearances (and, some would say, the *public* admission of what normally lies just below the spoken surface) so jolted the indigenous community that years later the episode remains a prime example for Tecpán Maya of what motivates ladino actions against the indigenous segment of the population: a desire for wealth, an elevated sociopolitical position, and control over others.

Maya Perspectives

Indigenous portrayals of the Indian range from a negative self-image that Maya see forced on them by virtue of their position in Guatemalan society to a positive view of a group of people practicing *costumbre*, holding responsible jobs, and attempting to create or maintain some sphere of action (albeit one limited in range) dominated by Maya values. Because all too often the former is the reality of highland life and the latter but an ideal, the most positive expressions of being Maya generally appear as individual acts, private interactions restricted to the domestic scene, and small public performances with no overt political themes. To that list should be added the work of the growing number of Maya professionals whose job responsibilities and civic activities give them a certain visibility at the regional and national levels, where they are seen as intelligent, skilled, responsible, *and* Maya.

Indigenous Guatemalans condemn the fact that all too often when ladinos appear to embrace the Indian, it is only their words that speak of some true union: their deeds, on the other hand, result in the hierarchical ordering of people. These sentiments are pronounced frequently in Tecpán and even appeared in a published interview with a Tecpán Indian fair queen. *Tecpanidad* (T), a local magazine that was published between 1977 and 1980, featured a conversation with the 1978–1979 Princess Ixmucané (P) in which the young Maya woman stressed the vacuousness of a ladino queen's claims.

T: What can you tell us about the Queen of the Franciscan Fiestas?
P: I can say that she is nice. I heard in her speech that she wants to work with everybody. Let's hope that's true. But, for example, last year's queen, from the moment that they're in front of the public they're claiming they really like Indians, that we ought to work together, but they're only words. When it comes down to what they do, they always try to marginalize [us].
T: Do you mean that there is racial discrimination?
P: We can't say there's a true union, although they claim there is

one, because, when it comes right down to it, it's another story.
(AJOZAL XUYÁ 1979-1980: 22, MY TRANSLATION)[15]

Maya feel that through their actions ladinos order the social world, and inevitably the position allotted Indians is a low one. Dress, seen in this context, does not function as it does in tourism—that is, as a commodity that entices foreigners to visit the highlands and buy into the whole image of Guatemala. Neither does *traje* stand for all Guatemalans as a visually beautiful statement of national heritage. Rather, it points to the class status of the wearer and marks him or her as someone less than the non-Indian viewers. This idea is made very explicit in the following passage, in which the editor of a Maya newspaper in Comalapa reacts to her treatment at a ladino event:

> Don't tell me that you don't look down on me, don't lie to me and tell me that my *huipil*, my skirt, my *tocoyal* [a woven band plaited into a woman's hair] and my sandals don't humiliate you and spoil your splendid gala balls. Don't you remember that you showed me how you felt? Yes, of course, you must remember it . . . my offense was so great, very great because I dared to tread on your impeccable floors with my Indian sandals, I committed the sin of mingling with you when I was dressed, not in a beautiful maxi, like yours, but in a *huipil* and *corte*. (MARÍA ALICIA TELÓN SAJCABÚN, IN ANTHONY 1974: 36)

While certain articles of women's *traje* can be selected to create or maintain a positive image of the wearer in many situations (high-quality *huipiles* and *cortes* tend to have this effect, though perhaps not in the Comalapa example), other items do not have this social flexibility. *Caites* (the Indians sandals just mentioned), made with leather straps and tire-tread soles, are one such item. While these are used to the person's benefit when the wearer wants to signal "traditional dress" (in a pageant or special celebration, for example), they are also associated with rural areas, more informal spheres, and "*abuelitas*" (little grandmothers, but here with the sense of "little old ladies").

As I have mentioned, Maya men in the Tecpán area, especially younger men, generally do not wear *traje*. One reason frequently given for this is that indigenous men are discriminated against in the workplace and that appearing in *traje* only makes the situation worse by making their identity explicit. It seems to me, however, that an explanation must go beyond this since most Maya women who work outside the home continue to wear *traje* and do not seem to think that abandoning indigenous dress would change their work situation.

I would suggest that the discrimination arises in part because of the differential assessment of *traje* in terms of gender: the image of a Maya man in *traje* is categorically different from that of a Maya woman in *traje*. Women's indigenous dress is thought of as extremely fine and thus is an admired expression of female beauty. Painstakingly handcrafted in a bright array of colors and complemented with jewelry, ribbons, and elaborate hair accessories, women's *traje* conforms to (or appears to make reference to) "Western" standards of femininity, female loveliness, and a nonproductive consumption of wealth. And, while ladinas do not wear it on a daily basis, they can admire it and even incorporate pieces (*huipiles* mostly) into daytime or evening outfits. Male *traje*, on the other hand, does not contain elements that resonate with the sartorial expression of masculinity according to the fashion hierarchy of *vestido*. Outfits incorporating such items as calf-length striped pants decorated with bird designs and multicolored woven cloth wrapped around the head contrast sharply with such preferred male items of common clothes as blue jeans, cowboy boots, and flannel, button-down shirts. The effect, then, is not only to label a man in *traje* as "Indian" but also to see him as one who is less masculine (even less adult) in a world dominated by non-Maya values.

But, as we have seen, Indian men in *traje* are not always portrayed negatively in ladino-dominated spheres. In tourist literature and festival presentations, the image of the Indian male in traditional dress gets special attention and abundant praise. However, this positive image, some Maya charge, is not what it seems on the surface. Rather, it points to a victimization of the people being praised, so Indians become commodities in the capitalist scheme of the larger world, an arrangement that benefits the non-Indian upper class and not Indians themselves. Thus, *traje* is or is not laudable, beautiful, and unique, is or is not dirty, crude, and lower-class according to how it suits the money-making situation. *Traje* on an Indian in one of the highland tourist spots is good because it is good for tourism; *traje* on an Indian working as a migrant laborer on the coast is, at best, irrelevant to getting the job done—but perhaps not irrelevant to supplying clues about the supposed (lack of) intelligence, sensitivity, or abilities of the wearers.

Maya commentators regularly claim to feel the presence and force of negative public images generated, instituted, and preserved by non-Indians, and they disagree heartily with these. In Tecpán, the most articulate and explicit pronouncements generally come from younger, more educated, more publicly active, and more nationally aware members of the indigenous population, individuals with a strong sense of how actions and the physical presentation of self can be perceived and interpreted by a wide range of observers. The most vocal are also those who often take the risk of damning the image-producers and the system that perpetuates a particular image or set of images of the Indian for its own ends. For example, a particularly strong statement was issued by a group of politically and socially active, indigenous Guatemalans who joined together at Iximche' shortly after the massacre at the Spanish Embassy. The massacre—the killing of thirty-nine people on 31 January 1980 after a delegation of Maya and Maya supporters went to the Spanish Embassy with a list of grievances—became a symbol for the general victimization of Maya by the government and its associated forces. In the following portion of the Declaration of Iximché, the authors—a number of whom were subsequently killed as part of the violence—protest the public portrayals of Indians and label their victimization a "massacre." The authors of the statement have a well-developed notion of how indigenous people are being used in the capitalist system, where being Indian is either glorified to turn a profit or debased to turn indigenous people into less-than-humans, good only for their labor.

> These rich and their government are the worse liars because they massacre us in various ways and still try to deceive us, setting up *"fiestas folklóricas"* such as the day of Tecún Umán, the [*Día de la*] *Raza*, festivals . . . like those of Cobán, and . . . giving out little medals, diplomas, pats on the back and little smiles to certain professionals and "regal" Indians. Their cheating ends in speeches filled with lies, and finally, the photographs which the INGUAT exploits for tourist trade. The INGUAT . . . paints Guatemala in a very romantic and picturesque way with its Mayan ruins, its weaving, dances, and traditions. The Indian becomes an object of Tourism, a commercial object. All the benefits of this business are for the hotel chains, transportation business, the middle men for the Indian crafts, and the government itself. But we, the Indians, are those who gain the least benefits from tourism, which in the last few years has been in second place [in terms of producing foreign currency].
>
> (GUATEMALAN INFORMATION CENTER 1981: 8)

In this passage, reference is made to several topics discussed earlier in this chapter, with emphasis now on the deceitful nature of the claims and the victimization of indigenous people within the national context.This theme of victimization is a common one, frequently made with reference to social and economic policies presented by the government as affecting all Guatemalans equally when in fact, Maya claim, they really sort out the indigenous population.

The question then arises as to what positive steps indigenous people feel they can take (or have taken) that would allow them to live as Maya in the larger world. What would the union between Maya and non-Maya be based on? And how would it look? The Declaration of Iximché offers a statement on this subject.

> To end all these evils perpetuated by the descendants of the rich invaders and their government, we must fight allied with workers, poor ladino peasants, committed students, townspeople, and other popular and democratic sectors, to strengthen the union and solidarity among the Indians and poor ladinos, since the solidarity of the popular movements with the Indian struggle has been sealed with their lives in the Spanish Embassy. The sacrifice of these lives brings us now closer than ever to a new society and the dawn of the Indian's liberty.
>
> May the blood of our Indian brothers and their example of a firm struggle and their valor strengthen all of the Indians in their continuing struggle to secure a just life: FOR A SOCIETY OF EQUALITY AND RESPECT; BECAUSE OUR INDIAN PEOPLES CAN DEVELOP THEIR CULTURE NOW BROKEN BY THE CRIMINAL INVADERS; FOR A JUST ECONOMY WHERE NO ONE EXPLOITS OTHERS, SO THAT THE EARTH WILL BE COMMUNAL AS OUR ANCESTORS HAD IT; FOR A LAND WITHOUT DISCRIMINATION, SO THAT ALL REPRESSION, TORTURE, ASSASSINATION AND MASSACRE MAY BE ENDED; SO THAT FORCED INDUCTION BY KIDNAPPING STOP; SO THAT WE ALL HAVE THE SAME RIGHTS TO WORK; SO THAT WE NO LONGER SERVE AS OBJECTS OF TOURISM; FOR THE JUST DISTRIBUTION AND USE OF OUR WEALTH AS IN THE TIMES IN WHICH THE LIFE AND CULTURE OF OUR ANCESTORS FLOURISHED.   (IBID.: IO)

The passage, then, combines a criticism of the ruling ladino elite—those affiliated with the "state"—with a vision of a new, Indian-inspired cultural order that harks back to what is envisioned as a preconquest order. While Maya are at the heart of the new order, this particular reconstruction of society does not exclude non-Maya. Rather, non-Maya members would be those who, with a similar ideological orientation and along with the Maya, would forge a society run by popular and democratic principles.[16]

But how is this vision played out in a society where, from the Maya perspective, the coming together of the two groups results in a domination of the indigenous segment? As some of the previous materials suggest, actual "solutions" are limited in the present-day world where even the smallest attempt to act publicly in accordance with Maya principles may cause the death of an indigenous man or woman.[17]

If action within the public sphere is dangerous, the home, by contrast, provides a protected space where the expression of Maya values can be strong and central. It is here that children are taught to wear *traje*, speak *lengua*, and practice *costumbre*. Included in *costumbre* are a number of traditional celebrations that families may organize for the sowing of crops, the harvesting of the year's supply of corn, the birth of a baby, and so on. All are organized by domestic units for the benefit of the family and, perhaps, close neighbors. Thus, the effect of these events is rarely felt beyond a certain small set of individuals or seen to intrude upon aspects of life that are of value to non-Maya.

Local and regional organizations with a strictly Indian membership are also involved in attempts to seize control of and separate out of the larger society what are seen as indigenous expressions of ethnic worth. These might be thought of as larger-scale efforts akin to family-based activities, and likewise aimed at strengthening pride in being Indian and fostering the practice of *costumbre*.[18] However, unlike activities centered in the home, these have a public following that extends well beyond some immediate group within the indigenous community. Thus, while the professed and, perhaps, most important goal might be to engage the local indigenous population in the active, public expression of what it means to be Maya, those who organize and participate in the events are also aware that they are addressing viewers from outside a strictly indigenous circle. The result is that complex patterns of meaning—intended meaning, supposed meaning, perceived meaning, meaning denied—can arise and surround the events. It may also mean that, depending on the larger, political circumstances, certain expressions of Indianness voiced at the community level will be read as public statements of autonomy and, consequently, seen as a challenge or threat to locally dominant ladino or government forces. The following case reveals some of the nuts-and-bolts difficulties experienced by indigenous people in trying to take control of the production of the image of the Indian offered for public consumption in Guatemala.

The *fiesta folklórica* in Cobán, mentioned in the Declaration of Iximché, refers to the occasion and site of the national Indian queen competition. Sponsored by INGUAT, the Folkloric Festival is billed as a colorful celebration of Guatemalan culture and includes among its events special handicraft exhibits and costumed dances, along with the crowning of the Rabín Ajau, or national Indian queen. In this competition entries from different highland municipalities vie to represent the entire Guatemalan indigenous population at local, national, and (sometimes) international events. This is how INGUAT envisions the event, at least.

Up until the mid-1970s, Tecpán and neighboring Comalapa, San Martín Jilotepeque, and Chimaltenango each sent a contestant chosen and sanctioned by a local indigenous group. However, when participants started coming home with reports of how corrupt things were and how the contestants were being used to further non-Indian economic ends, the local Indian selection committees began to reassess the matter. They concluded that the festival hierarchy was dominated by ladinos who treated the queen contest as a sideshow rather than as a respectful tribute to the beauty of Maya women, traditions, and *traje*. In one case, the young women were encouraged to participate with promises of accommodations during the festival week and a prize trip to the winner. However, the accommodations turned out to be in a tent in the local park (where the contestants were expected to sleep "like animals") and the winner was not the prettiest, but rather the one whose family was said to have paid the most money to the festival committee. What is more, the winner never got the promised trip abroad. Had it occurred, it might have been less than desirable, however, as an earlier queen had found when she was taken to a Miami tourism convention and spent the week promoting Guatemala. Because of this, the four towns in the Chimaltenango area stopped sending locally sanctioned candidates, and groups from other highland towns soon followed suit.[19]

This reaction to the festival situation was not the only one, however. A group of Maya from the towns that boycotted the INGUAT event met in Tecpán to make plans for an Indian-run queen contest to take place at the time of the annual Tecpán fair. While the event would be similar in form to the Cobán affair—various Indian representatives in municipal *traje* competing for a single crown—its goal would be to provide the proper context for the appearance of each municipal representative and to focus on Indian culture in and of itself. Instead of subverting the expression of Maya identity to monetary ends, the indigenous production would match professed goals with actual ends and thereby underscore purely Maya values.

Plans for an Indian-run competition, however, never got off the ground. At the start of the first planning meeting in Tecpán, a suspected government *oreja* (ear—i.e., spy) appeared, wanting to participate and the meeting was quickly adjourned. Any further thoughts of continuing with plans were dashed as *"la situación"* worsened and key individuals of the nascent committee were killed or forced into hiding. In private, Maya commentators charged that this incident was yet another in which Indians, attempting to participate in the wider Guatemalan society as a group in possession of their own cultural identity, had been dominated and forced to give over to ladinos and the national government what, at heart, is theirs alone.

The final image I want to mention is that of the Maya professional, since it offers something of a bridge between the image of the land-poor *"indio"* damned to the lowest level of Guatemalan society and that of indigenous Guatemalans practicing *costumbre* within the closed ranks of family or small local groups. Professionals, by virtue of training, are often able to secure employment in respected community positions (as teachers, home economic agents, agriculture specialists, and the like). At the same time, being Indian means that he or she will have some small influence in the community, as a role model for other Indians (assuming placement is in a town with a Maya population) or, perhaps, even as a policymaker. Here I also include individuals who are working in organizations that promote Maya culture. Being professional as well as Maya, these people redefine the image of the Indian as competent in the ways of the larger world and possessing the "special talents" (e.g., language and familiarity with local customs) to work with individuals who might be, but are not necessarily, Indian.

Not all readings of the work and images of active, educated Indians are this positive. While Indian professionals might like to see themselves as intelligent, resourceful human beings in a biethnic world, the threat always exists that the person will be defined by a hostile individual or group as a subversive. There is enough of a history of this sort of redefinition to move some parents to admit to being glad that their sons never went on in school. Their thinking is that a young, educated man (much more so than a woman) with a "strong character" and the tendency to speak out is more likely to hold a public position where his actions are highly visible. In this position he is always in danger of crossing the fine line between balanced participation in the larger social world and advocating Indian interests that run against the dominant national grain. Individuals heavily involved in revitalization issues can also draw criticism, some of the sharpest being from other Maya. Points of contention often revolve around who has the right to define what it is to be Maya and the use of (academic) knowledge to elevate oneself and claim superiority. As one person commented about townspeople involved in revitalization activities: "They're more Maya than the Maya."

Contrasting Images of the Indian

Discussion in this chapter has centered on conventional characterizations of the Indian as they relate to indigenous and nonindigenous perspectives. The set of images, in turn, translates into a model of the construction of Guatemalan society and, in particular, focuses on relationships between ladinos and Indians or between the indigenous population and the government. In the cases examined, the images of the indigenous population shifted dramatically according to the "work" to which each was being put. These shifts, however, are not without their logic.

In Table 2, I present a four-part grid that summarizes important dimensions of the materials just presented. In particular I want to emphasize the fundamental differences in how indigenous and nonindigenous peoples assign values to images of the Indian—images used to characterize the population as an integrated, interrelated group, on the one hand, or as autonomous, unique, and discrete units, on the other. An important fifth dimension falls outside this neat schemata and has to do with indigenous

Table 2. Images of the Indian

	Images presented nationally by government and locally by ladinos	Images presented by the indigenous population
Indians and ladinos as interrelated peoples	+ the notion of "we Guatemalans"; some notion of a common history and heritage	− a unity characterized by conflict and domination
Indians and ladinos as autonomous units	− Indians as mysterious others and a source of labor for the market	+ a people practicing *costumbre* in their homes or in small groups

efforts to build a positive image of Maya within the broadest sphere of Guatemalan national life. In the Tecpán case, Maya professionals most clearly fall in this group, although the actual status or positive valuation of people in these positions is far from secure.

In closing, I want to focus on a few examples having to do with clothing and examine how Guatemalans acting within a given social moment can contemplate and adjust their own appearance (if only momentarily and on an extremely small scale) and hence the social role assigned to them. It is within such concrete situations that people have to weigh their desires, abilities, and expectations against the expectations and perceptions of others. In these cases, it is also a matter of anticipating others' reactions—what image is brought into being by one's presence—and, in cases that are not purely routine and ordinary, taking the risk of standing out as "different" or, even more extreme, being the target of negative comments and actions.

For example, young Maya women contemplating careers outside the home must consider whether they will be able to wear *traje* in certain positions and, if not, whether they are willing to abandon it to pursue a certain line of work. One young woman explained that she would have liked to become a secretary in the capital; however, wearing *traje* in that situation would have been nearly impossible, and she was unwilling to give up indigenous dress. The image required in the business world of urban offices (excluding the tourist business, perhaps) and that created by a secretary in *traje* have no common ground, so the combination is unthinkable. The woman, instead, chose a career in rural education, a profession in which *traje* is acceptable.

Another instance involves a group of young Maya women in a vocational school in Guatemala City who approached their graduation date with the knowledge that they would be obliged to abandon *traje* in order to don *togas* (graduation gowns) for the evening ceremony. Three of the group—two of whom were from Tecpán—exerted what they felt to be their right and petitioned the administration for permission to wear *traje* during the ceremony. Their reasoning was that *togas* are not part of *traje*. And, besides, if they wore the graduation gowns, people would not be able to see that indigenous students were part of the graduating class.

Despite some initial resistance from administrators, the three succeeded. The rest of the Indian graduates, characterized by one observer as fearful of negative reactions from the audience, opted for graduation gowns. In the end, however, the audience was extremely sympathetic: they gave the Maya women in *traje* standing ovations in recognition of their special achievements as Indians. The Indian women in *togas*, of course, did not get the same recognition and later regretted their decision to give up *traje* for the "safer" act of hiding their ethnic identity behind graduation robes.

As this example shows, the public presentation of self is often precisely calculated; the wearer chooses to emphasize one aspect or another without always knowing the full consequences of the act—particularly when the situation is not routine and when it is not obvious which image of the Indian will come into play for any particular circumstance. However, people do not simply let the assignment of one image or another fall to chance, nor do they always passively accept the available images if they feel that none does justice to their "true" nature. In the highlands today, Maya are striving to do away with stereotypes that they see as untrue and damaging, and, in their stead, to reenforce the image of the Indian as wise in the ways of the world, competent, responsible, and yet tied to ancestral values.

FOUR

BETWEEN BIRTH AND DEATH
Traje and the Human Life Cycle

[Giving birth] is just a minute, but a minute between life and death.

TECPÁN RESIDENT, 21 JUNE 1980

You live and you die. [sentiment expressed about the recent murder of a local Maya leader]

TECPÁN RESIDENT, 24 MAY 1980

A child is born into a world already made, one with ongoing social practices and a local culture that gives meaning and value to actions. This system, however, is hardly rigid and unchanging. What are seen as enduring and sometimes abstract themes have contemporary interpretations and applications within a very real social world inhabited by very real people. The socialization of a Tecpán child takes place within such an active, contested, and yet established world, in the company of individuals—parents, siblings, grandparents, and other relatives as well as neighbors, teachers, classmates, and local merchants—who make up the community. Despite real instances of violence around them, residents of Tecpán enjoy a stability and richness of life that give them a sense of identity, of being Tecpanecos or having "Tecpán-ness" (Tecpanidad—also the name of the local magazine).[1] This sense of identity, security, and belonging develops gradually, and socialization takes many forms, a significant dimension of which is the socialization of the body by means of clothes.

Terence Turner argues that the surface of the body and its "social skin" operate so effectively as a socializing agent because of its mediating position: it serves simultaneously as "the common frontier of society, the social self, and the psycho-biological individual" (1980: 112). Through clothes or their "symbolic equivalent" (ibid.), a wide range of meanings and values are physically imposed on the body—by parents and other family members, principally, when the child is young—and then learned, rejected, forgotten, or reconceived by the child as he or she matures. In this way the clothed body (and other learned, bodily forms) becomes "a memory," a "mnemonic form" that reflects "the fundamental principles of the arbitrary content of culture," but at a level "beyond the grasp of consciousness" (Bourdieu 1977: 94). Socialization through clothes thus leads to a set of seeming contradictions: it entails a process of learning-but-forgetting as the "natural" body becomes "social"; it gives bodily form to "a whole cosmology, an ethic, a metaphysic, [and] a political philosophy," though people usually cannot articulate these; and it taps into what is essential to a culture, yet is seen as trivial and insignificant (ibid.: 78, 94–95; Turner 1980: 112).

In this chapter, I focus on the life course of indigenous Tecpanecos and the use of clothing during different phases of their lives. The sequentiality of this life cycle is constructed largely from the simultaneity of events (relatively speaking) that I have observed in Tecpán since 1980. Thus, the stages of life discussed here cannot possibly belong to any one person, for they describe what it means to be born in the 1980s, to be a young adult in the 1980s, and to be an old person in the 1980s. Nevertheless, a sense of process should emerge—what earlier I called "stereotypical change"—with *traje* the focal point.

Birth and Childhood

As the first epigraph of this chapter suggests, childbirth is considered a period of liminality for both the mother and child, a potentially fatal point in their shared existence when events can bring life anew or death. Present at this time are trained personnel (a doctor or midwife, depending on whether the birth is in a hospital or at home) as well as family members (such as the woman's mother, mother-in-law, husband, children, other relatives, and close female neighbors) who help with the birth or lend a hand with domestic chores.[2]

Concern for the baby, however, precedes its birth. During the prenatal phase, the developing child can be affected by the actions and conditions of others. Though my data from Tecpán are not elaborate on this point, other highland studies note that the unborn and newborn are considered "cold" on the hot-cold continuum, a classificatory system that "structure[s] 'natural' principles, . . . social forms, and values" (Greenberg 1984: 4). In this extreme "cold" state, the individual is characterized as being weak, vulnerable, and not fully formed as a social being. He or she also contrasts with those persons at the other extreme. People believed to be "hot" or to have *sangre fuerte* (strong blood—a term that is more frequently used in Tecpán) are considered powerful, domineering, rigid, and able to do harm: they exert themselves in the world and, in doing so, ignore proper social relations and appropriate social boundaries (ibid.: 82). The harm brought by these actions can be especially damaging to those beings (and animals are included here) who, by their very weak constitution, are least able to cope with the force. For this reason, newborns are especially vulnerable, particularly so when the person with *sangre fuerte* is physically or relationally close (a neighbor or sibling, for example). People talk of infants born with a cat's head or with two heads, one black and one white, and blame the parents. "They aren't good," one woman said, explaining that the parents drink, the husband beats the wife, and they engage in other equally unacceptable activities. These actions constitute socially repugnant behavior that can be transformed into socially repugnant forms in the flesh of the transgressor's offspring.

During and after childbirth, the new mother is also extremely vulnerable. In some highland communities the woman, considered "hot" and supersocial throughout her pregnancy and with a potential to affect those weaker and colder than she, is suddenly reduced to a state of being "cold" and vulnerable (e.g., Greenberg 1984; Neuenswander and Souder 1977: 115). In Tecpán, too, a woman experiences a change in body constitution following parturition. Typically, for forty days after *dando la luz* (giving birth, but literally "giving the light"), the mother's diet consists mainly of chicken and other foods considered "hot" while it lacks "cold" foods such as potatoes and avocados. This diet, prepared for her by family and friends, brings the woman back to a normal state now that she is no longer *enferma* (pregnant, sick). She also avoids certain activities that would expose her to the cold or cold elements: needlework, for example, with its cold, metal needles is not recommended by some even though, as one new mother put it, the forty days following a birth is a time when a woman actually has some free moments and might enjoy the activity. Likewise, she wraps herself to keep warm (the head is often covered with a kerchief or towel, as it is when one is ill). The intention is to keep the new mother warm so that, among other things, her milk will flow. In this case in particular, the woman's return to a normal social and physical state has a direct effect on the well-being of her infant.

The *tuj* or *temescal* (sweatbath) is a small chamber made of adobe blocks that stands in the backyards of a number of Maya homes.[3] Bathing in a *tuj*, a traditionally Maya activity, with its steam and tubs of hot and cold water, is another way in which new mothers have their heat restored. As it was described to me, the new mother enters the *tuj* the day after giving birth and, with the help of the midwife, rubs the stomach area so as to *subir la matriz* (lift the uterus). Her clothes are also changed, and a cloth belt, which functions to lift and control the uterus, is wrapped around her. This belt is worn under her clothes and, unlike the elaborate woven belts used with *cortes*, is plain and often made of store-bought cloth. She wears the belt for the prescribed forty days of recuperation.

Despite its association with the "traditional," the *tuj* is not for everyone. Some women say that they never use a *tuj* because the intense heat and steam makes them dizzy or the closed, little room makes them feel claustrophobic. (People also discussed whether I, a foreigner whose body has not been trained over a lifetime, could tolerate these same conditions.) After childbirth these women bathe in a shower or tub and care for their bodies in ways that they see as equally appropriate as the *tuj*.

The treatment the mother receives parallels in significant ways that of the infant. The child is also bathed in the *tuj* or tub and afterward his or her stomach is wrapped, this time with a cloth called an *ombliguera*. The *ombliguera*, a square piece of cotton, is folded into a band and then wrapped over the *ombligo* (navel) so that the body is held in place. The bodies of both mother and child are thought to be particularly plastic at this time, and the *ombliguera* aids in the (re)shaping process just as woven *fajas* (belts) will later contain, constrain, and thereby help socialize the growing child.

The newborn, though still in a vulnerable state, is now also visible to the world. Because of this, she or he is directly available to those who, by virtue of their strong constitutions, are most able to inflict harm. Because the initial moment of exposure to the world at birth is crucial, some people withhold the birth date from anyone but the most intimate of family members and medical specialists. They believe that indiscriminate broadcasting of such sensitive information could mean that wrong-minded outsiders, armed with a precise date, would be better able to focus their powers on the moment of birth and to perpetrate *malhechos* (bad deeds) on the mother and child.

This view was described to me as a "traditional" attitude toward birth, and a fairly extreme position on the issue of privacy. Over the years, these beliefs have been challenged by new, school-based knowledge and the demands of salaried jobs. People who received sex education in school have a significantly different attitude than their parents on this subject, and it is a much more open topic. For example, women who have become pregnant while holding office jobs mention how their male colleagues openly ask them the anticipated date of the baby's birth. This information is fairly public anyway since the women need to provide dates to their employers in order to schedule maternity leaves.

Clothing, coverings, and their symbolic equivalents protect the newborn child. Caps, blankets, shawls, and the like afford reasonable protection from inanimate, largely undirected, and potentially dangerous elements such as *aire* (wind), which can reach the child's body and cause, or perpetuate, sickness. Animate sources of harm, which can be further divided into intentional and unintentional forms, can also be thwarted by body coverings and adornments. Here, again, wrapping is important in separating the child from harmful outside elements; clothing and blankets, for example, inhibit the ability of the inflicting person to see the child, an important function in light of the belief that eye contact can be the means of contagion of the common disease *mal de ojo* (evil eye) or, more simply, *ojo*. Likewise, anything red, itself considered a *fuerte* (strong) color, affords protection much like clothing does, although its strength appears to lie not in blocking vision but in neutralizing or countering forces. Thus, for example, the ears of baby girls may be pierced within days of birth (when, I was told, they feel little pain) and studs with small red beads are put in place; baby boys, on the other hand, may be given red bracelets; and small animals (puppies, lambs, calves) may wear red ribbons, collars, or tiny crocheted bags around their necks, the latter carrying splinters of *ocote*, the resin-rich pieces of pine that provide a ready flame for the hearth and are thus associated with fire.[4]

What all of these—babies, puppies, lambs, and calves—have in common is such a susceptibility to animate forces outside their bodies that they can be *ojeado* (eyed) and made to suffer negative effects from persons with strong blood or a strong negative character. However, within this broad category of "strong forces," there is a range of causal agents: (1) those who are aware of their powers, capitalize on them, and direct them toward other, weaker souls, as in *brujería* (witchcraft); (2) those who are strong-blooded by nature and who, in clashing with other strong-blooded persons in the course of daily life, can inadvertently cause ill health in spatially or relationally close individuals with weaker natures; and (3) yet others who, by virtue of a temporary state (the "heat" of pregnancy, for example), are potential conveyors of harm. While all these dangers are real, in my experience the actual instances of *ojo* are relatively rare and parents are diligent in but not overly preoccupied with protecting their child. Rather, it is the more mundane concern over *aire*, coughs, and colds as well as a general interest in keeping a baby warm during cold, high-altitude nights that moves parents to bundle their children with layers of cloth and clothes.

Plain cloth diapers cover the lower body, either by being folded into multilayered squares, pulled between the legs, and pinned on both sides of the hips or, more simply, wrapped around the waist and secured with a belt. Disposable diapers are virtually unheard of because of their cost, though people are certainly aware that they are popular in Guatemala City and the United States. It is also common to see a second cloth—a towel, *servilleta*, or any cloth roughly one and a half feet by three feet—wrapped around the child (boy or girl) and secured by a belt, *corte*-style. The upper body is covered with a store-bought undershirt or some home-made equivalent, and this is often topped by another small, plain shirt. Finally, the whole body is wrapped in a blanket or shawl, often so that the child can be carried on the mother's back. Wrapping the baby with plenty of thick coverings at night is also considered prudent because a warm baby is less likely to urinate and wake up crying. In recent years I have also noted (and been asked to bring with me from the United States) such "new" items as fleece baby sacks and sleepers. I attribute the presence of these articles to changing fashions in baby clothes, greater wealth to buy manufactured items, and changing attitudes toward the body (and here I am thinking of parents' increasing willingness to dress girls in what might look like pants).

Because ladino clothing is cheaper than articles of *traje* and because babies cannot yet control their body functions, the expressed reason for the abundant use of common clothes is that it is simply not worth the money or effort to dress essentially messy babies in better (i.e., indigenous) clothes. Another reason that makes sense but is not explicitly stated is that infants are not yet fully constituted human beings with a public, social identity. Thus, both Maya and ladino babies appear in essentially the same clothes—if anything, economics rather than ethnicity is marked according to who can afford new clothing or higher-quality items. As one indigenous woman put it, "Ladinos use baby clothes just the same as Indians do."

Soon after birth, the family begins planning for baptism, an event that focuses attention on the child and solidifies his or her place in the spiritual community (principally the Catholic church). According to perceived church standards, the baptism should be performed when the child is about six months old, but in my experience children are generally much older when they are baptized. This discrepancy can be explained by the fact that baptism is not simply an act performed in church (for which a small fee is paid), but also a celebration of family and friends. Delays, therefore, are commonly attributed to the lack of funds for an adequate celebration. When a baptism is finally arranged, the child's *padrinos* (godparents)—who may be Maya or ladino—mark their special relation by sending a gift of clothing in honor of the day. A shirt, jacket, hat, booties, and blanket are common for a boy, while pieces of *traje* or a dress with a hat, booties, and blanket are appropriate for a girl.

While her baptism might be the first place that a Maya girl appears publicly in *traje*, other special occasions are also appropriate. From as early as three months, a holiday celebration such as Christmas is occasion enough to dress a baby girl in a small embroidered or handwoven blouse and a *corte* made from a *retazo* (scrap; more specifically, the remnant left after a Tecpán woman's skirt is cut from the standard *corte* length). While this outfit might remain on but a few hours, the family can publicly display their pride in being Maya and the fact that they have every intention of having their child follow *costumbre*.

During a child's early life, attentive parents and older siblings allow the *nene* (young child) to play at length and make excessive demands on the family. The child is not seen as responsible for his or her actions and, hence, cannot run afoul of the household rules by which older children must abide. The child's obliviousness to forbidden substances, like forbidden actions, is also excusable at this age. Indeed, in the early months and years, a child's growing awareness of and control over unclean substances—things described as *sucio* (dirty) or, more colloquially, *chuco*—is something of a gauge by which progress in socialization is measured. A control over body excrements comes first at around the age of two, with a change in clothing to mark this transition. While the everyday clothing used up until this point is not entirely unisex, a stricter differentiation between the sexes by means of dress is maintained from this point on. Boys go from wearing diapers and rectangular cloths wrapped around their waists to sporting *pantaloncitos* (little pants); no Tecpán boys wear *traje típico* on a daily basis.[5] Girls, on the other hand, continue having their lower bodies wrapped, now with *corte* cloth, though recently it has become increasingly common to see girls dressed in sweat suits—presumably because they are warmer, although it seems to me that the shift also relates to the growing acceptance of exercise and recreational clothing among females. Regardless of shifts in fashion and leisure activity, changes in clothing due to toilet training continue to mark a transition from external, though intimate, parental control over the child's growing body to the child's own increasing self-control.

Children are also seen as developing an awareness of dirt in the physical environment, although their control over this factor is slower in coming (perhaps because it is less socially offensive). In a world marked by the omnipresence of cultivated land, packed earth yards, and dirt roads, not to

29. Children with their grandparents, 1990. The girl, like her grandmother and grand-
father, wears Tecpán's *traje tradicional*; the boys wear *vestido*.

mention the more than occasional use of packed earth floors and adobe
bricks within the home, adults struggle hard to keep clean. This can take
the form of regular bathing for both sexes, taking care to turn the flap of
one's skirt out before sitting on a dusty bench (for a woman), or frequent-
ing the shoe-shine boys in the park (for a man). Because children are
perceived as still lacking any heightened social awareness of dirt, the situation is extreme. Parents anticipate an excessive level of grime to accumulate on their children during the course of the day and hence continue to
dress them in inexpensive clothing. For girls, especially, this seeming con-
tradiction—the use of clothes that are both *típico* and cheap—calls for
some creative solutions. For example, small blouses are made from a single
lienzo (a woven length of cloth) of the mother's unfinished *huipil* (in Tecpán
virtually all adults' *huipiles* are made from two *lienzos*), or from cheaper
threads; in the case of one girl whose mother wove for a living, a patchwork blouse was made entirely from the neckhole squares cut out from
scores of commissioned projects.

With a growing control over the body comes a growing sense of what
failure to do so can mean. A seven-year-old girl, for example, took great
pains to explain to me the utter mortification she felt in school one day

when, in going to the bathroom, she soiled her *corte*. Her primary concern was her own image among peers, which was tied closely to a concern for her clothes that she recognized as being her responsibility to maintain.

At the same point that children are gaining some control over bodily functions and their outside environment, parents note their rapidly developing language ability and rational processes. These two, in fact, are often thought to go in tandem. Thus, for example, one couple refrained from cutting their young son's hair until he was two and they could explain their actions to him. This explanation would be in Spanish, the first language taught in virtually all the homes I frequented, although the intention is often to teach children Kaqchikel, too.

Along with language acquisition comes an increased capacity to learn or, as one woman explained, to have knowledge *pegar en la mente* (stick in one's mind). At approximately six years of age, parents and academic insti-

30. Patchwork *huipil* made from the square neckhole cutouts of ninety-six different *huipiles*, 1990. (Field Museum of Natural History catalog number 236822.)

tutions deem children ready for formal instruction, which, according to one child development theory that was explained to me, is taken as having a set level of difficulty that the child's mind must develop to meet. School is also generally the environment where children first interact for sustained periods of time with people outside the family and begin to acquire a better sense of their own social identities.

Virtually all Tecpán children—referred to as *muchachos* (boys) and *muchachas* (girls) at this age—enroll in school. Indeed, pressure is so great for local families to better themselves through education that, a year or more before a child comes of school age, parents begin weighing the educational offerings of the various local institutions, the estimated capabilities of their offspring, and the desires and financial means of the family. The local preschools and schools are judged in terms of such factors as the quality of educational programs, emphasis on discipline, and cost. For the two private schools in town, church membership is not required, although most students in the Catholic school are Catholic and those in the Protestant school are members of some of Tecpán's many Protestant churches.

Unlike the public schools, the private church schools have monthly tuition fees of around Q3.00 per month. Because many consider the education received in either of these institutions to be superior to that of the public schools, families are willing to set aside a portion of their scarce resources for school fees. Scholarships are available for the needy, and, as part of the application materials, a photograph is required. For this picture, I have known parents to dress their offspring nearly in rags so as to emphasize the poverty of the family and the need for financial aid.

Another consideration in choosing a school is the dress code. Indian girls are allowed to wear *traje* in the public and Catholic schools, but not in Bethesda, the Protestant school. The restriction causes something of a dilemma for indigenous families who consider wearing *traje* an important aspect of being Maya and at the same time believe the Protestant school to be the best academic institution in Tecpán. Academic superiority notwithstanding, some indigenous families, charging discriminatory policies, do not enroll daughters in Bethesda's program specifically because of its dress code.

Between the ages of eight and ten, when young girls are in the early to middle years of primary school, their mental and physical abilities are considered developed enough so that they can begin learning to weave on the backstrap loom. Generally their mothers are the teachers, but on occasion instruction is available (though less and less frequently) from other female kin, neighbors, church members, or close associates of the family. While it is unusual for non-Indians to have any knowledge of backstrap weaving, the "ethnic purity" of the instructor does not seem to be a central issue. For example, I was asked by one of my neighbors—the mother in a family of skilled weavers—to teach her teenage daughter a weaving technique that was currently popular in Tecpán but that no one in her family knew. The daughter learned quickly, surpassing me in speed and technical ability almost immediately, and used the new *cruceta* technique (which I discuss in the next chapter) on items she was making for her wedding trousseau.

Boys also learn to weave, though in much fewer numbers and generally at an older age than girls. Furthermore, in contrast to women, who almost always weave *a mano* (by hand) on the flexible backstrap looms, men in Tecpán generally weave *a maquina* (by machine) on large *telares* (treadle looms). While this gender division of production techniques is not without exceptions, the overwhelming majority of Tecpán weavers fit into this pattern. Young men begin mastering treadle loom techniques by apprenticing themselves outside the family or by learning from an older family member. Once proficient, a man may weave as his primary income-producing activity or work less frequently at the loom to supplement other income. In addition, he may sell his labor and weave for someone else's textile business, or produce items on his own loom and sell these outside his home.

The initial project for a young girl learning to weave is generally something small and simple: a plain belt or small *servilleta*, for example. At this point the most important function of the exercise is to educate the hands and mind, and to get the two working together. Experienced weavers comment that beginners' hands "*no saben todavía*" (don't know yet, in the sense that they are not educated) or that, like school-learned facts, the weaving steps have not yet had time to "stick in the mind." People learning to use floor looms and sewing machines are said to have the same problems. In all cases, practice, aided by occasional physical persuasion (one woman remembered how her mother would rap her knuckles with the weaving batten), is considered key to learning.

Despite the fact that weaving is characterized as traditional Maya woman's work, not all Indian girls learn to weave. While some nonweavers claim that they have no interest in it, or prefer other handicrafts, or had no one to teach them when they were young, a more common explanation is that as youngsters they spent their time in classes and doing homework instead of learning to weave. The situation does not change after graduation when young women with degrees pursue careers while their less educated, generally poorer counterparts weave.

Weaving, however, is only one type (albeit the most technical and time-consuming) of a range of arts that girls can learn in order to make articles of *traje*. Embroidery, for example, is a common, more portable, and generally simpler alternative. And while embroidered blouses are not considered part of Tecpán *traje*, they are nonetheless marked as "Maya" and are appropriate and popular attire for Indian women and girls. Since embroidery is also a culturally appropriate skill, families that do not teach their daughters weaving are not necessarily seen as being remiss in the cultural education of their children.

Youth

Juventud (youth) refers to a group of individuals as well as a culturally defined stage of life. While the end point of *juventud* is contextually defined and depends more on economic and social conditions than on being a certain age or reaching sexual maturity, all Tecpanecos are first labeled by the term at roughly the same age—that is, when the balance of control of an individual's life tips away from his or her parents. At the upper limit, marriage, with its new relationships and extra responsibilities, generally marks the end of youth and the start of adult life. However, with a growing number of persons postponing marriage in order to go on in school and start professional careers, the sense of the term is shifting slightly. For that reason, I have included material on young unmarried professionals in this section.

Starting at about the age of ten, young Tecpanecos find their lives controlled less and less by parents, older siblings, and resident relatives. They can take on such simple personal responsibilities as, one woman recalled, choosing what *huipiles* she wanted to wear and not being forced to use the pink and yellow favorites of her mother. Nowadays young Tecpanecos also have greater freedom in deciding their futures. Fewer and fewer marriages are planned by families, and advanced schooling is a definite possibility for many. Faced with this latter opportunity, students must balance the availability of classes and their personal preferences against educational expenses, family resources, and the degree to which Indians (especially Indians in *traje*) are accepted in certain jobs.

Along with greater personal freedoms come more formal responsibilities in the household and community. While children of seven or eight regularly help around the house in small ways, the chores are rather ad hoc (often spur-of-the-moment errands). Older children, however, are assigned regular tasks, and it is their sole responsibility to carry them out.

Growing up also means leaving aside children's games and toys—making mud tortillas or mud houses from tiny adobe blocks, racing around with hoops and sticks, or caring for dolls (usually plastic and imported, but sometimes homemade and complete with *traje*). This is not to say that youth leave behind all idle pleasures. As critical parents and neighbors often point out, many young people, increasingly aware of themselves and others in their age group, indulge in elaborate self-beautification schemes and lengthy social visits with friends. These actions relate to changing male-female relations and the growing elaboration in the presentation of one's public self.

While the state-run primary school system in Tecpán segregates boys and girls into separate school buildings located on opposite sides of town,[6] the two private grade schools and most classes beginning with the seventh grade are coeducational (home economics, for example, is not). Children who play together in the streets before they are old enough for school therefore often find themselves attending class together or, at least, participating in townwide events in which all schoolchildren have roles.

31. Students from the secondary school marching in Tecpán's Independence Day parade, 15 September 1980.

But very young children have always been playmates and fairly unrestricted in their play relations. I imagine this is why I heard little comment about differences between childhood experiences today versus those of twenty-five or fifty years ago. The situation, however, has changed for the older students, principally those who go on to *básico* (the first three years beyond primary school) and who find their social opportunities substantially different from those of their parents' and grandparents' youth. For the older generations, social interactions with the opposite sex were relatively limited during their youth: smiles exchanged while passing in the street or, at the extreme, illicit meetings in cornfields were the stuff of premarital contacts. Although those two forms of interaction still exist, for Tecpán students today there are more legitimate opportunities for extended interactions between the sexes without immediate family supervision. In classes and away from direct parental supervision, boys and girls collaborate on school projects, exchange tips on homework, and chat between classes with relative impunity. The opportunity afforded by supervised course instruction has made it permissible for adolescents to be together on a regular basis without thoughts of marriage being foremost in everyone's mind.

Within the sphere of expanded educational opportunities, patterns of friendship emerge. A young person's closest friends are always of the same sex and usually, though not necessarily, of the same ethnicity. Cliques of friends, in turn, allow members of one sex to approach those of the other, either en masse (e.g., a group of girls go off together to watch a boys' basketball game) or individually, but under the watchful eye of the group (e.g., one boy runs across the schoolyard and delivers a message to a girl or girls while his friends watch and comment). These friendship groups are particularly important for girls, the more closely guarded members of the household who, even in this "progressive" social environment, risk being labeled someone's *novia* (girlfriend) after just one brief, unaccompanied interaction with a male. Yet even for young men, who are generally allowed more freedom to flirt and remain uncommitted, the implication of a *novio* relationship is not something to be avoided at all times. Young people in their mid-teens are increasingly mindful of their appeal to the opposite sex as well as what is appealing in others, both in friendships and in amorous relations.

While people would tell me that the goodness and appeal of a person is separate from physical attractiveness, I never got the sense that the physical aspect was unimportant. Quite the contrary. Young Maya women, for example, are concerned with a whole set of beauty standards that focus on outward appearances. (To a certain extent, Maya men are, too, as I discuss later.) As far as physical attributes go, they lament not having thick, shiny black hair with no split ends, clear skin without pimples, or nice teeth, and turn to consumer products to aid them. Cosmetics—lipstick, eye shadow, rouge—are not generally among these, as they are labeled "ladino." Differences also come out in clothing: ladinas were said to emphasize sex appeal when they wear tight clothing, articles that accentuate breasts, and items that supposedly entice males for lustful pleasures. Despite what I sometimes felt to be a sensual riot of colors and a sexually appealing presentation of the body in *traje* (not to mention the fashionable tightness of *cortes* and belts for young women), I do not remember any instances where Maya explicitly noted the use of *traje* as blatantly and unambiguously "sexual" in its message.

The clothing prohibitions articulated by different Protestant churches in town overlap but do not completely coincide with a general Maya sense of what should and should not be worn. According to church proscriptions for women (I am unaware of similar ones for men), slacks, tight clothing of any sort, and jewelry are among the forbidden items because they have the potential to excite men and to be used for vain purposes. More positively expressed, moderation in clothing and adornment reflects well on the person as well as on those around her. When I asked indigenous Protestants—churchgoers but not church specialists—what biblical passages supported these ideas, no one had immediate answers, but, after being pushed on this point and searching scripture, they sometimes referred to verses such as the following one:

> You [wives] should not use outward aids to make yourselves beautiful, such as the way you fix your hair, or the jewelry you put on, or the dresses you wear. Instead, your beauty should consist of your true inner self, the ageless beauty of a gentle and quiet spirit, which is of the greatest value in God's sight. For the devout women of the past who placed their hope in God used to make themselves beautiful by submitting themselves to their husbands.
>
> (GOOD NEWS BIBLE 1976: I PETER 3: 3-5)

Backed with such biblical authority, some pastors encourage women to stop wearing jewelry (wedding rings are the exception), although I never heard a prohibition against beautiful indigenous dress. For some Maya women even the jewelry proscription is a problem because such items as earrings and necklaces are considered elements of traditional *traje*. The

Protestant proscription against pants for women (and the Maya tradition that does not include pants as women's *traje típico*) likewise runs into trouble with the increasingly accepted use of shorts and pants for school sports and recreation. To my mind this situation has changed quite dramatically since 1980, when during basketball practice for teenage girls the Maya players all wore *traje*. That has completely changed today, with the nearly universal use of sports clothes and sneakers.

Skin color and facial features are also points of conversation for Maya. With ladinos, skin color is usually a matter of "the lighter, the better," with "refined" facial features also carrying a high status. For the indigenous population, both female and male, the high, angular cheek bones, broad and downwardly sloping nose, and dark "*morena*" skin of the "pureblooded Maya" (direct descendants of whom, I was told, still live in isolated villages, though not in Tecpán proper) are the inherited features of the race and, hence, like municipal *traje* from throughout the highlands, valued in traditional Maya contexts. But these are not features that get a positive reception in the larger world; there darker skin and "coarser" features are not only viewed negatively on "aesthetic" grounds but also equated with less intelligence. This double reading of a classic Maya "look" is, I believe, the key reason why indigenous Guatemalans are much less likely to pass judgment on skin color and facial features. "Looking Maya" cannot be deemed "bad" if the judge has the least bit of pride in cultural roots. At the same time, though, Indians recognize (consciously or not) that *not* looking Maya has its advantages for persons constantly bombarded with U.S. and European notions of beauty and for those trying to operate successfully in an essentially prejudiced, ladinoized world.

No matter how much attention is paid to physical appearances, it is the rare person who in all seriousness does not claim—about friends, family, and self, at least—that the true worth of a person transcends flesh and is reflected in "one's character" and "one's manner of thinking and being." While this public attitude might hide a whole range of private thoughts to the contrary, a person's character and actions are nonetheless important in the creation of one's social persona; and Tecpanecos in their late teens begin consciously and critically to assess the personal, spiritual, and moral dimensions of themselves and the people around them.

Inner goodness relates to the balance between one's own needs and desires and a sense of what ought to be done for one's family, neighbors, townspeople, or other groups that are important to the person. The community as a whole is preserved when this balance is maintained and respect is exhibited. Youth, of course, has its role. The Princess Ixmucané

(P), mentioned in the previous chapter, speaks on the subject in an interview in *Tecpanidad* (T):

> T: What can you tell us about young people [today]?
>
> P: It strikes me as fitting to mention and it saddens me that among us, the students, we feel ourselves superior to those who haven't studied. One of the serious mistakes is the respect that we've lost for our elders. I've heard many complaints from our parents, that children don't respect them any more, Indians as well as ladinos. And another thing is that we've forgotten how to work, the males especially shouldn't forget to take up the *azadón* [a large hoe used in agriculture throughout Mesoamerica] because we also live thanks to mother nature and we all need our daily tortillas.
>
> (AJOZAL XUYÁ 1979-1980: 22, MY TRANSLATION)

Such concerns are reiterated by parents, grandparents, teachers, and church leaders (i.e., the people most concerned with the social and moral development of children). They claim that it is all too common for a young person to go to school and develop into someone who is haughty, never helps around the house, and dresses in an elegant manner for vainglorious purposes. In contrast, the "ideal student" in this public model of civic and familial propriety goes to school, but also maintains ties with friends and neighbors and shares work within the family. While the former is motivated by egotism and selfishness—inward-looking forces—the latter enters adulthood looking out toward the community and sensitive to the needs of others. A person's physical appearance—parts of which can be controlled and manipulated but which inevitably includes "natural" attributes, too—is the visual complement and material reflection of this outward concern for community.

Young women who wear *traje*, especially those who wear fine and very expensive pieces, are particularly aware of how different interpretations of dress can reflect positively or negatively on the person. On one hand, *traje*, as the principal visual element of Maya identity, is seen as something to be worn proudly and in a manner that reflects not the person alone but the larger theme of cultural heritage. From this perspective, wearing indigenous dress is a selfless act: the more beautiful the *traje*, the more honor and respect the wearer pays to Maya traditions and the more opportunity the community has to live with an active visual expression of cultural pride. Cultural pride was, after all, a major point of Tecpán's 1980 *traje* presentation, described in Chapter 2.

At the same time, however, Tecpanecos realize that *traje* is an enormously expensive item and a burden to any family's budget. Unmarried Maya men joke that they are looking for ladino wives so they can avoid spending large sums of money on clothes. The fact that many families cannot afford fine *traje* pieces points to economic differences among Maya as well as the general level of poverty of all Maya within the larger class-based, national society. To insist on buying and using fine *traje* to the detriment of others reflects poorly on the wearer.

A few concrete examples illustrate how these different interpretations come alive within particular social spaces, with different social actors wearing and judging *traje* for specific social reasons.

Adolescent females—ladino and Maya—are frequently referred to as "flowers" in contexts that emphasize their beauty. However, Maya (most often school-educated younger adults with at least a slightly sharpened political perspective) point out that while ladino women all too often are treated as substanceless ornaments and passive sex objects in roles subservient to males (their frequent media appearances as props in skimpy, seductive outfits is pointed out as proof of this), indigenous women are men's equals, with complementary but active and important roles in life. A young woman in *traje* is seen as taking an active role in indigenous cultural expression, and a family that supports this expression is understood to be keeping *costumbre*. However, rationalizing the purchase of expensive *traje* has its limits.

In one instance, I learned of a teenage boy who was about to graduate from school and whose family had decided to organize a large celebration for the occasion. Despite their bragging about the upcoming affair, they were short of money and so had to humble themselves by borrowing a fairly large sum from relatives. In the end, however, the money did not go to pay the costs of the celebration, an event that the lenders had deemed appropriate given the boy's hard work in school. Instead, much of the loan was used to buy new *traje* pieces for the teenage daughter of the family, the mother's claim being that it was only proper to dress a young woman of that age in the finest clothes. As for other members of the boy's family, the mother went to graduation in old clothes and the graduating son was described as having scraped together something to wear. Afterward the lenders deemed the fiesta adequate for the occasion, but they were definitely not pleased that their money had gone for the daughter's clothes. To them it was not a matter of spending money to support the cultural vitality of *traje* or to increase the visibility of an unmarried daughter at a large social event or even to assure that male and female children of the family received roughly comparable "goods." Rather, their criticism was directed at the deceptive nature of the loan request and what they saw as an inappropriate ordering of priorities by a controlling mother and daughter.

Queen contests are omnipresent in Guatemala and are seen by most as a legitimate way to have the "flower" of local youth represent different sorts of groups. The wide range of titles hints at this diversity: Princesa Mam (Mam being a Maya language group), Flor de Durazno (Peach Flower), Señorita TV, Reina del Banco de Café (Queen of the Coffee Bank), Señorita Guatemala (Guatemala's representative in the Miss Universe pageant), and scores more representing geographic units, companies, and social organizations.

Generally speaking, queen contest winners are picked in one of two ways. More commonly contestants face a panel of judges and, based on criteria internal to the event (e.g., appearance in *traje* or evening gown, poise, and intelligence demonstrated by answering questions), a winner is selected. Alternately, contestants are ranked according to how many tickets (referred to as "votes") they sell in the weeks preceding the coronation; the contestant selling the most tickets wins the crown. While this procedure is good for the finances of the sponsoring organization, it reduces the meaning of the crown to a matter of economics. In the 1970s, an Indian fair queen in Tecpán was selected in this manner. Though the queen was reported to have said that she won because of personal qualities— "beauty, body, and height"[7]—everyone knew her rich father had bought enough tickets to hand her the title. Thus, the Indian queen, whose personal attributes were being promoted as representing those of all indigenous Tecpanecos, was seen instead by some as a conceited, self-serving individual who would not acknowledge the true (economic) means by which she attained her prestige. Not even her appearance in expensive *traje* brought positive comments from her critics on the beauty of local dress. Rather, the outfit signaled the wealth of a family that could buy a competition; for her critics, the *traje* simply underscored the fact that it was wealth and not any cultural interpretation of being Maya that had won her the crown.

In my experience, Indian women change from *traje* to *vestido* most frequently in the years preceding marriage, a period when all young people are actively defining their social persona through dress and other public emblems. For example, it is not uncommon for indigenous girls who go to secondary school in Guatemala City to switch to *vestido* there. They may not want to stand out and risk being labeled "*indio*," or they may seek the more glamorous, urban lifestyle that is perceived to go with *vestido*. Because they are mindful of what friends and family at home will say, they commonly switch back to *traje* for visits. An exception was one woman who claimed access to the "highlife" of the capital through *vestido*, which she also wore in Tecpán. As a consequence, she was snubbed by her Maya friends. Their reaction was considered harsher than it might have been in another case because she had previously been affiliated with local Maya youth groups. Given the groups' dedication to indigenous culture and what seemed to be the woman's earlier adherence to the ethnic cause, her independence from the clothing norms promoted by the group was particularly annoying to them. Her change back to *traje* in 1980 did not bring totally positive comments, either. Some saw this move as self-serving because it was becoming fashionable to be "Maya" and to participate in pan-highland Indian activities, dangerous though some of these were.

Changing from *traje* to *vestido* is not always criticized, however. Sometimes the negative comments are aimed instead at the social system that makes the change necessary. For example, one young Tecpán woman was involved with social service projects in neighboring Comalapa, a town that witnessed a number of killings and intense army occupation very early in the 1980s. Her work included helping to distribute U.S. aid supplies to the needy. However, individuals within the local government claimed that these supplies were Cuban in origin, and so she and her fellow workers were immediately suspected of ties to communism. (This and similar charges were common appropriations of global Cold War terms and were used to interpret local conflicts and discredit individuals or groups.) After a brief and unpleasant encounter with army soldiers, who questioned her on her work, the young woman fled to Guatemala City, where she cut and permed her hair and began wearing *vestido*. Sympathetic Maya recounting this and similar episodes felt that the change to *vestido* was necessary for the individual's personal safety and had nothing to do with personal preference or lack of respect for one's culture. In fact, the forced change in dress was interpreted as yet another example of how the government strips away personal freedoms and acts prejudicially toward Indians.

Finally, recall the three young Maya women who were granted permission to wear *traje* for their graduation ceremony in Guatemala City, while all the other students (including other indigenous students) wore graduation gowns. All three appeared in *huipiles* and *cortes* from their hometowns, and all three received standing ovations when they were presented with their diplomas. *Traje* had identified them as Maya, while the professional degree labeled them as intelligent, hard-working individuals who had gained access to the educational system in the capital. The three women were proud to represent their families, their towns, and the Maya community on such a special occasion, while the Indian women who opted for *togas* were said to regret their decision and the lost opportunity for personal praise. Of course, there was no way of predicting this exact outcome, and the young Indian women who had abandoned *traje* for *vestido* earlier in their school careers had reason to believe that they had suffered less persecution by not being visibly identifiable as "Indian."

These examples show a range of instances in which young Maya women exercise the signaling power of their "social skin." But what about young men? As far as their physical bodies go, they express some of the same concerns that young women do for clear skin, good teeth (including replacing any that have been pulled), and strong, well-cared-for hair. In addition, a good physique with well-developed muscles signals more than long hours spent laboring in the fields; today this physique bears status among Maya youths and links them to other males with great bodies—Rambo, Bruce Lee, various sports stars, and the male models in jeans advertisements. And while young Tecpán men know that their bodies are generally not judged in situations such as movies, magazine ads, or queen competitions, they *are* aware of being subject to a constant stream of judgments from people, both acquaintances and strangers. An example of this is what I always felt were dubiously affectionate nicknames like Gordo (Fat Boy) or Canche (Blondie in other contexts but here more like Light-haired One). On a much more damaging plane are the ethnic stereotypes that equate "Indian" with, for example, "coarse black hair that sticks out," a characteristic that feeds easily into the image of a country bumpkin unfit to function in the larger national society.

As I noted earlier, Tecpán men do not, by and large, wear *traje*, especially younger men, perhaps because there is a distinct but largely unspoken feeling that a man wearing *traje* is less masculine according to the standards of the larger social world, while the femininity of a Maya woman is preserved and even enhanced by indigenous dress. The phrase *tener pantalones* (to have pants—i.e., to be a real man, to be unafraid) calls up the image of a rugged individual in blue jeans and a plaid flannel shirt (the preferred outfit of many young Tecpán men, Maya and ladino) rather than of someone in loose white pants, with a wool *rodillera* held at the waist by a pink striped belt. The *traje* of young Maya women, on the other hand, elaborates on more "universal" themes of feminine beauty. That non-Indian women, Guatemalans and foreigners, admire Maya dress to the point that they wear *huipiles* both for daily use as well as for more elegant nighttime affairs seems to support this idea.

After months of living in Tecpán and hearing little direct commentary on why women wore *traje* but men generally did not, I began asking people directly for their thoughts on this matter. They talked about the prejudice of non-Indians toward Maya dress, the expense of *traje*, men's contact with a wide range of institutions where they felt they could not appear as "Indians," and the fact that *traje* identifies the ethnicity of its wearer on occasions when that is undesirable (e.g., during times of military "recruitment" when Indians are more likely to be forcibly picked up and "drafted" from the street or field). One man, who is active in Maya affairs and who left Tecpán in the early 1980s after being threatened, initially responded that it was a matter of prejudice that Maya men would not be accepted in the working world outside a strictly indigenous environment if they wore *traje*. Besides, he added, women are "*más valientes*" (braver).

This last observation deserves further attention for a number of reasons. First, the use of *valiente* here is somewhat ironic since the term connotes a daringness usually associated with men. Men, more than women, are generally the ones involved in potentially dangerous activities that could result in injury or death. In 1980, "valiant" Maya men from throughout the region were being pursued and sometimes murdered for actions aimed at securing more rights for the indigenous population. Their actions often entailed speaking out against injustices and organizing movements to right perceived wrongs.

But speaking out, taking a public stand, and acting politically in institutionalized roles historically have been male-dominated activities. Nevertheless, it is men, and not women, who have ceased the very public and political act of wearing *traje* in Tecpán. If this move on the part of the men is seen as succumbing to the pressures of the non-Indian world, women then emerge as the more *valiente*—especially young, professional Maya women whose domain of action is often far from the home. These women appear in the workforce in significant numbers, hold respectable jobs in which they interact with a wide range of people, and yet continue to wear *traje*.

Marriage

A generation ago, young people regularly wed at sixteen to eighteen years of age in marriages arranged by parents. However, townspeople reaffirm the center-periphery distinction, as well as class differences among Indians, when they claim that arranged marriages are now more frequent in the *aldeas* than they are in the municipal center and are more likely to involve children of poorer families. Romantic love, on the other hand, seems to be the accepted grounds for most marriages in town, and even those unions that neighbors suspect of being arranged are treated publicly as if they had been formed by two freely consenting individuals. Arranged marriages may be seen as a "traditional" Maya practice (meaning that it has a long history in the indigenous community), but in the common pattern of courtship today the *novio* and *novia* initiate their relationship and the parents give their approval.[8]

These changing marriage patterns and the trend toward higher education and professional careers mean that many Tecpanecos well into their twenties—both males and females—are not married, nor do they have any intention of getting married in the near future. The period I have perhaps stretched to call "youth" has certainly ended by the time many people wed and form new family units. Members of certain Protestant church groups, in fact, have an evening of celebration the night before a wedding that is called the *despedida a juventud* (farewell to youth).

Despite the fact that the arranged marriage is not very common in Tecpán, many young Tecpanecos who decide to marry nonetheless formally commit themselves to each other by means of some form of *pedida* (from the verb *pedir*, to ask for), a process of marriage negotiation associated with Maya tradition and the past. The *pedida* generally involves a visit to the house of the young woman by the young man, his family (including perhaps a dozen or so relatives beyond the parents), and their *suplicante* (suppliant) or *pedidor* (petitioner). The young woman's family, having been warned beforehand, have their *recibidor* (receiver) present. During the course of the evening (or several evenings, if details get involved), arrangements for the marriage are debated and, if all goes well, settled upon; then the food and drink that the man's family have brought as gifts are consumed.

The wedding follows the successful *pedida*. By federal law, a civil wedding is mandatory, but most people also marry in a religious context. Festivities leading up to the wedding day can include, for a Protestant bride-to-be, the previously mentioned *despedida a juventud*, complete with testimonies of religious conversions, singing, preaching, and quantities of food. For Catholic couples, the family of the *novio* visits the home of the young woman the day before the wedding and brings more baskets of food. As before, these are divided up among family members. The *novia's* family, expecting the visit, has a meal prepared to offer guests. At this time, a short prayer session led by laypersons may also take place. Typically the meal and prayers are offered in the family's *sala*, the room in which guests are received. For the occasion the floor is swept clean and perhaps covered with pine needles (a common way for marking a special space), and a table may be set with candles and religious articles.

For the prenuptial events, the *novia* dresses in an outfit that her family has purchased for her, that she might have helped make, or, for salaried women, that she herself bought or helped family members purchase. It generally consists of a new *huipil*, *corte*, belt, sandals, underwear, shawl, and apron, with one or more large wedding *servilletas* woven or commissioned for her at the same time. With these pieces, the family signals, in a sense, the fulfillment of their obligation to raise, feed, and clothe their daughter until maturity, and they send her off ready to assume her position in a new household and to take up the role of a wife. After marriage, most women return to their family's home only for visits, and economic (if not emotional) relations shift.

For the wedding itself, the young man or the man's family provides the *novia* with a complete set of clothes. Along with their immediate use value for the day's events, the clothes are seen as a reflection of how well the woman will be treated in her new role as wife. If the wedding *traje* is exceptionally fine, her parents are relieved to think that their daughter will be well taken care of. Even less expensive outfits can signal the future well-being of a bride if a family of modest means takes care to buy the best that they can afford. However, clothing that is inferior or below the standard that the family is able to afford does not bode well for the marriage. For example, a *huipil* with relatively few designs or one done with long, loopy brocade stitches and poor-quality thread is regarded as a public announcement of bad things to come. And it is embarrassing for the bride's family to realize that all who attend the wedding will see from the clothing the potentially unhappy situation that the young woman is entering.

If one or both of the *novios* hold a salaried position and the marriage is based on romantic love, the couple generally takes responsibility for many of the financial details of their wedding, including buying their own wedding clothes.[9] Marriages between professionals, who might have met in a regional secondary school or on the job, are also more likely to involve individuals from two different municipalities. In the cases with which I am familiar, the brides wore *traje* from their towns (and some even went so far as to help select the style of clothing and weaver), although the grooms still paid for the clothes and presented these to their future wives.

32.   Woman with her wedding *huipil* and *corte*, 1985. Both pieces of *traje* were bought
by her husband as a wedding gift. Note the *huipil*'s abundance of roses in *cruceta*,
with rows of doves and curls at the bottom edge. Special floral tape decorates the
neck and armholes.

On the morning of the wedding, the groom's family rises early to begin food preparation for the feast that takes place at their home after the wedding ceremony. In the house of the bride's family (assuming they are near), one of the major tasks that needs overseeing is the dressing of the bride. Of all the women present, it is the future mother-in-law of the *novia* who has the most interest in the activity. Besides arranging all the gathers and pleats of the new clothes, she is also interested in seeing that the young woman's "look" befits a married woman—making sure that the skirt is sufficiently long, for example.

The activity also gives the young woman an opportunity to see how her new mother-in-law will treat her. This is especially important if the new wife moves to the home of her husband's family after the marriage. In her in-laws' house, the young woman is under the eye of her mother-in-law, especially if the two have to work together in the same kitchen, wash dishes and clothes at the same sink, and use the same patio area. Here she is also subject to the older woman's orders, criticisms, likes, and dislikes. The mother-in-law's treatment of the bride on the morning of the wedding is therefore a taste of what the bride can expect in the weeks and months to come.

In the early 1980s, when the economy was good and Tecpanecos were feeling richer than they had in the decade before, the norm for attire at a Maya wedding was *traje* for the woman and a suit (usually in a dark, solid color), white shirt, tie, and dress shoes for the man. With the possible exception of the pastor at a Protestant service, the groom was often the only male dressed in that style of formal attire. By 1990, economic conditions in Guatemala had deteriorated so that the purchase and use of such "special occasion" clothes was deemed impractical or impossible by a wider range of people. For example, that year I attended a double ceremony in which two unrelated couples were married by the local priest. Both couples appeared to be of extremely modest means (which the double wedding indicated). The brides both wore Totonicapán *huipiles*, the type woven on treadle looms and costing a fraction of the backstrap-woven Tecpán blouses. Both also wore the less expensive acrylic *cortes*. As for the men, both wore what looked like new clothes—and ones that were fashionable for streetwear—but items that were not as formal or marked for special occasions as a suit. In particular, one of the men wore a yellow sweatshirt with an advertisement for a bus line on the back while the other wore a brown cloth bomber jacket with plush "fur" collar. Although suits are still worn for wedding ceremonies, changing fashions and economics influence clothing decisions.

33. Bride and groom, 1981. The couple are on their way from the civil ceremony to the wedding service in a Protestant church.

34. Wedding procession in Tecpán following a marriage ceremony in the Catholic church, 1990.

A woman's wedding *traje* is distinguished from other new outfits by details and items that may be removed, ignored, or never worn again after the wedding day. For example, wedding *cortes* often have a length of white lace sewn about six inches up from the hemline selvage. White shoes and veil, neither of which are socially obligatory or "Maya," are used only for the wedding. And, finally, the *huipil* is often one with white as the base color underlying the supplemental weft designs. Because this feature is also common among nonwedding *huipiles* from Tecpán, a wedding blouse worn for any other occasion would probably not be recognized for its original function. In fact, unlike the white wedding dress of the ladino world, wedding *traje* is worn repeatedly after the woman marries, first for special events such as holidays and Sundays, and then as everyday attire until it finally ends up as a rag.

These descriptions of wedding clothing apply to the majority of cases, though certainly not all. Couples (and their families) select clothing according to what they see as appropriate for the occasion, and sometimes this choice runs counter to the general trend. In one instance in 1980, a couple, both university students studying in Guatemala City and both activists in the early cultural revitalization efforts, made the joint decision to celebrate their wedding, not only as the union of their two lives but as an opportunity to honor Maya traditions. For the occasion, the young man, who otherwise did not wear *traje*, wore the traditional Tecpán outfit with white pants, a *rodillera*, a white shirt, a black jacket, and sandals. Together the couple had bought a *ri'j po't* for the young woman, and she wore this with a fine cotton *corte*, one with elaborate *jaspe* designs, and a *su't* folded on her head. The *padrinos* (godparents) of the wedding couple were likewise dressed in traditional *traje*, as were the two boys and two girls who served as attendants. Officiating at the ceremony was a recently ordained priest, an indigenous Tecpaneco, who conducted mass in the Kaqchikel language and encouraged the couple to preserve Maya ways in their home and with their children.

Weddings can also be opportunities for Maya women to abandon *traje* and wear the long, white wedding gowns that they see promoted and romanticized in the ladino media. In extreme cases, a woman may use this occasion to make a permanent switch to *vestido*, as in the case of an Indian woman who anticipated moving to the capital, where her husband was employed, and working as his secretary. In other cases, the woman wears the white gown for her wedding day but then reverts back to *traje* the next. Here *vestido*, in the form of the wedding gown, may be seen as a costume, appropriate as one element of this special event, but not something to be used for everyday life.

For the wedding itself, relatives, neighbors, and other invited guests gather at the bride's home, then follow the couple to the municipal building where the civil ceremony takes place. In an inner office and in the presence of a municipal representative (often the mayor), the *novios* sign the official register (or press it with a well-inked finger if they cannot write). From the town hall, the group then walks to a local church or chapel for the religious portion of the ceremony.

Inside the church, family members are seated in the front rows with guests behind, with men on the left and women on the right. With this arrangement, the two families are brought together to witness the wedding and, in turn, be watched by those in attendance. Occasionally, however, one or both of the parents—mothers more often in the cases I heard—disapprove of the marriage and stage a protest either by not attending the ceremony or by attending in old and dirty clothes and sitting at the front of the church where everyone can see.

Wedding ceremonies, Catholic or Protestant, stress the complementary roles that the young couple will have during their life together, the husband in his work role outside the house and the wife in her domestic labors. Specifically, the groom is charged with earning enough money to take care of expenses at home and may be warned not to hang out on the street looking for other women. The bride is told that her responsibilities lie in the home, and she is encouraged to work hard so that she contributes to the well-being of her family. (In one service, weaving was specifically mentioned as an example of a useful, home-oriented, female occupation.) The couple are expected to consent to having sexual relations, and together they must provide for and educate their children.

After the service, it is usual for the wedding party and guests to proceed to the home of the groom's family where women (relatives and neighbors) have been busy preparing a nuptial meal. Guests who have not already dropped off their gifts at the home of the bride's parents now deposit them at the groom's. Wedding presents include practical items destined for use in the new home: glasses, dishes, baskets, and kerosine lamps.

In situations where religion does not forbid it, the wedding meal is followed by dancing, drinking, and the distribution of cigarettes. These activities can continue far into the night, but in the end the bride and groom are left alone. At this point the flirtations and excesses that characterize courting and wedding-day celebrations end, and married life begins.

Married Life and Parenthood

December is known as the month for weddings. The long school vacation begins at the end of November, the corn crops drying in the fields need little tending, and a number of offices close for the holidays, thereby giving individuals the extra time needed to go forward with marriage arrangements. December is also one of the coldest months of the year, when temperatures in the highlands can dip to the freezing point early in the morning, causing frost to form in the cornfields. It is this combination of weddings and the cold that motivates the joking objectification of new wives as *ponchos con tripas* (blankets with guts).

But sleeping with one's spouse for the first time can be an almost terrifying experience, especially for women, whose bodies have been wrapped and covered from the eyes of even other female family members since they were young, to the point that even the exposure of a knee cap can cause embarrassment.[10] The experience can be particularly difficult for women whose mothers have said little or nothing on the subject and who have had little schooling and, hence, no involvement in sex education classes. While young men are thought to be savvy on the subject of sex, owing to their relative freedom to leave the house and socialize with other men (on street corners or soccer fields, in cornfields or bars), young women are expected to live under the careful watch of their parents and other family members until they marry. Even trips to public sinks (if there is no running water in the home), the market, or a family garden—which allow for moments to gossip or exchange messages—may be monitored or the young woman accompanied by other family members. Not all families, however, are so diligent or concerned, nor do all young women put up with this situation. Whether in Tecpán or farther from home (while working as a domestic in Guatemala City, for example), they may find or create opportunities that allow them a kind of independence. Thus, while parents might wish for a respectable marriage in order to pass along a daughter to her new husband or in-laws, elopements, out-of-wedlock births, and single parenthood tell of conflicting interests and actions by the different parties.

Some mothers claim to have *vergüenza* (a term that covers a range of states from shame to shyness to humility) when it comes to educating their children on the facts of life. (I never heard this term used by or for fathers.) *Vergüenza*, they say, prevents them from informing their daughters about menstruation and intercourse or keeps references brief and veiled. Because of this, many girls enter puberty with only scant knowledge of sex, and that gleaned from assessments of actions taking place within the close confines of the family home, conversations with older siblings, or snatches of suggestive conversation that they might overhear. Other young women have more involved discussions with their mothers, with conversations focusing on emotional states of a newly wed woman (confused, afraid, lonely, sad), the asymmetry of the marital roles, or embarrassment and coping during the first years of marriage.[11]

In her work on the highland community of San Pedro la Laguna, Lois Paul (1974) refers to the "mystery of sex" that characterizes the central years of a woman's life and that is opposed to her "mastery of work" in the household regimen. Paul writes:

> In the matters of sex [as opposed to those of work] . . . , the relationship between men and women is much more asymmetric, and marked by mutual distrust and anxiety. In work women command their bodies, but in sex their bodies are commanded not only by men but by mysterious powers that periodically cause bleeding and gestation. Barriers of shame leave the maturing female unprepared

for the crises of first menstruation, her wedding night, and the birth of her first baby. But each experience admits her by stages to the inner arcanum of female secrets, which unites her with other mature members of her sex. (IBID., 299)

Paul's comments are based on field data collected in 1941. While her insights still demand consideration, changes regarding (re)production have occurred in the intervening half century. What is seen as altering this division of labor, as it were, is the growing importance of formal education.

As I explained earlier, school attendance provides girls, especially, with a type of freedom that was largely unknown to women their mothers' age. Because of classes, girls can leave their homes on a daily basis and associate with other people, adults as well as students their own age. The educational environment is sufficiently goal-oriented and controlled that going to school is generally approved of by families, in contrast to an activity like *paseando* (hanging out or, more literally, strolling around town in an idle manner). The information passed along in classrooms, moreover, has an assumed "correctness" about it because it is considered scientifically based. The category of scientific or technological knowledge, is, I believe, taken to be essentially neutral with regard to ethnic categorization. Thus, for example, parents do not feel they are giving up anything "Maya" at heart by having their children receive sex education in school. Sex education, like televisions and blenders, is a "good" that comes with the other benefits of higher education and the adaptation of a more "modern" lifestyle.

The effect of this education, however, is to contribute a new element to the relationship between men and women as sex partners, because it changes their views of themselves, their bodies, and their spouses. In earlier times men were stereotypically the experienced, knowledgeable initiators of intercourse, to which women passively resigned themselves, hardly knowing (in the early days of marriage, at least) what to expect. Nowadays, many young men and women are schooled in the biological aspects of reproduction. For women, perhaps more than men, this information can change attitudes toward the body: it rationalizes processes with biological explanations, makes these part of a public system of information, and allows a person to compare his or her body and its functions with those of others.

Young indigenous women are aware of the contrast between their own situations and those of their mothers when they married, and consider themselves fortunate. For example, one unmarried woman mentioned her mother's account of the unexpected onset of menstruation and the difficult first days of her arranged marriage. In contrast, the daughter felt that, because she had continued in school and received sex education, she would enter marriage with an educated person's knowledge of human reproduction, a knowledge that makes for a much more equitable relationship with a spouse and thoughtful planning for children. Such a vision of one's future, however, can clash with what actually happens. Although the sex education taught in schools is socially acceptable, it is introduced in a rather antiseptic environment, without a great deal of consideration of the cultural assumptions on which it is based, the cultural context into which it has been brought, or the past history of sexual relations between couples. In fact, I often felt that the images carried away from these school lessons were overly Americanized, with access to a certain type and level of health care seen possible and certain gender relations assumed. (A number of people asked me about topics such as birth control and gender relations in the United States, as if they were checking their understanding and comparing it with that of a genuine specimen from the north.) What I witnessed were young, educated women—relatively confident in their knowledge of sexual relations, the size of the family they wanted, and the idea of family planning—meeting and marrying young, educated men who, in my estimation, also seemed to be aware of issues concerning gender relations and sexual reproduction and who were ready to participate in a marriage that redefined local gender roles. However, the resulting union often did not measure up to expectations, at least as far as the woman was concerned. Issues having to do with birth control were harder to discuss than expected, the authority of the new husband was more "traditional" (like her father's) than anticipated, and the burden of the "double day" of salaried work and domestic responsibilities was not significantly reduced by the all-too-infrequent helping hand from her educated spouse.

In an expanded sense of social (re)production, a wife's traditional responsibilities—as these are spelled out in contexts ranging from marriage ceremonies to playlets performed at public events—center on the family, the home, and the local community. She buys and prepares the food, washes clothes, cleans house, bears and raises the children, monitors the family water supply, tends the animals raised at home, and oversees any domestic help. Her apron, an article of clothing that a girl learns to wear from an early age, marks her as a hardworking woman who is serious and capable in her efforts. In addition, she may weave and sew clothes for her

35. Shoppers at stalls selling shawls and *corte* cloth in Tecpán's Thursday market, 1990. Shawls with pom-poms and *jaspe* designs hang from the stall at the center; folded *corte* cloth is piled on the table and hangs from the stall on the right.

family or for extra income, produce handcrafted items such as embroidered pillowcases or artificial flowers to beautify the home, and help run a family business. She may also leave the house regularly to help in the fields, tend the family garden, buy or sell in the market, decorate graves in the cemetery, or participate in church events. Some of these individual activities are seen as particularly Maya in nature: for example, making and wearing *traje* or teaching her children to speak Kaqchikel (though the latter is not something that a woman does alone).

In fact, taken as a whole, Maya women's productive activities and reproductive powers are central in defining them as the embodiment of Maya culture and Maya community. Kay Warren (1993a: 46) expands on these ideas when she writes:

Women are powerful metonymic representations of community because they are felt to be central to the continuity of Mayan culture in their roles as the bearers of the next generation and the socializers of children in Kaqchikel culture. They stand for the essentialist construction of Kaqchikel identity—that there is an intrinsic uniqueness to being Kaqchikel—in the face of rapid social change. As Mayan men often put it (and even the urban ethnic nationalists assert this), it is more important for women to wear traditional dress than for men, who in many communities have adopted "ladinoized" clothing, because women perpetuate the culture.

But if women are seen as perpetuating indigenous culture, what are the roles of Maya men and the significance attached to these? Men's activities often move them away from the heart and hearth of the domestic sphere. Many men spend the better part of the day away from home, laboring in the fields, gathering firewood, operating a knitting machine in one of the local sweater workshops, or working in an office or classroom in Tecpán or in another town. Even if a man's work is centered in his home, his work space (a barber's chair, treadle loom, or dying vat, for example) is generally set off from the rest of the house. It is a site of relatively uninterrupted activity, and yet it is also generally more public (i.e., accessible to a greater range of people outside the immediate family) than many of the household spaces where women work. As members of the larger Tecpán community, men are integrally involved in agricultural cooperatives, church organizations, cultural committees, special interest groups (e.g., a truck drivers' club), sports teams, local politics, and social campaigns. Women join some of these groups, but often their participation is dependent on their husbands' lead and their level of participation more restricted than the men's. There are also single-sex groups in which married women participate (e.g., cooking and crafts clubs, church choir groups, and weaving cooperatives). As I encountered numerous times while working with 4-S clubs in Tecpán, permission to join such groups is usually granted by the husband, or, at the very least, the couple discusses the matter before the woman joins. In these ways, male authority can limit and define women's actions in the community at the same time that men praise women and their activities as essential to the preservation of Maya culture.

One reason given for treating women deferentially or restricting their activities (and this refers to Indians and ladinos alike) is that they are *delicadas* (delicate, weak, or frail), a term that can refer to the physical, emotional, or rational dimensions of being female, depending on the circumstances. Furthermore, embedded within this notion of *delicada* is a conservative and slightly nostalgic image of a chivalrous world where peace reigns and harmonious social relations are the norm. However, apart from the changing social norms that are making this concept seem dated, the various forms of violence in everyday life often make it impossible for Maya women to express or take advantage of their "delicate" natures, even if they are so inclined. For example, in a world of extreme ethnic prejudice, ladino women with children (especially wealthier ones) can quickly find seats on crowded buses while Indian women with children (especially poorer ones) are more likely to be instructed to push to the back where they can hunt for a space. In situations such as these, particularly when the people involved are strangers, clothing is the clearest signal of ethnic identity. The country's poor economic conditions also conspire against the expression of women (here, again, Indians and ladinos) as "*delicadas*." Women who would rather not work outside of the home, in situations that they see as possibly dangerous, feel forced to keep their jobs because of their families' economic needs. This might mean long walks to schools or health clinics in rural areas known to be the sites of guerrilla and army activities. Of course, men, too, are victims of violence in such situations, but, along with being less "delicate," they are more likely to have access to vehicles, which would at least make the journey faster and less physically grueling.

The idea of the "*valiente*" woman that I mentioned earlier is striking because of the contrast with the more common label "*delicada*" and because men are the ones expected to act vigorously and bravely. Men serve in the military, argue politics, and shoulder large financial decisions. When women cross these boundaries, as they do to a greater or lesser extent all the time, they may gain a type of power not permitted women in more "traditional" roles and they can throw their observers off guard, but they also run the risk of being abused like men. An instance that Rigoberta Menchú describes for the Quiché region illustrates this poignantly:

> I remember when my little brother disappeared, our whole community united and joined together in a protest, after my mother had gone to enquire after him at the police, and the army, and had received no reply. So, they all went, all of them. The community acted together for the first time; the majority of them were women. We knew that if the men went, they'd be kidnapped and tortured. So my mother said it would be better to hold a demonstration of women and children to see if the enemies, the army, were so shameless, so cowardly, that they would massacre women and children.
>
> (1984: 196–197)

While the public is horrified and saddened by political violence to men, this horror takes a quantitative leap when women are the victims. A woman's death or disappearance in a political context signals that something is very wrong with society.

A related example, which came to my attention while I was in Tecpán, involved a ladino journalist kidnapped in October 1980. An editorial in *El Gráfico* stated:

> It is not the first time women have been victims of the violence. We have seen how, recently, the bullets have cut short the lives of women professionals, without thought of their positions as mothers and wives. The values of those [women] who, up until just a little while ago filled us Guatemalans with pride, given our heightened sense of chivalry [*caballerosidad*, from *caballero*, meaning "gentleman"], have been trampled once and again by clandestine forces.
>
> (1980A: 6, MY TRANSLATION)

Here violence to women—wives and mothers—again reflects the ills of the world, although in this instance blame for this situation is explicitly assigned to the guerrillas.

The case of the journalist is also interesting because her work lies in the realm of words. Gender roles are characterized by their different modes of public presentation, and the artful manipulation of words throughout Guatemalan society (especially in public forums) is generally associated with men. Within the Maya community, men display their specialized gifts in oral performances as *aj q'ij* (diviners) for traditional Maya religious practices, as members of *cofradías* within the Catholic church, and as ethnic spokesmen on political issues. Some of the older schoolgirls and female professionals with whom I worked noted the relative absence of women in public-speaking roles and worked to counter this situation: they said they tried hard to master the verbal skills needed to speak articulately and move their audiences, whether in their roles as teachers, Indian queens, or members of a local organization. Some also commented on the lack of training and practice that their mothers and grandmothers received at comparable times in their lives, and encouraged the girls and women with whom they worked to improve their skills.

The use of very expensive *traje* often wanes as women grow older, especially if their work is centered in the home and they are not weavers (and hence dependent on having cash to buy new clothes). These women may continue to "perpetuate the culture" (in Warren's words) by wearing

36. Mother and daughter, 1981. The mother wears a blouse woven on a foot loom; the daughter wears a *huipil de Tecpán*.

traje neatly and with pride, but they do so in clothing that may be faded and threadbare. Not all women in worn-out clothing, however, are thought of in such kind terms. According to a number of Tecpanecos whom I came to recognize as thoughtful social commenters, some women quickly abandon any effort to make themselves and their clothes the least bit attractive once they have married. This poor appearance reflects antisocial behavior on a number of levels. Prior to marriage, they may have passed considerable time in front of mirrors while, afterward, their *cortes* are sloppily wrapped, *huipiles* left bunched up around the waist, hair uncombed, and bodies in need of bathing. The feeling expressed to me was that women such as these use good looks and neat appearances to deceive potential husbands and advance their social agendas and that their appearance before marriage, no matter how beautiful, is tantamount to a lie.

Less harsh criticism falls on families, the parents of which sacrifice everything (including improvements to their own wardrobes) for their children. While some couples, especially those with salaried positions or a successful business, accumulate considerable wealth as they grow older and can afford costly material goods for themselves and their children, many families find that money remains scarce throughout their lives. In the latter case, especially, trade-offs have to be made regarding the purchase of items as expensive as *traje*. As I mentioned earlier, one common solution is for mothers to forgo new clothes so that older daughters can dress in style. Such behavior on the part of the parents and children is considered appropriate as long as it is not taken to an extreme; daughters in their teens, after all, have career and marriage opportunities coming their way that will shape the rest of their lives, while mothers' lives are essentially set and, in general, will not be changed by more elaborate dress. However, daughters with excessive demands for new clothes are considered selfish and the parents who powerlessly provide them pound-foolish.

Los Ancianos

As an *anciano* (old person, elder), a person is a living link to the Maya ancestors and a focus of respect that derives partly from his or her personal contact with the relatively distant past. As repositories of knowledge and wisdom, *ancianos* are sources of special information about natural phenomena (e.g., eclipses, unusual geological formations, or the weather) or conditions that befall humans (e.g., illnesses along with their cures), as well as tales about events that no longer occur and beings that no longer exist in Tecpán (at least not in the center of town). They also provide descriptions of *costumbres* that are no longer practiced and of *traje* pieces that have fallen into disuse.

Confined to the home more and more with age, elderly grandparents, parents, aunts, and uncles have an important role in the socialization of the young children living in the household. With written and photographic records of the town scarce or nonexistent, they are consulted as a prime source of historical knowledge: they are like living encyclopedias on Maya culture. In Comalapa, for example, where there is a large indigenous industry in oil paintings of local scenes, older members of painters' families are often asked to delve into their memories and recall visual details of dress, buildings, and rituals. In Tecpán, mothers and grandmothers are consulted for descriptions of *traje* pieces that are seen only rarely or are no longer woven. Likewise, older men and women are consulted, and their clothing sometimes borrowed, when schools hold *traje* or "folkloric" dance contests. As part of the competition, a brief speech on "traditional life" is generally de rigueur and so, again, grandparents become important resources.

Older people are also known to retain preferences for earlier forms of clothing as well as earlier habits of dressing. As previously mentioned, a small number of older men continue to use *traje*, but, to my knowledge, no items of the *vestido* used by younger Tecpanecos make reference to it. (For example, the white pants sometime worn by young men do not seem to refer to the white pants of *traje*, but more to the white-denim look of ladino clothes.) In contrast, the *traje* worn by and associated with older women is different from that favored by young women, but the different styles are related. For example, belts approximately six inches wide, in multicolored stripes or brown with woven figures emblematic of Tecpán, are generally associated with older women. In contrast, younger women may purchase narrow versions (one to two inches wide) that give them the same, time-honored municipal *traje* "look" but allow them to show more of a waistline. In this and similar instances, styles of dress associated with old people are adapted so that references to the past remain, but an awareness of contemporary fashion (one that often extends well beyond a Maya-centric world) is also conveyed.

Other examples support the idea of the active trafficking of *traje* ideas through generations of Tecpán women. The dark blue-black, indigo-dyed skirts with white pin-striped checks, for instance, are associated with older women and the past. Known as *morgas* in general and *penecitas* more specifically for the Tecpán style (see Photos 18 and 20), these older types of skirts were criticized for their stiffness and course texture and virtually never used for daily dress in the early 1980s. During my year of fieldwork, for example, I only observed old *penecitas*—family heirlooms worn for a special event—on girls in parades and in enactments of Maya *costumbres*. A few older women in Santa Apolonia also preserved that town's style of *morga*, and occasionally I would see one of them in Tecpán on a Sunday or Thursday. Since 1980, however, the situation has changed, driven in part by the cultural and political dimensions of Maya revitalization efforts. Now *penecitas* are purchased by families wishing to express pride in their Maya heritage, and these skirts are used regularly for ceremonial purposes—a school play, a town parade, the inauguration of a weaving shop, a Maya blessing ritual, or a Catholic church event. As they are worn and washed, they become less stiff (less likely to rub raw the backs of a woman's legs) and hence more appealing for daily use.

Cotton *cortes* with *jaspe* designs come in a wide variety of colors. One combination of white, black, and green (the tone of green being like that of the leaves of a mature corn plant) is also associated with very old women. Their preference for this style comes across in their urgings to granddaughters to buy "a nice *green* one." That the granddaughters, in turn, are not pushed by their families to do as their grandmothers suggest is likewise telling. Grandparents may hold considerable sway within the family and home; however, people realize that clothes must function in a wide range of contexts and impress a wide range of people. The authority of elders, then, is tempered by a range of considerations.

The major piece of *traje* associated with older Maya women—and the single item of clothing that most embodies Maya identity—is the *ri'j po't* or *sobre huipil*. It is distinctive for several reasons. It is enormously costly: a *ri'j po't* made from handspun natural brown cotton, with silk designs, costs the equivalent of about one month's salary for a schoolteacher. It is worn loose over another blouse, with the wearer's arms held inside or emerging from under the bottom edge. In addition, it is used only for special occasions such as town festivals, Maya rituals, church masses, and *cofradía* activities.[12] Guarded carefully throughout a woman's life, and by her family after death, *sobre huipiles* may also be borrowed by younger family members for special contests and school competitions that focus on traditional Maya culture. It is my impression that weavers are much more cautious when it comes to innovating with the *ri'j po't* than with any other item of municipal dress. Of course, *ri'j po't* change over time, but any attempts at innovation are always checked by the desire to strengthen and reproduce material ties with the past. An example of the changes in the use of *ri'j po't* over a ten-year period will illustrate this fact.

In the early 1980s, interest in the town's *cofradías* was low. The 1976 earthquake had destroyed or seriously damaged the sacred spaces housing the *cofradía* figures, and some of these had never been reconstructed. Members of the existing religious brotherhoods were generally older people. In contrast, the attitude of a significant number of younger Tecpanecos was reflected in a comment by one young man who said that he had no interest in carrying around those "*palitos*" (little sticks—referring to the saints and the custom of carrying them around town on religious holidays). By the early 1990s, however, the sentiments of many younger Catholics had changed. Middle-aged couples who earlier said that they would not join *cofradías* have now become active participants, with thirty-year-old women eager to wear *sobre huipiles* for official church functions. Other women (or sometimes the same ones), those involved in the renewed or reinvigorated practice of Maya rituals—planting or harvest rituals, property transfer rituals, and so forth—also want to wear *sobre huipiles*. Thus, those not fortunate enough to have inherited a *ri'j po't* must find the money to buy one or the time and money to weave one. Either way it is an expensive proposition. A solution settled on by many has been to use cheaper threads for some of the most expensive materials: for example, respun brown acrylic thread is popular for the base cloth of the *sobre huipil*, as it more or less successfully imitates the "hardness" and luster of natural brown cotton. The resulting piece is not an exact copy of an earlier one but rather an object that replicates an "original" to a degree that is acceptable for contemporary use, as discussed in the previous chapter.

In connection with *ri'j po't* and its association with older Maya women and Maya tradition, I want to mention a survey on *traje* that a local Maya woman administered for me. My aims were multiple: to tap into a different pool of respondents, to check the general accuracy of the data I had collected, and to see what additional information might arise from having a local woman ask the questions in Kaqchikel. By and large, the effort supported what I had already found. In fact, the most interesting finding arose from a misunderstanding concerning the preliminary question of whether the respondent wore *traje*. When I reviewed the completed questionnaires (which had been administered orally and filled out by the young woman), I became confused. In some cases where I was sure the woman wore *traje*, the response was "no," she did not. When I talked about this discrepancy with the young woman who had collected the data, I learned that, not surprisingly, she had not asked the respondents what she felt was too obvious a question but, rather, had answered the question herself, based on her own observations. Moreover, her notion of *traje* was not simply that of "Maya dress" versus "*vestido*" (as I saw the matter), but rather one that varied according to the age of the respondent. Thus, for young and middle-aged women who wore the sorts of *cortes* and *huipiles* commonly available in the market or made at home, she wrote "yes"— those women did wear *traje*. However, for older women who wore the same sorts of clothes, she wrote "no." Her reasoning followed a logic that paired age with types of Maya dress. For older women, "*el mero traje*" (the real *traje*) includes not simply a "regular" *corte* and *huipil*, but rather the *penecita* skirt and especially the *ri'j po't*. If the older woman in question did not adhere to these standards (and, specifically, if she did not wear a *ri'j po't*), she was categorized as not wearing *traje*—that is, *traje* proper to or associated with her advanced age.

In addition to their different clothes, the power and prestige of the *ancianos* are in a different realm from that of younger people. If the strength and contribution of younger generations lie in their ability to look out beyond their own community and their own ethnic group to create and perpetuate an active Maya identity, then the strength and contribution of the older generations lie in their ability to preserve and perpetuate the links with the past. Once again, the 1980 *traje* presentation in Tecpán provides a good illustration. While the male emcees, fair princesses, and young women in different municipal *traje* were featured on stage, a group of *ancianos* occupied a place of honor at the front of the audience (Photos 37 and 38). The men—in white pants, *rodilleras*, dark jackets, and hats—and the women—in *sobre huipiles* and *cortes*, with *servilletas* folded on their heads—were being honored because they had continued to wear Tecpán's

37.   Women in *sobre huipiles* at the Tecpán *traje* presentation, 28 September 1980. Older men and women who had continued to wear "*traje tradicional*" were seated in front as guests of honor.

"*mero traje.*" In one respect, the *ancianos* held a role structurally akin to that of the young women: both groups were asked to be silent but visible emblems of *costumbre*. But age and the type of *traje* added a further dimension for the *ancianos*. While some of the young women, whose social personae were still in the making, played the roles of Maya from other municipalities, the older person represented only themselves, the embodiment of Tecpán's living Maya past.

Death

Death is taken as an inevitability, even for someone who has not lived long. "*Pero que va a hacer*" ("But what are you going to do"), uttered by friends and acquaintances of the deceased, expresses the sense of futility over a person who died "too young"—struck down by illness, accident, or murder. The general sentiment is that a mother should not live to see her children die, that the correct order of things is for death to follow old age.

When people die, in all but exceptional cases, they are entombed. In preparation, the clothes of the dead person are washed, the traditional course of action being to take them to a *tuj ya'* (literally, "sweatbath water"), one of the special springs associated with this activity and covered by a *tuj*-like adobe or cinderblock structure. The spring water allows for abundant rinsing of the fabric—an action that is very important for all cleansing and purification procedures.[13] The body itself is washed and then dressed in clean clothes that, while generally not brand new, are still in good condition. An older woman, for example, might be buried in her *sobre huipil*, though it is possible that her family would dress her in a fine *rupam po't* and keep the *sobre huipil* for future use. Because of the strong association between the dead and their clothing, some people are very much set against this practice of reusing garments of the deceased and express surprise that foreigners buy used clothing without even knowing whether they once belonged to a dead person. In some cases the head is wrapped, both around the crown and around the face; once in the coffin, shoes (and in the case of some men, hats) are placed to the side of the body. Families may also include other items associated with or of value to the person (e.g., cigarettes, a Bible, or additional clothing).

For those mourning the deceased, black and purple are appropriate colors. Maya women wrap themselves in a black or purple shawl, the colors that are also used during Holy Week. Men wear dark pants and a dark jacket. And the exteriors of homes and places of business of the deceased may be draped with black cloth or crepe paper. Members of the Catholic church can also request special masses and have black gauzy curtains draped from the church rafters. A special bell with a low, mournful tone is rung to announce a death shortly after it occurs and before the funeral mass. In this way news of the passing and the church ritual circulates in the community.

Starting at the home of the deceased, the funeral procession proceeds on foot, women in a column on the left and men on the right. A stop may be made for a religious service, but all processions end in Tecpán's cemetery on the east side of town. Inside the gates and flanking both sides of the path leading in, one encounters first a long wall of small crypts facing the large, above-ground mausoleums of Tecpán's wealthier families. Beyond these structures lie the smaller, underground burial spots of the majority of Tecpanecos. These are less lavishly marked by mounds of earth and perhaps cement and plaster crosses or plaques, generally painted turquoise, that bear the name of the dead, his or her birth and death years, a biblical verse at times, and, more often, the initials D.E.P. or E.P.D.—for *Descanse En Paz* or *En Paz Descanse* (Rest in Peace). At the far end, where the cemetery begins to be overtaken by a field, there is a long trench in which scores of local victims of the 1976 earthquake lie buried together. In all sections of the cemetery graves are decorated with flowers, both real and artificial; and on special occasions—after the burial itself or for November 1 and 2, All Saints' Day and All Souls' Day—pine needles may be strewn on top of the grave plots. Both forms of decoration are believed to beautify the space and honor the deceased. They also reflect well on the family that remembers and cares for its dead.

There are various interpretations—sacred and secular—of the fate of the person after death. Since all the churches in Tecpán are Christian, every churchgoing Tecpaneco is familiar with certain very basic allusions to dress in the afterlife. The uniform word on heavenly attire is that it is white and composed of light. As one hymn puts it, "White clothing bathed in light! . . . Beautiful robes! (Dress of light you will have.)" (Castillo 1980: 133, my translation). This vision, of course, is generic: Christians around the world hear similar lines and connect it with the purity of the divine.

While I now realize that I neglected to ask Tecpanecos what they themselves thought they would be wearing in heaven, I can testify that it is not something they discuss with frequency. The soul, spirit, or essence of the person is thought to survive the earthly body, but the notion of "soul" as it is discussed in Tecpán does not have a significant visual or material component. The visual and material seem to be reserved for life on earth.

38. Audience at the Tecpán *traje* presentation, 28 September 1980. The elders are seated in the front row; men sit on one side and women on the other.

The volatile political situation in Guatemala in 1980 was forcing many Tecpanecos to reassess their valuation of life. While the politically motivated deaths of prominent Maya leaders from throughout the highlands generally produced fear and concern in the Tecpán population, in certain individuals it produced a determination to fight harder for social justice. As one young Maya man said when asked if the recent murder of a local indigenous social worker scared him, "*Me da más cólera*" ("It makes me angrier"). To him, the proper response was to meet continued injustices and the threat of death with actions in the social sphere. These actions would push for the establishment and protection of indigenous rights within the structure of a truly democratic national government by changing the current offending, ladino-controlled regime. While I was told that it is more common for Tecpanecos to work for such a change through educational channels and not armed resistance, violence all too often is the offspring of social action. In the early 1980s it was not uncommon for death to come to those inspired by others' deaths and for members of the indigenous community to feel even more polarized against a government that it saw as non-Maya and essentially unjust.

FIVE

THE CULTURAL BIOGRAPHY OF *TRAJE*

To weave traje *is to write our past history and our contemporary culture.*

CHOLB'ÄL SAMAJ
(EDITORIAL MAYA WUJ 1991, MY TRANSLATION)

Weaving, that is my job.

TECPÁN WEAVER, AUGUST 1980

I started weaving in Tecpán in August 1980. Up to that point I had completed a number of sewing and knitting projects that I had worked on whenever I had spare moments—at meetings organized by the Ministry of Agriculture, on buses, or waiting in the park for friends. As part of my plan for doing fieldwork, I had gone to Guatemala with a modest library of needlework and weaving books, expecting to create a number of pieces and exchange ideas with people. During my academic training I had been surprised to learn that not all anthropologists who had done arts-oriented fieldwork had tried their hand at making the objects that they were studying. To me that seemed to ignore an obvious way to learn about the subject, especially about information that is contextually bound and not easily articulated in the abstract. I was set on continuing my backstrap weaving efforts in Tecpán, a learning process that I had started in Comalapa six years earlier.

An opportunity arose with an offer from a member of one of the 4-S clubs, a woman who wove her own clothing and also sold commissioned work. Under her tutelage, I worked for several hours each week, first on a simple *servilleta* and then on one panel of a *huipil* that was referred to as my "wedding blouse." I spent close to two hundred hours on the panel and completed only half of it (one-quarter of a finished *huipil*) by the time I returned to the United States. Nonetheless, the exercise was an extremely valuable one. It showed me that the production process is not one that is narrowly focused on technical problems nor is it complete when a piece comes off a loom. Instead, my experience convinced me of the validity of an approach that, in the words of Nancy Munn (1977: 39), sees "making processes not simply . . . , for instance, technological construction, but rather . . . developmental symbolic processes that transform both socially significant properties or operational capacities of objects, and significant aspects of the relations between persons and objects, between the human and the material worlds." Seen in this light, a "cultural biography of things," as Igor Kopytoff (1988) puts it, needs to move beyond the "mere" making of objects and include a consideration of their symbolic values, the relationships between objects and humans, and the larger social processes in which they are involved. In this chapter I examine the production and use of *traje* in this broader sense, and organize the sections in terms of temporal processes of socialization of thread and cloth from the embryonic loom stage to completed and, ultimately, well-worn clothing.

Thread-Level Decisions

The first step in the production and use of dress comes with a decision to wear something new, produce and sell a piece, or give the gift of clothing to another person. Often this decision is prompted by an upcoming event and concerns the person or persons for whom the event is particularly important—a bride and groom, a child having a birthday, a baby being baptized, or a student who is graduating. In the case of Tecpán *traje*, the "cultural biography" of a *huipil* is the most lengthy because of its size and complexity and the fact that it is made locally from the thread level up. What is more, *huipiles* are the most municipal-specific and symbolically dense of all *traje* pieces. For these reasons, I concentrate on their production.

In each measure of thread there are a number of culturally recognized characteristics that contribute to the nature of the finished cloth. When particular thread is bought, important qualities of the finished cloth become unalterably fixed. The choice of a particular thread, therefore, can help determine how the finished piece will look, how it will be used, who will use it, and on what occasion. What is more, not all possible characteristics of thread are given the same (or any) cultural weight. Thus, for example, while the S or Z spin of thread (i.e., the left or right twist given to fibers during the spinning process) relates to good luck and protection from evil in Andean weaving (LeCount 1990: 62), it bears relatively little cultural importance in Tecpán and the surrounding Guatemalan highlands.[1]

All the materials necessary for weaving a Tecpán *huipil* can be bought in the large Thursday market: thread, sticks for the backstrap loom, backstraps made from leather and maguey, and ropes for lashing the loom to a house beam or tree. If a weaver needs a new backstrap, the vendors selling rope products over by the post office have a wide selection. The sticks for the loom are harder to find, but then weavers rarely need to buy new ones. Threads, on the other hand, are prominently displayed and always in great supply in booths managed by local and traveling merchants. These items can also be purchased in a local shop any day of the week, but prices might be higher and the range of choices more limited.

Although decisions made in the marketplace are not restricted to the economic, in this early phase of production the monetary dimension is a prominent one. The buyer needs to take into consideration the financial resources available and the current market costs for the raw materials. These factors set bounds on the kinds and quantities of threads that the weaver can buy and limit the possibilities of the finished product.

Money, however, is not everything at this stage: even with a modest budget, weavers still have a wide range of options, but they need to purchase materials carefully in order to achieve the product they desire. For example, in the case of the fastness of color, it is common to hear people lament that even a few extra cents spent on higher-quality thread or a different brand would have saved a piece from being ruined by colors that bled in the wash.[2] Similarly, an awareness of local color aesthetics and a knowledge of the range of threads offered by different manufacturers allow weavers to buy materials that will result in a more beautiful piece than a similarly priced garment that has been less thoughtfully planned. Called by one man "*la mera flor de esto*" (the true flower of this [weaving]), color is important in terms of not only individual hues but also the combinations created by contrasting colors or delicate shadings, depending on the types of figures woven.

Aside from their hue, colors are classified in terms of their saturation, value, and consistency of shade. On the whole, colors classified as *fuerte* (strong or strongly saturated) are generally preferred for the figures that are "traditional" Tecpán designs. Included among such *fuerte* colors are ones that are further classed as *encendido* (afire, bright): red, orange, and yellow. These, in turn, contrast with "opaque" or dark hues. A strong dark blue, emerald green, or maroon would fit into this category and be satisfactory for traditional Tecpán designs or the ground fabric of a blouse. Black, another dark color, is rarely used in these two contexts. Rather, it is incorporated sparingly on portions of *huipiles* with woven designs executed in *cruceta* (cross-stitch), whereby small groups of warp threads are wrapped with supplementary weft threads. This technique, introduced fairly recently, is used to produce naturalistic designs, including flowers, fruit, and birds. Here colors described as "pale" or "pallid" are also employed. Variegated thread, referred to as *manchado* (stained or spotted), is sometimes used for the decorative figures, but sparingly.

The concept of "color symbolism," labeled per se, is at least vaguely familiar to most school-educated Tecpanecos from presentations in school, lessons in a home economics class, or newspaper articles. One version of this idea, as applied to clothing, is that colors and emotions are related: a particular color in a person's clothes implies or reflects the emotional state of the wearer. Thus, according to one schoolgirl, "red is for passion" and "green is for hope." A newspaper article entitled "*Lo que simboliza cada color*" (What each color symbolizes) gives a more elaborate list:

WHITE: Loyalty, justice, cleanliness, wisdom, purity.
BLACK: Sadness, death, pessimism.
RED: Passion, power, strength, and determination.
ORANGE: Happiness, ambition, appetite, pride.
YELLOW: Infidelity, wealth, health, intelligence.
GREEN: Hope, fortune, calm, activity.
BLUE: Tenderness, skill, calm, virtue.
INDIGO: Ardor, humanity, healing, resolution.
VIOLET: Jealousy, education, sleepiness, goodness.

(*EL GRAFICO* 1980B: 20, MY TRANSLATION)

Generally seen as emanating from sources of "scientific" authority (books, newspapers, magazines, etc.), "facts" such as these are considered by some Tecpanecos (e.g., home economics students) to be knowledge that should be learned without question.

All Tecpanecos, however, show some level of awareness of a localized sense of color symbolism. Whereas the newspaper list articulates symbolic associations apart from any sort of context in which these might operate, color symbolism, as it is "lived" in Tecpán, is very much embedded in particular events and instances of use. Thus, people find it difficult to articulate the range of meanings signaled by a color or to remember the different contexts in which a particular color bears symbolic importance. A few examples have already been mentioned: white for weddings, black or purple for funerals, and red on babies and young animals. Because red has such powerful meanings and is so popular for *traje*, I discuss it at greater length here.

As I stated earlier, red is considered a *fuerte* color, with the double meaning that it is strongly saturated and that, in certain social contexts, it has a force or power to *do* something. In general, the emotions associated with red fall in the superlative bracket, whether on the positive or negative side. For instance, in the Dance of the Conquest staged for the 1980 fair, the Indian *brujo* (magician, wizard, witch) was dressed entirely in red and held a red cloth doll. A trickster, he roamed the town and stole things— a pair of shoes from one shop, some bread from another (all arranged with prior consent)—and was mean to children and made them cry. Among the children I polled, he was considered to be not just bad, but incredibly bad. But red does not always clothe the evil force. As mentioned previously, it can also counter negative forces like *mal de ojo* by protecting the person or animal wearing it.

Red is also a predominant color in the *traje* of a number of highland towns. Although it is not used so extensively in Tecpán, in the neighboring communities of Patzún and Patzicía, red is the principal background cover for the traditional municipal *huipiles*. While the Patzicía blouse was rarely seen in the early 1980s, Patzún's traditional blouse has been a habitual favorite and is worn by women widely throughout the Department of Chimaltenango.[3] Several reasons are commonly given for its popularity: (1) the embroidered designs (often flowers) that encircle the neck are especially beautiful; (2) the blouse is generally cheaper than those from surrounding communities; and (3) the color red is thought to go well with Maya skin tones and to make the wearer look healthy.

Along with decisions about thread color, the buyer needs to consider the permanence of the dye. Because the saturation or intensity of colors—its vividness of hue—is such an important factor in Maya dress, the fastness of the dye used to color the thread as well as the color that the cloth will have after being washed a dozen times are prime considerations. The objective is to choose a color that "*no destiñe*" (doesn't fade or discolor), that retains its full, original color as long as possible.

One way that weavers can select thread and still feel confident that fastness and color intensity are guaranteed is to adopt a routine of buying particular brand names. While there is general agreement as to the superiority of a select group of brands, these are also the most expensive and not always available in town. Among those brands and colors that are available, different people swear by different brands, although often for the same reasons. Along with fastness of color, weavers and seamstresses are quick to point out the brilliance or shine of thread—its ability to reflect light—as an extremely important feature: "*porque brilla más*" (because it shines more) is a very common reason why one brand is preferred over another.

The threads used for weaving a *huipil* are broadly divided into three categories: those used for the warp, the weft, and the designs. Three primary varieties of cotton thread are considered suitable for the warp or weft: *hilo, mish,* and *carriso. Hilo* (thread) is single-ply unmercerized cotton—the thinnest, lightest-weight thread. Tripled (by hand, by means of large chain loops similar to those done in crochet) or quadrupled (the triple strand plus one), it is used primarily for the weft or horizontal threads. *Mish,* a two-ply mercerized cotton thread, is used for the warp or vertical threads (though some women complain that the cloth that results from using *mish* is limp and looks ugly), for weft threads, or for the design motifs added as supplementary weft. *Mish* is used extensively in the last of these roles, for it shines more than *hilo* or *carriso. Carriso,* on the other hand, is a three-ply thread and is thicker and stronger than *mish* and considered by many to be the perfect warp thread for *huipiles.* Because of these qualities, *carriso* warp threads can better withstand the friction involved in the process of weaving and are less likely to pill—that is, to form the linty nubs that are referred to locally as *piojos* (literally, lice) and that interfere with weaving. If a finer thread is used in place of *carriso* (*mish,* for example), it is often sized with a preparation of either starch or corn masa boiled with water until thick.[4] The sizing helps strengthen the thread and prevents it from pilling and breaking so easily.

In terms of the finished woven product, *carriso* also rates high praise as a warp thread. Its extra ply and tight twist make for a stiffer thread and a crisp, almost starched quality to the finished cloth. These characteristics are especially apparent in Tecpán's *huipil* cloth because it is warp-faced, meaning that only the warp threads of the foundation fabric show. As it was explained to me, the body that *carriso* gives to the vertical line of a *huipil* (i.e., the cloth does not sag) combines with the suppleness that an *hilo* weft gives to the horizontal line to make the garment easily gathered around the waist). Thus, the cloth helps create a look that is desirable to Tecpán women, one that clearly displays the *traje* designs but also curves with the body. The finished fabric, however, is heavy, a common complaint about all Tecpán *huipiles.*

Besides these three kinds of thread commonly used for the base cloth, there is also *k'aqo'j,* the handspun thread from natural brown cotton, as well as *lana* (acrylic thread). The first is used exclusively for the *ri'j po't* but, as I mentioned earlier, it is very scarce and expensive. Acrylic thread, on the other hand, is relatively inexpensive and considered warmer than cotton, a factor that is especially relevant to *cortes* in the cold season. However, its suppleness and the fuzzy finish characteristic of a number of brands are not to the liking of many women, so acrylic threads are generally avoided if the person's weaving budget allows for a costlier variety.[5]

Of all the threads used for design motifs, *mish* and *sedalina* (pearl cotton) are the most common.[6] While both are mercerized (a chemical process that increases the durability and luster of the thread [Anderson 1978: 38]), *sedalina* has greater sheen and is considered superior. Because of its cost, however, people carefully consider its expense versus its appropriateness and desirability when planning a weaving. One common solution is to use the pearl cotton for design figures in the very public chest and shoulder areas and to use *mish* for the figures that end up gathered and partly obscured at the waistline and below.

Threads that are less frequently used for designs include silk, *bricho*, and acrylics. Silk is the high-status natural fiber prized for its rich luster. However, it is expensive and hard to find, its colors are often not as fast, and it frays easily, even in tightly woven designs. Because of this, silk is used only rarely in Tecpán weavings and then largely in the less frequently worn *sobre huipiles*. *Bricho*, a metallic thread, is a more literal attempt to give woven surfaces a shiny quality. However, while it regularly shows up in the acrylic *cortes* bought in the market, it is rarely woven into Tecpán *huipiles*. The same is true for the bright Day-Glo colors that are available in acrylic yarns. Even acrylic threads in a more subdued palette of primary colors are still considered less desirable by many weavers and their use for design motifs is restricted.

While these are only the most commonly used types of *hilo* (the generic term for thread, fine yarn, or string), they nonetheless embody the full array of meaningful properties associated with thread. For weavers and consumers of weaving, these properties are important social facts that are discussed in detail at home, in the market, and in ritual contexts. While perhaps not as all-encompassing as the "bovine idiom" that Evans-Pritchard (1969: 19) claimed dominates the lives of the Nuer, the concerns reflected and created by *traje* saturate highland Maya life. Through thread, an elementary component of *traje*, people express concerns about economics (cost), the visual (color, shine, thickness), and the temporal (the retention of color, durability of thread, trends in the use of particular types of thread). These concerns are elaborated upon and grow more meaningful as slender threads gain another physical dimension—width as well as length—when woven into cloth.

The Woven Dimension

Weaver, Loom, Weaving

While the neat formula that equates Maya women with backstrap looms and Maya men with treadle looms does not hold for all highland communities, it does, in fact, provide a reasonable image of the gender division of weaving activities in and around Tecpán. What is more, the image of a male seated at a floor loom weaving *a máquina* (by machine) is one of an individual at his place of employment. This workplace may be a space in a weaving cooperative where a number of looms are operated in the same room (Comalapa had such a place in 1980); it may be several looms in one room of a large family compound where hired weavers come to work on a regular "factory" work schedule; or it may be a special portion of a weaver's own home devoted to a large loom, with the man (or men) of the household devoting long, uninterrupted stretches of time to making cloth. Tecpán has relatively little floor loom production, but what exists generally falls into the last category.

For women, on the other hand, the financial aspect of their weaving, while often extremely important to their families' financial well-being, is not the cultural focus of the activity. Rather, the image of a Maya woman at a backstrap loom weaving *a mano* (by hand) is given a higher value than that of a man at a treadle loom, not simply because the pieces she makes are generally more expensive but because her work has such important cultural associations. As I noted in the previous chapter, the image is related to the notion of females as guardians of Maya values and as the central domestic force binding families together. This binding force takes on concrete form as Maya women alternate weaving with childcare, washing, cooking, and other home-based chores. What is more, the image of woman as weaver is specifically linked to ancient, preconquest times through the goddess Ixchel, whose verbal or visual reference appears in contemporary contexts that are markedly "Maya."

Gender differences in weaving are also reflected in the stage at which men and women learn to weave and the ways in which they incorporate the activity into their lives. While a man might take up treadle-loom weaving well into adulthood as something of a career change, I know of no local women who began learning backstrap weaving once they were past their early teens. In Tecpán, indigenous men are not assumed to know how to weave (agriculture would be the assumed area of expertise), while Maya women are stereotyped as experts. It is almost as if women as a group are expected to be born weavers while men may choose weaving as an occupation, just as they might also choose to make bricks, repair cars, or cut hair for a living. This attitude, I believe, is reflected in women's responses to the question "Do you weave?" Virtually without fail a woman who does not weave offers some rationalization for why she does not: because she went to school and had homework that consumed all her spare time, because she has a salaried job, or because she thinks weaving is boring and prefers crocheting (a typical reply) or another type of hand-work that "grows more quickly," something that weaving is not thought to do.

Although weaving often reflects positively the competence of women as skilled and talented workers,[7] weaving and, by association, weavers also suffer from negative images related to them. Many of these images—both positive and negative—are extensions of those discussed in Chapter 3. On the positive side, praise is lavished on the art of weaving as the essence of Maya culture—how weavers preserve traditional Maya customs with their nearly sacred work and how weaving makes manifest the soul of the Maya. This message comes from both indigenous and nonindigenous sources. On the negative side (and typically from non-Indians), there is the asso-ciation between weaving and backward rural life and the characterization of weavers as unschooled automatons with clever hands.

Because weaving is learned outside the national educational system, weavers do not receive the benefits of diplomas and other officially sanc-tioned academic props to document their knowledge.[8] In an effort to convey the idea that activities learned outside of school are still informed by the same human intelligence, one social worker talked about the meaning of "talent" with a group of young women in a 4-S club. He explained that talent meant using the head first and then the hands and mouth. Without the mind, he stressed, the hands would work like parts of a machine, but informed by the mind, the hands can fulfill their function in "thought-full" actions.

And, indeed, Tecpán women talk of educating the hands and minds together when it comes to learning to weave, as these examples show:

1. "*No pegó en la mente*" (It didn't stick in my mind). This statement came from an accomplished weaver who found she could master the full range of techniques used for Tecpán designs save one, which she claimed she simply could not remember. As I noted before, this phrase is also used with reference to the material learned in school.

2. "*Las manos no saben todavía*" (Your hands don't know [how to do it]

yet). This comment was made about my own ineptness in changing sheds when I first began weaving.

3. "*Es en la mente*" (It's in my mind). This statement was the response when I asked an experienced weaver how she arrived at decisions about design arrangements, their spacing across the width of a weaving, and the modification of designs that fell at the edges.

Learning is, therefore, a matter of coeducation—of mind and body—and when weaving succeeds it is because of the coordination of the two. Taking this a step further, I would argue that weaving is a means for making public Maya intelligence. That the larger world does not always conceive of it this way is a point of frustration and conflict.

The hands and mind get their first real chance to work together in preparing the threads, warping the threads, and arranging them on the loom sticks (Photos 39 and 40). Because the general process has been well documented elsewhere and because of its technical nature, I refer the reader to *Guatemalan Backstrap Weaving* by Norbert Sperlich and Elizabeth Katz Sperlich (1980) for a step-by-step description.[9] However, particular details of the weaving process are relevant here and warrant discussion.

Handwoven blouses in Tecpán are made from two nearly identical lengths

39.　Preparing warp threads for a *huipil*, 1990.

40. Setting up the backstrap loom, 1990.

of woven cloth, or *lienzos*, each approximately three and one-half feet by one and one-quarter feet, and each generally with four selvage edges.[10] In the beginning, when the weaver sits at a newly warped backstrap loom, she faces a large expanse of warp threads neatly arranged along two slender cords that have been lashed to the lower and upper loom bars. These threads, which angle up and away from her lap, have been further manipulated so that half of them are looped around the heddle string (the heddle stick and heddle string enable the weaver to raise every other warp thread and make a "shed" or space through which the weft thread can pass). In addition to the heddle, there are other sticks with important roles: the bobbin carries the weft thread back and forth in the weaving; the shed roll, or *ruk'u'x* (center; literally, "its heart"), maintains a cross in the vertical warp threads and enables the weaver to form the second shed; and the batten serves to beat the newly woven threads into place (Figure 6). The weaving takes shape as first one shed and then the other is

opened, and the horizontal weft thread (or threads) is laid in with a bobbin or by hand.

In Kaqchikel the word for "weft" is *ruway* (literally, "its tortilla"). When
I commented on this term, people would respond with something like,
"Yes, you can think of it as the weaving being filled with its food." This
kind of statement led me to think of the *Popol Wuj*, the sixteenth-century
K'iche' text that is now taken to be a general statement of Maya origins by
many indigenous Guatemalans. In the *Popol Wuj*, the successful creation
of human beings is accomplished by combining water and corn, which
Ixmukane grinds nine times:

> the making, the modeling of our first mother-father,
> with yellow corn, white corn alone for the flesh,
> food alone for the human legs and arms,
> for our first fathers, the four human works.   (TEDLOCK 1985: 164)

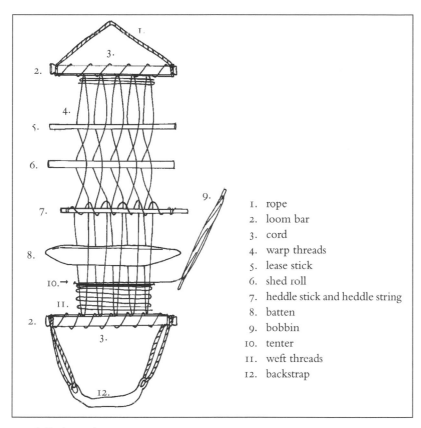

1. rope
2. loom bar
3. cord
4. warp threads
5. lease stick
6. shed roll
7. heddle stick and heddle string
8. batten
9. bobbin
10. tenter
11. weft threads
12. backstrap

FIG. 6. Backstrap loom

Nowadays, the principal use of ground corn is for *way* (tortillas), the staff of life in the highlands and something that, like weavings, all young women are supposed to be able to make before they get married. Just as the early Maya were made from corn/food and the Maya living today are filled with corn/tortillas, warp threads become cloth with *ruway*.

A woman sitting at a newly warped backstrap loom does not face several feet of undifferentiated space on which to create patterns of colors and shapes. Her work is limited and simplified by formulas that she may call upon to help her structure threads into a blouse. By this I mean that weavers have as a resource conventional methods of dividing up the surface of the warped loom, methods that are learned and modified by each person. An experienced weaver "sees" these as she faces a new weaving: she sees *lienzos* of past *huipiles* reflected on the surface of the newly warped loom and she has a sense of the possibilities for change that are open to her.

The first segmentation of the surface is physical and comes in the form of a smudge of dirt, pencil lead, or charcoal from the cooking fire at a point halfway up the loom. This mark indicates the part of the weaving that will fall at the top of the shoulder—the *ruk'u'x rutele'n* (center of the shoulder; literally "its-heart its-shoulder"). The goal in executing the piece is to weave a set of patterns up to this point and then produce a mirror image of those patterns on the upper half. When the piece is finally worn, both halves appear "right side up," one on the wearer's chest and the other on her back.

Other broad divisions are mentally noted and only take physical shape in their woven form. In Kaqchikel, the three basic areas of *rupam po't* (*huipiles* that are worn tucked into skirts) are labeled: (1) the *ruxe' po't* (literally "its-base blouse"), the unadorned area that falls below the waistline of a blouse and is tucked in; (2) the *ruwäch ruk'u'x* or *ruwa ruk'u'x* (chest; literally "its-face its-heart") or *chuwäch ruk'u'x* ("in front of the heart"), the area of adornment that centers on the chest; and (3) the *rutele'n* (literally "its-shoulder") or *ruwi' rutele'n* ("on top of the shoulder"), the band of designs that covers the shoulder area. These areas are woven in the order listed, the height of each being calculated so that half the *rutel'en* is done when the weaver reaches the smudge on the warp threads marking the midpoint of the *lienzo*. Here she begins reversing the order of designs and weaving the figures upside down (from her perspective, at least). Further divisions of the woven surface are possible, both in terms of named areas and the elaboration of visually distinct design areas (Figure 7); and, like poets with their rhyme schemes, weavers manipulate these areas to

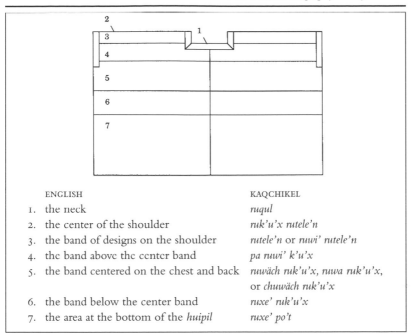

	ENGLISH	KAQCHIKEL
1.	the neck	*ruqul*
2.	the center of the shoulder	*ruk'u'x rutele'n*
3.	the band of designs on the shoulder	*rutele'n* or *ruwi' rutele'n*
4.	the band above the center band	*pa ruwi' k'u'x*
5.	the band centered on the chest and back	*ruwäch ruk'u'x, ruwa ruk'u'x,* or *chuwäch ruk'u'x*
6.	the band below the center band	*ruxe' ruk'u'x*
7.	the area at the bottom of the *huipil*	*ruxe' po't*

FIG. 7. Parts of the *huipil*

create different overall effects.[11] Blouses with particularly elaborate structural schemes are often made for special occasions; however, whatever the blouse or its intended use, a basic principle remains: each *lienzo* is structurally divided into two halves along the central shoulder line, with each side a mirror reflection of the other. In addition, the designs above the *ruwäch ruk'u'x* are often repeated below it.

This information is interesting from a broader cultural viewpoint for several reasons. First, the physical and mental divisions of the woven surface map directly onto the human body. The "shoulders" of the two lengths of handwoven cloth eventually lie on the shoulders of the person, and the "chest/heart" of the blouse encircles the chest and heart of the wearer. The weaver weaves a two-dimensional object and imagines how it will cover, enhance, and perhaps even mimic the three-dimensional body.

Second, a conceptualization of these divisions is important as the time, effort, and materials put into the different sections of each *lienzo* vary according to where they fall on the cloth and, subsequently, on the body. The upper part of the finished blouse is the most public part and, hence, the area most likely to be thickly and painstakingly woven with expensive threads. The bottom part of the blouse, on the other hand, is tucked into the skirt and is out of sight, so designs located there are often woven in less expensive thread.[12]

Finally, while there are significant differences between the ends and the center of the *lienzo*, its symmetry around the *ruk'u'x rutele'n* means that there is no distinction between the front and back of a finished blouse. The weaving designs run across the entire width of the loom, with threads laid in place row by row, band by band. In the completed *po't*, these rows of figures join end to end and become circles that encompass the whole upper body. The designs are situated not only on the front of the body, as is sometimes the case with *vestido*, but all around the upper trunk, much the same way as the designs of a *corte* encircle the entire lower body.

Design Motifs

To weave patterned figures on a backstrap loom, a person needs good eyesight, excellent manual dexterity, some facility with numbers, and an ability to manipulate spatial concepts mentally. While these are the minimum requirements for the manual and technical aspects of the craft, to be fully informed of the cultural dimensions requires a great deal more local knowledge. Two designs might look alike to an outsider, but to the local eye subtle variations in weaving technique, scale, material, or color scheme can signal different municipal origins or production at different points in time.

In highland towns like Tecpán a core set of designs has been associated with the community for as long as people can remember. While these "traditional" municipal motifs are sometimes described as if they were unchanging (e.g., in school presentations and at certain cultural events), existing patterns are, in fact, regularly modified in terms of scale, spacing, quantity, placement on the blouse, and color combinations, and the popularity of particular motifs waxes and wanes with time. These traditional *etz'ab'äl* or *figuras* (figures, designs) also have names in Kaqchikel and Spanish, some of which are known by nearly everyone in town—for example, curl, star, comb, scissors or lightning, and flag (see Photos 23 and 32). Others, however, are not so easily labeled. In fact, in one case no agreement could be reached by the group of weavers I queried, and a couple of people even said they had no idea what the thing was called, though, yes, it certainly was a design used in Tecpán and, yes, they themselves could weave it.

In addition to these older, time-honored patterns, there is another set with much more contemporary origins. In Tecpán this class of figures is known by the name of the other art form that it closely resembles as well as the weaving technique used to produce naturalistic representations of fruits, flowers, birds, and other animals. *Cruceta* (cross-stitch) designs are formed by wrapping small bundles of warp threads with supplementary weft threads according to patterns found in cross-stitch magazines and other, gridded design sources. These often lavish figures are commonly used for the wide *ruwäch ruk'u'x* band that appears prominently on the upper chest and back. Referred to as *marcador* (marker) in other towns, this style of *huipil* design is also currently popular in Chichicastenango, Comalapa, and San Antonio Aguas Calientes.[13]

Design patterns are conventionally associated with particular regions of a *lienzo* and the finished *huipil*. For example, the motif known as *kumätz* (snake, in Kaqchikel) or *arco* (arc or arch, in Spanish) is a popular choice for the wide *ruwach ruk'u'x* band.[14] On *sobre huipiles* this design can take an exaggerated form, with the zigzags rising and falling more than six inches, whereas on everyday *huipiles* arcs are generally only three to four inches high (see Photos 12, 23, and 37). In 1980, this central band was also an important space for showcasing ornate *cruceta* designs, as were the shoulder areas and the spaces immediately above and below the *ruwäch ruk'u'x*. *Cruceta* designs, however, are considered too time-consuming to weave and too beautiful to fall below the waistline. Rather, this seldom-seen space is covered by small, quickly woven "filler" patterns, often done in cheaper thread. These patterns generally have few historical or municipal associations, a status reenforced by their position on a blouse.

Finally, I want to consider the representational dimension of design motifs. As mentioned earlier, virtually all of the figures used in Tecpán have labels, and these labels, by and large, are the names of things. Some of these terms seem to reflect an iconic relation between the name and the woven design (i.e., the dove design looks like a bird, the *jicha'n* or *peine* could pass for a comb, and so on), while other designs appear to have a more nonrepresentational, symbolic relationship with the object named (e.g., it would take some imagination to see scissors in the *tijeras* design). Although non-Guatemalans who learned of my research seemed excessively interested in knowing the stories behind these design motifs, weavers virtually never told stories when I talked to them about these patterns. For them, the labels seem to refer most directly to the designs themselves and not to what the designs resemble or represent symbolically (cf. Forge 1973). The representational dimension becomes important only within certain contexts—particularly the academic or folkloristic. For example, during the Concurso de Vestidos Tipicos de Guatemala (Contest of Typical Dress of Guatemala), held among the town's secondary schools in July

1980, one contestant in Tecpán *traje* claimed that the *arco* was a road while the *paloma* stood for liberty.[15] I was reminded of this interpretation months later, when the questionnaire I described in the previous chapter elicited this comment about the same *arco* design: "It is said that they [Maya weavers of the past] invented it because of the volcanos." When I showed this comment to other Tecpanecos, it roused little interest and was generally dismissed as but one individual's interpretation. A response to the contestant's interpretation of the *arco* figure likewise seemed aimed more at the person making the comment than at what was said. In the course of judging the event, one of the two ladina judges (I was the third "expert") complimented the contestant on her knowledge of "*traje* symbolism" and then gave her points under the category "originality" on the score card. But was this simply a ladino response? I see parallels here with the reactions to another event in which the participants were Maya.

At the 1980 *traje* presentation, one of the two emcees from the Instituto Indígenista Nacional recounted a story about the origin of the curl design. The story concerned a girl who came upon a boy in a cornfield one day. She was so nervous at this chance, quasi-illicit meeting that, while they talked, she twisted off a leaf from a corn stalk, played with it by folding it into quarters, and then began nervously chewing on the folded corner. When the conversation ended, the girl tucked the leaf into her basket and returned home. Later, when she sat down at her loom, she began thinking about a new weaving design. At this point, she spotted the leaf of corn in her basket, unfolded it, and discovered that her teeth had made an interesting pattern that she turned into what is now the *colocho* design.[16]

After the story was told, just after the significance of the teeth marks was revealed, the audience laughed heartily. I noted the incident with amusement but did not give the story a great deal of weight. Afterward, however, I was surprised to find myself approached by people who wanted to make sure I had heard the tale because they took it to be just the sort of information I wanted about weaving patterns. Yet, when I tried to make sense of the story itself as information about the particular design or its symbolic content, I was at a loss. At that point my assumption was that the content of the story and its relation to woven figures was the appropriate point of interest.

Now, however, it seems to me that the reason the story was embraced had less to do with what was said and more to do with the authority of the emcees—their status as academically trained experts from a government institution whose official capacity is to record and convey knowledge on indigenous culture. Furthermore, the authority of their explanation contrasted sharply with the local and particular knowledge advanced on other occasions by "ordinary" individuals with their homegrown theories. Thus, while ostensibly an account of the origin of the curl design, the episode is more telling if seen in terms that include the storyteller's identity and the audience's reaction. The broader frame of reference allows for a different understanding of the systems of authority and the sources of authentic knowledge about traditional Maya culture.

Color Considerations

If considerable thought goes into the selection of design elements and their distribution on the surface of the *lienzos*, the same has to be said of the use of color. To produce a weaving with "well-coordinated" colors, the weaver must take care to follow certain principles. In all figures, except for parts of the naturalistic *cruceta* designs, the object is to achieve the maximum contrast in colors. Just as thread is chosen in the marketplace for its shine, different colors are juxtaposed to achieve the optical sensation of sparkle or vibration. Such combinations are thought to be *alegre* (cheerful or merry) color schemes, in contrast to *triste* (sad) ones. Accordingly, it is appropriate to place an orange figure next to one that is blue, purple, or magenta, but not next to one that is yellow. Similarly, blue can be placed next to red, orange, yellow, pink, or white but not next to green. In fact, as my weaving teacher told me, when it comes to selecting colors for these designs, blue and green can be considered the "same color."

For figures done in *cruceta*, on the other hand, blue and green are definitely not the same, as I learned in an embarrassing incident that occurred while I was weaving my *lienzo*. I had just completed one row each of dove and curl designs. Having been told that blue and green are "the same" and sensing that I had come across an instance of cultural sensitivity to color that was very different from my own, I enthusiastically launched into weaving a band of flowers in *cruceta* based on my new understanding. If blue and green are "the same," I reasoned, I could use navy thread to create darkly shadowed portions of the foliage. I had no sooner begun when my teacher asked me what on earth I was doing. No, she said, blue was not an appropriate color for leaves; I should use dark green. Our conversation ended there, but what had started out as an attempt to be culturally savvy ended abruptly with a feeling of ineptness.

Blue and green are "the same" only in instances where the figures are *not* rendered in *cruceta* (i.e., they are not portrayed naturalistically) and where maximum contrast in color is desired. With *cruceta*, on the other hand, shades of the "same" hue are considered distinct and can be used to render subtle variations in the shadows and reflections of woven flowers, fruits, and foliage.

Weaving Techniques and the Classification of Rupam Po't
Surprisingly, Tecpán *traje* is seldom mentioned in the textile literature on Guatemala, perhaps because of the many *huipil* "looks" that make it difficult to summarize a municipal *traje* style. In my own work, I was eager to document this variety but found myself trapped by some of my own cultural assumptions about what I was looking at and how different blouses are classified and labeled. For example, motivated by an interest in the different types of *huipiles* and guided by the assumption that there must be a neat set of labels to match all these differences, I began to ask people for the names of the various forms of finished blouses. I was somewhat perplexed when they were not able to respond readily; in most cases, they appeared to be struggling to come up with some term that would satisfy my curiosity. For instance, I would point to a blouse covered entirely with geometric shapes and ask, "What do you call this style of blouse?" Pause. "*Huipil de Tecpán.*" "Then what do you call this?" I would ask next, pointing to a blouse covered with dove and curl designs. Pause. "*Huipil de Tecpán.*" Several examples that I thought were stylistically distinct prompted the same generic label, and I was left with the feeling that I either was not asking the question clearly enough or was asking the wrong question. With time, however, I became convinced that the "truth" is located somewhere in between.

Much of the information that revised my thinking emerged during sessions focused on learning Kaqchikel Maya, when I was conversing with Maya teachers skilled in fathoming the meaning of foreigners' questions and illuminating cultural activities through language. On these occasions, when I pointed to design motifs of *huipiles* and asked the names of the different styles, I was told that I had to understand how the different designs were woven. I was given the names of three different weaving techniques and shown examples of each.[17] In essence, the three techniques divide motifs into three separate groups, each one with a distinct appearance created by the addition of supplementary weft threads to the weft threads that form the ground fabric. Because the additional thread is laid into the sheds along with the regular weft thread, some tourists think that the figures have been embroidered onto the finished cloth, but the design motifs are actually created as an integral part of weaving *lienzos*.

41. *Huipil de Tecpán*, 1992. Note the geometric shapes of the *jun ruwa kem* technique at the top of the shoulder and bottom of the blouse (scissors with stars and little rings respectively), the wide, floral band of *cruceta* crossing the chest, and the *ka'i' ruwa kem* technique used to form curls above and curls and stars below the chest band. The V-neck *huipil* became popular in the 1990s.

The three techniques used to make the designs on Tecpán *huipiles* are *jun ruwa kem*, *ka'i' ruwa kem* or *ka'i' nitzun*, and *cruceta* or *ka'i' rupalaj* (Photo 41). *Jun ruwa kem* (one-sided; literally, "one its-face weaving") is single-faced supplementary weft patterning; the additional thread appears only on the surface of the finished cloth and not at all on the back. Figures formed by this technique are what I call geometric shapes (flag, scissors, arc, comb). In many instances, they are woven in rows that completely cover and hide the foundation fabric. *Ka'i' ruwa kem* or *ka'i' nitzun* (two-sided), on the other hand, is a two-faced supplementary weft technique whereby pattern threads appear on both sides of the weaving—as a "positive" image on the front and a "negative" image on the back. The figures formed by this method (dove, curl, star, fan) are more "free standing" in that the background cloth shows around each motif.

As I have mentioned earlier, *cruceta* or *ka'i' rupaläj* (two faces) has entered the repertoire of Tecpán weaving techniques fairly recently. With this technique, warp threads are wrapped, but they do not form double-faced or identical patterns on both sides of the cloth (as is done in some towns). *Cruceta* is used to depict realistic representations of flora and fauna. Moreover, while the shapes, thread counts, and embellishments associated with the two older methods of weaving produce a stable and fairly predictable assortment of designs, new *cruceta* patterns appear all the time (though the themes tend to be focused within a certain "organic" range). *Cruceta* is also considered the most time-consuming of the three weaving processes and is generally reserved for special projects.

An additional set of terms distinguishes types of striped cloth that form the foundation fabric of some Tecpán *huipiles*. The general labels for this cloth and style of blouse are *kajin chij* and *xilon* (striped). The former term can be further modified by adding colors to denote two distinct styles of blouse known as *kajin chij säq* (literally, "stripes thread white") or *kajin chij k'aqo'j* ("stripes thread brown"). The striped *rupam po't* with a predominance of brown was also described to me as a *pequeño ri'j po't* (a mix of Spanish and Kaqchikel meaning "small *sobre huipil*") because it is an "inside blouse" that resembles the ceremonial *sobre huipil* (see Photos 5 and 12). The white striped blouse, the one commonly labeled *xilon*, is said to be related to a traditional style of *servilleta* associated with Tecpán weddings and ceremonial occasions (Photo 42). While the blouses with a solid ground cloth are woven with the full range of motifs and feature a wide selection of design combinations, all the striped blouses I saw were adorned with patterns executed in the two older styles of supplementary weft work but not with *cruceta*. This practice seems fitting, for the striped blouse styles are referred to as extremely old weaving forms, unlike the "newer" solid-base *huipiles* with their "modern" designs and creative sequencing of bands.

While all the *huipiles* I have described so far are made with two *lienzos* and have design motifs that extend across the entire width of the blouse, there is one style of Tecpán *huipil* that is made from three *lienzos* and has short rows of *ka'i' ruwa kem* design motifs (e.g., doves, curls, stars) confined to the areas around the neck and armholes (Figure 8). Woven with a solid brown ground fabric, the restricted placement of *figuras* means that relatively large spaces of coffee-colored cloth are visible. This arrangement of design motifs at the neck and armholes and solid brown cloth in between is also very different from the structure of the horizontal bands of motifs that I described earlier for other Tecpán blouses (cf. Figure 7).

I first saw one of these *huipiles* in 1980 at the home of my weaving

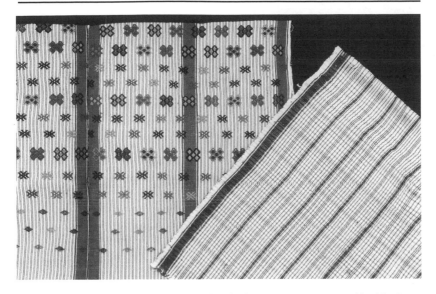

42. *Xilon*-style cloth, 1983. Left: *huipil* with dog pawprint patterns (double figure eights) and stars; right: *servilleta*.

teacher. She had made what to me was a very different sort of Tecpán blouse following a description of clothing that her mother had seen when the older woman was very young. Later I located two instances of the blouse in different textile collections and have since learned that the *huipil*—referred to as a *tyoxi'b'äl po't* (saints' blouse)—was a type worn by women involved in *cofradía* activities. Though the blouse I saw in 1980 was made with acrylic thread, it seems likely that, in the past, *k'aqo'j* was the principal material for the warp and weft threads, given its use for other ritually significant garments (e.g., the *ri'j po't*). By 1990 more women—*traje* vendors and active participants in revitalization activities—were weaving these *huipiles* based on verbal descriptions and, in a couple of cases, aided by photographs that I had taken of the older pieces.

Completing the Project
In the minds of Tecpanecos, a weaving becomes more beautiful as qualities of individual elements are tastefully combined during the production process. The color and shine of thread, for example, join to create intense contrast of colors and subtle shadings on the woven plane. Additional indicators of a particularly fine and well-conceived weaving are the complexity of the motifs, the number of colors combined in a given figure,

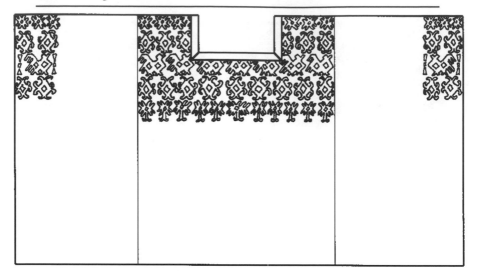

FIG. 8.   Tecpán *huipil* with historical ties to *cofradías*

the fineness of the handwork, and the creativity displayed in appropriately recreating older styles.

Shaping the completed *lienzos* into a wearable, three-dimensional form provides another opportunity to add more textures and significant details. For example, pleats or, occasionally, decorative smocking are positioned over each shoulder and run vertically down the front and back of the blouse, from the shoulders to the waist. They help square off the shoulder area and give the upper body an erect look that bespeaks proper posture and alertness. Pleats also stiffen the cloth and help the bands of designs lie horizontally across the upper trunk, often beyond the shoulder blades, which enables viewers to see clearly and, hence, appreciate the designs and handwork on the front and back of the body. In addition, velvet ribbon or cloth tape with floral designs finish off the neck and arm openings. The floral tapes are associated with older styles (the *ri'j po't* and the striped *huipiles*). Similarly, the cut of the neckline is charged with meaning: round necklines were used on *ri'j po't* while square necklines were standard on most *rupam po't* in 1980. Within the past ten years, however, V-necklines have become increasingly popular, especially among girls and young women.

It is important to remember that the garments described in this section are worn by women and contribute to the qualities that are thought to be

quintessentially female. Their bright, contrasting colors are seen as especially appropriate when worn by young Maya women whose physical
appearance likewise is often described in terms of shine—such as "*ojos
brillantes*" (shining eyes) and "*pelo liso y brillante*" (smooth and shiny hair)—
whose nature, like that of *traje*, is flowerlike, whose visual beauty attracts
public attention, whose creativity and innovativeness parallels the creative
potential of *traje*, and whose presence in Maya dress helps signal the con-
tinuation of indigenous culture.

Clothing the Body

At the start of the *traje* production process, thread and other "raw materials" leave the public space of the market or store and enter the household
or other private workplace where they are woven, pounded, sewn, and
otherwise manipulated. They eventually reappear in public, transformed
into the articles of *traje* worn by Tecpanecos. This process—going from
raw materials to clothing—is also a transformation from an inanimate
object minimally charged with meaning to an animated object that is
dense with cultural significance. *Traje* here is animated not only by the
person wearing it, but also by the spirit of Maya culture reflected in its
designs, colors, and shape. In addition, the person wearing *traje* is engaged
in an exchange of sorts, although the transfer is visual rather than material. Tecpanecos in *traje* "give" members of their community, especially
Maya members of the community, the "gift" of presence. By actively wearing *traje*, indigenous Tecpanecos signal to the world that they intend to
preserve *costumbre* and participate in a dynamic Maya community.

But wearing *traje* in a meaningful, active manner is conditional on a
knowledge of what to wear and how to wear it properly. Summed up in
the process of dressing—in the seemingly trivial details of arranging a skirt
or fastening a belt—is a universe of meanings that are mastered, manipulated, argued about, and exalted by members of a society. In this section I
will explore some of these meanings in the process of examining individual elements of *traje* and the act of dressing and undressing.

For indigenous Tecpanecos, not wearing clothing in public is inappropriate for all but the smallest of children. In fact, under certain circumstances, merely seeing people with insufficient clothing can cause illness.
A Maya woman explained to me that there are indigenous people of "*una
otra mentalidad*" (another mentality, meaning less educated in the ways of
the world and less progressive than she considered herself and her family

to be) who are so sensitive that, if they see men and women together in bathing suits, they can become *asustado* (frightened, in the sense of being affected by *susto*, a disease characteristically brought on by violent transgressions of social norms). As she explained, these people think that "*el cuerpo es de uno*" (the body belongs to the individual) and is not for others to see. She, however, sees herself as more worldly and would not avoid beaches simply because people in bathing suits are present. However, she would not necessarily wear one: there is a significant difference between accepting an action in others and actually doing it oneself.[18]

In another beach episode, the division between ladinos and Indians was drawn by differences in what were considered acceptable displays of the body and clothes. During a Ministry of Agriculture trip that I made with a group of 4-S women and girls from Tecpán and Patzicía, the ladinas in the group stripped down to their underwear to bathe, shampoo their hair, and wash a few pieces of clothes at a popular lake resort and in the presence of strangers.[19] The indigenous women, on the other hand, paid little attention to their minimally attired traveling companions, but they were greatly concerned about exposing their legs above their calves as they waded deeper into the pool. While some of the Maya hitched their skirts up over the knees, others, amid great laughter and blushing, got their clothing soaked rather than exposing more of their bodies in public.

Whether in thigh-deep water or on dry land, a Maya woman typically appears in public completely covered, with the exception of her head and neck, arms below the biceps, and legs from the calves down. Exactly how much of an arm or a leg shows depends in part on municipal styles (e.g., the Chichicastenango *corte* is notably shorter than that worn in Tecpán), attitudes about skin color (e.g., so as not to show bands of whiter, untanned skin on the arms), and a sense of proportion (e.g., the balance between areas above and below the waist), to name but a few factors. Women nursing babies freely expose portions of their breasts, although those with more schooling and higher-status jobs are less likely to do so in very public spaces. Exposing the breasts at other times, however, is not considered normal or in good taste but rather the actions of women who are mad or promiscuous.

For Maya men the norms for exposing different body parts are basically the same as those for ladinos. Scantily clad male bodies are routinely seen at sports events—soccer, basketball, cycling, and running are all popular—where the appearance of bare legs and the occasional bare chest is accepted almost without comment (except, perhaps, by an admiring observer). For the vast majority of public appearances, T-shirts and button-front shirts clothe the upper body and all or part of the arms, while long pants cover the lower body and legs. Despite this coverage, clothing can be worn to reveal the body underneath, though the meanings associated with tight shirts and pants, say, differ according to whether the wearer is identified as sexually flamboyant, a growing youngster, or too poor to afford anything else. Among young Maya men, the exposure of feet—in sandals or because the person has no shoes—is a mark of low economic status, although some men involved in Maya revitalization now wear the types of sandals that are seen as "Indian" to express ethnic pride through "traditional Maya footwear."

For older Maya men who wear *traje*, the degree to which they cover or expose body parts seems to parallel that of older ladino men, but here I am less sure that the two standards have been historically motivated by the same cultural concerns. The white pants of men's *traje* are cut wide at the seat and legs, with the front of these pants covered further by the *rodillera*. Because the woven belt used to secure the *rodillera* is the wide variety and over two yards long, even wrapping this tightly around the waist does little to reveal body contours. Though the exposure of feet in sandals goes with the use of this footwear for *traje*, closed shoes are preferred by many because of their warmth and what they signal about wealth and "civilization."

As with men's traditional clothing, Tecpán women's *traje* of the past is said to have revealed little of the body's contours. With six *varas* of skirt cloth wrapped around her waist, some two yards of blouse material gathered inside, and then all of this held together by the long, wide belt common years ago, a woman ended up with more or less equal measurements at the bust, waist, and hips. This, in fact, is the image projected by many older women who still wear the wider belt.

While younger and middle-age women use many of these same elements of *traje*, a narrower belt (one to two inches wide) has helped them alter their body silhouettes and achieve today's preferred look. The narrower belts are wrapped even more tightly around the waist, cinching in the area between the rib cage and hips. The desired body shape, as humorously described by one young woman when she was five years old, is "*delgadita de la cintura y abultadita del pecho*" (slender of waist and bulky of chest). The curious phrase "bulky of chest" does not refer to accentuated breasts per se—which is associated with ladina clothing. Rather, it describes the way the whole upper body fills a *huipil* so that the woven surfaces of the front and back lie square and flat and, hence, can be "read" by the viewer. Correct posture—standing up straight and rolling the arms in slightly so that the shoulders are square—and choosing blouses made with *carriso*—so that the cloth stands stiff and does not drape—allow for optimal display of the *huipil* and its designs, not to mention the wearer herself.

But how exactly does a Tecpaneco bring together all the various articles of *traje* to achieve a socially appropriate and culturally meaningful look? How, through the act of dressing, does a person create a particular social persona? Because the clothes and the process of dressing vary depending on the individual, I describe the situation for a young, single woman in her late teens or early twenties, the age when appearances are important in presenting oneself publicly to possible marriage partners, in community events, or on the job.

Women's undergarments are commonly used and consist of underpants—jokingly labeled *jaulas* (cages)—and brassieres (used mainly by younger women). In the larger, ladino-dominated world a great deal of attention is given to the role of women's underwear in intimate male-female interactions and in provoking male lust. For example, in the *fotonovelas* (romance comic books with photographs instead of cartoon drawings) that are so popular throughout Guatemala, pictures and storylines generally have fully clothed men pursuing women in various states of undress, with the emphasis on lingerie and acts of undressing. Among the indigenous population there is no emphasis on such public displays, and suggestions of how the body might be undressed emerge more in private, often ribald joking situations.[20]

The first outer garment to be put on is the *huipil* or *po't*, whose principal function was described to me as covering the upper body and keeping it warm while, at the same time, allowing for the free movement of the arms for work. Despite the bulkiness of Tecpán *huipiles*, women believe it is important to have the entire two yards of cloth evenly gathered around the waist. Given that the six *varas* of skirt cloth must be folded, wrapped, and adjusted a great deal to position them correctly, keeping the gathers of the blouse neatly in place during the process can be an exasperating task. One woman solved this problem by first securing her blouse with a slender string tied around her waist and then wrapping the skirt material. The string did not show after the skirt was in place and yet it gave the blouse a neat and orderly look. Her "invention" proved so effective that a number of other women inquired about her technique, proving that the problem was definitely a matter of importance to the women.

Similar technical problems exist at the skirt level and these, too, relate to larger questions of personal presentation and identity. Before *corte* cloth is ready to wear, the six *varas* of fabric are sewn to form a tube. Flattened, the tube of cloth is reduced to a three-*vara* length, double in thickness. At this point, the length of the skirt is also adjusted. If the meter or so of the *corte* material's width (what will become the length of the skirt) is too long for the wearer, the cloth is simply folded. Folding raises additional concerns—whether this folded edge should fall at the waist or the skirt hem; whether the double thickness of cloth should fold in toward the waist or inward to the center of the tube; how these tucks differ for acrylic versus cotton materials—that are believed to influence the appearance of both wearer and the *corte* cloth.

After this preliminary preparation, a *corte* is ready to be worn. How tightly the material is wrapped around the hips, thighs, and knees depends on personal taste expressed within a culturally appropriate range. A very tight wrap gives the woman a look described as "rolled" or, jokingly, "cigarlike," and makes walking, running, and boarding buses difficult. A *corte* that is too loose, on the other hand, is like "a flag"—that is, the material flaps around in an uncontrolled and unseemly manner. In addition, a woman needs to pay attention that no single layer of her skirt cloth falls below the others, thereby creating an unsightly "tongue."

Whatever the wrapping technique used, all *cortes* in Tecpán are held in place by belts, the current trend being toward narrower ones that are wrapped tightly around the waist to produce an hourglass shape. This shape has probably been adopted to conform to a more contemporary aesthetic in women's wear, one that spans ethnic boundaries. As I pointed out earlier, Maya women's dress, while distinct from the *vestido* worn by ladinas and foreign visitors, nonetheless accentuates the femininity of the wearer in ways that relate to a non-Maya aesthetic. The use of narrow belts to produce a cinched-in waist helps create an image of the Maya woman that overlaps with and accommodates this other concept of femininity at the same time that it marks a difference between younger and older Maya women.

An error in the proper fastening of one's belt can cause an embarrassing situation. If a belt is loosely or improperly secured, a *corte* may slip down and expose the woman's lower body—one of the most private parts of the body. Even a hint of exposure—not to mention the inference that an adult had still not mastered the basics of putting on clothes—would be devastating.[21]

But why is this part of the body considered so private and stigmatized? As I mentioned earlier, from an early age children—especially girls—are toilet-trained to understand the private and polluting nature of the lower body and the act of relieving themselves. A certain association with pollution also carries over to the clothing that covers the lower body. For example, I was talking with a Maya woman about tourist goods made from used *traje* pieces. One of us brought up the subject of jackets made from used *cortes*, especially the indigo *cortes* that age to resemble stone-washed denim. The woman made a sour face and explained that she never could understand why a person would want to wear a shirt or jacket (i.e., something for the upper body) that had previously wrapped someone else's rear. Even washing and refashioning the form of the cloth could not remove the stigma of its former use.

These issues of privacy also relate to women's reproductive functions. Drawing on research that she conducted in San Pedro la Laguna, Guatemala, in 1941, Lois Paul distinguishes between production and reproduction and, what is particularly important here, the role of different parts of the body in performing these activities:

> Female tasks in San Pedro not only are arduous but require a high degree of motor skills ranging from the refined wrist and finger movement required for weaving and making tortillas to the control and balance of the whole body. . . . [The Pedrano woman] glides gracefully up and down the paths to the lake balancing a heavy pottery water jar on her head. She pats and twirls corn dough into perfect tortillas with the motions of a skilled craftswoman. And she weaves handsome textiles with fingers deftly shuttling the weft back and forth across the warp. (1974: 285–286)

These same sorts of skills are part of women's work in Tecpán today and emphasize active hands, feet, and heads. In contrast to this competence in work, Paul discusses the mystery and uncontrollability of the body—here represented by the lower body or just that part covered by the *corte*—when it comes to matters of sex and reproduction (ibid.: 299). While sex education today prepares girls to enter puberty with more awareness of biological processes and the functioning of their bodies, the lower torso and thighs remain a very private domain, not the public, erotic sphere that is more likely to characterize a non-Indian woman's lower body.[22]

The area covered by a *corte* is also the part of the female body that receives the most conservative treatment. For both Maya and ladino women, a change in the type of clothing that covers the lower body is considered much more extreme than a change in clothing on the upper body. For example, it is not uncommon for certain ladino women—those who are wealthier or more educated and perhaps those who feel some sense of solidarity with the indigenous population—to wear *huipiles* with slacks or skirts. Likewise, an Indian woman may wear a cheap, ladinoized blouse around the home (a garment that becomes more inappropriate the further she ventures from home or, in contrast to the ladina use of *huipiles*, the wealthier she is). However, a ladina in a *corte* or a Maya woman in slacks or a skirt indicates a much more serious break in form and a greater transgression of categories—unless, of course, the situation is unusual (e.g., a play or, for Maya, gym classes).

Besides the *huipil, corte,* and belt, other major elements of women's *traje* are worn as situations demand them. At home, a woman is virtually never without an apron. The apron, in fact, is something of a symbol of the wearer's domestic role and the hard work that comes with being a woman. In a Mother's Day morality skit put on by a group of young Maya women, the lazy, selfish daughter was portrayed as sitting around the house in "good clothes," without an apron, and reading a *fotonovela.* The hardworking, thoughtful daughter, on the other hand, wore an apron and older clothes and worked with her mother, who also wore an apron and an even more tattered *huipil* and *corte.* As part of the preparations for a wedding, the family of the bride provides their daughter with a new outfit that often includes an apron. Wearing this, the young woman takes on her newly acquired domestic duties and shows her intention to be a hardworking wife. A multipurpose item, an apron serves her as a towel, a potholder, a carrying cloth, a hand wiper, a nose wiper, a place to carry money (in the zippered pocket), and a protector of *cortes.*[23]

Another sort of apron, one not found in a bride's trousseau, is meant to be worn in the public square more than in the kitchen. Short, generally made from costlier materials, and lavishly adorned, these are typically worn by young women with less schooling who see them as elaborate and fashionable (though not purposely ironic) symbols of their knowledge and preparation to assume responsibilities in the home.

When women think of keeping warm, shawls—especially ones with traditional tie-dyed designs—are the historically and culturally appropriate Maya articles of clothing. Sweaters, however, are common and said to be much more convenient when a woman needs her arms free for cooking, washing, sweeping, and caring for children. Towels, too, have served as wraps. A type of Cannon-brand towel with large printed floral designs was a favorite some years ago, but I did not see them worn in Tecpán in

1980; however, I remembered their popularity in Comalapa in 1974 and noticed some well-worn floral towels still used as wraps in San José Poaquil six years later.

Shoes, hair ribbons, and jewelry complete an outfit. As I mentioned earlier, the debate surrounding shoes turns on whether *caites*, sandals marked as "Indian," are necessary wear for all who claim to follow *costumbre*. Those who say no argue that *caites* are too unfinished and old-fashioned. Instead, they prefer shoes (either enclosed ones, often with heels, or sandals) that look less "homemade" and that bespeak the user's awareness of dress codes of the larger, multiethnic world as well as the competency of Maya in general.

Hair ribbons fall into two categories and are marked for the age of the wearer and for ceremonial versus everyday use. First, there are the *tocoyales*—long, thin bands of cloth woven with bright multicolored designs and with pompoms at each end. These are used almost exclusively by younger women in *traje* presentations or other public events of a "folkloric" nature. They are not associated with the Tecpán municipal *traje*, and no one in town wears a *tocoyal* on a regular basis. Second, there are *listones* (ribbons) in a range of pastel colors. These are made of four- to six-inch-wide strips of factory-made, brocaded satin cloth. Older women regularly braid these into their hair, the midpoint of the five-foot-long strip positioned at the nape of the neck and each of the two halves substituting for one of the three tresses of braided hair. The ribbons make thin hair look more substantial and attractive, as a head of thick, shiny hair is a much-admired attribute for women (cf. Firth 1973: 262–298). Younger women, with their fuller heads of hair, wear *listones* only occasionally to participate in a folkloric event or dress up for a special celebration.

And, finally, jewelry—earrings, necklaces, and rings. Based on the materials from which it is made, jewelry is classified into four broad types: (1) *de oro* or *de plata* (made of gold or silver), the finest variety; (2) *de fantasía fina* (made of a fine, common material), made from nonprecious metals (brass, copper, etc.); (3) *de fantasía* (made of a common material), or cheap jewelry made from "any old wire" and very prone to discolor; and (4) *de fantasía barata* (made of a cheap, common material), which includes the cheapest sort of unidentifiable metal that is sure to discolor as well as plastics covered with metallic paints. The type of jewelry bought and worn depends on such factors as the occasion, the wealth of the buyer, and the personal preferences and religion of the wearer (evangelical Protestants shun the use of jewelry on biblical grounds). Furthermore, for jewelry, as with shoes, locally made varieties that are markedly "Maya" (e.g., older pieces with coins and glass beads or newer creations in traditional designs made from silver and colored glass) are passé for many women.[24] Instead, pearl and gold loop earrings, rings with hearts and rhinestones, and gold mesh necklaces are the styles preferred and worn by the majority of Maya women in Tecpán. As a result of this system of preferences, I found myself in the position of bringing friends in the United States the "traditional Maya jewelry" they requested and, at the same time, taking friends in Guatemala the contemporary jewelry from the United States that they desired.

In these pages I have described the items of a young woman's *traje* one by one, more or less in the order she would dress herself. However, to discuss the act of dressing as if one were clothing a naked mannequin for the first time ignores the fact that people wear clothing pretty much all of their lives and only pass from one stage of dress to another at very specific times in the day or week. Thought of as a regular activity, the act of dressing and undressing can be seen as dividing up and giving shape to time in Tecpán.

Clothing is routinely changed after bathing and between activities that call for markedly different sorts of public appearances. Washing in a *temescal*, shower, or plastic tub takes place in the early morning (among office workers), during midday when the sun is high and the day warm (especially among children, who are susceptible to cold), or late in the afternoon (after a day of labor in the fields or at home). Virtually without exception, a complete change of clothes is called for at this point.

To a lesser degree, a marked change in activities calls for a change in dress. A trip to the capital, attendance at a special town event, or an opportunity to have one's photograph taken, for example, necessitates anything from a simple change of shoes or the removal of an apron to a more complete changeover involving pants, shirt, or blouse. People who live in the center of Tecpán tend to treat the difference between home and the streets of town (especially the streets immediately surrounding their homes) as minimal and do not change clothes if they simply need to run to the local thread shop or bakery for a small purchase. However, people who live in Tecpán's outlying villages and who journey long distances into town for the large Thursday market or church on Sunday see this occasion as a more dramatic shift in their daily activities and dress accordingly. I recall following an elderly man in *traje* in from the edge of town one Thursday as he finished his early-morning hike to the central market. As he neared the edge of the plaza and the first of the market stalls, he stopped, hid his walking stick in a clump of bushes, and pulled the cuffs of his clean white pants out from inside his muddied rubber boots. With clean clothes visible and properly arranged for his urban outing, he proceeded into the market square.

Bedtime is also marked by changes in dress, for some more than others. Before retiring, many women simply loosen their belts and *cortes* and sleep almost fully dressed. I have also seen women remove particularly fine *huipiles* and sleep in their *cortes*, undergarments, and sweaters. Among younger, more worldly women, nightgowns are worn to bed. However, for Tecpán males—ladino or Indian—*piyamas* (pajamas) are not considered masculine attire, though some exception is made for the rich in Guatemala City, who are thought to have different habits owing in part to their proximity to European and U.S. fashion circles. In general, Tecpán males sleep either in the clothes they wear during the day or in their underwear. In the morning, they put on more or less the same clothes, unless they bathe and dress for the new workday.

Garments that are deemed dirty are put aside until washday. Because washing is believed to rejuvenate clothes, the act of washing is seen as similar, if not identical, to making brand new clothing. On this subject, I overheard a young man telling a young woman that he would not attend an upcoming event for lack of a new outfit. The young woman said that this was silly—if his clothes were "very clean and well ironed," they would serve as well as new.

The notion of the rejuvenating powers of washing figures heavily in religious imagery, too. Religious texts not only speak of the cleansing of the body (as in baptism) but also use the cleansing of clothes as a metaphor for the purifying powers of God and God's ability to make people "new."

Laundry methods vary, depending on the material conditions of people's lives as well as their attitudes about which method produces the cleanest clothes. In Tecpán, the most common place to wash is in a *pila*, a large, shallow cement sink with a corrugated bottom that serves as a washboard. The majority of families in the center of town have running water and *pilas* in their yards (sometimes sheltered but, more commonly, open to the elements). For those lacking this convenience, the municipality also maintains several large public sinks where women can meet and socialize as they do their wash. Families living in some rural areas may not even have the luxury of a communal *pila* and, instead, may have to wash clothes in a river, using large, flat rocks for scrub boards.

A woman starts her wash by scooping little plastic tubfuls of water onto the clothes to soak them thoroughly. She then rubs cylinders of soap, purchased at the market or from a store, vigorously on the cloth, giving special attention to soiled spots. To work the soap and water through the clothes, the cloth is squeezed, rubbed, and turned. Throughout the washing and rinsing, quantities of water are poured over the pieces so that clean water runs through the cloth until the soap and dirt are removed.

Because local notions of correct laundry habits are so strong, Tecpán women visiting a distant highland town were appalled to see the residents there washing laundry in large wooden washtubs. Because the water could not flow through the fabric and away, the visitors felt that these other women were just washing their clothes in dirty water. As for washing machines, people like the idea of pushing a button and having the wash done automatically; however, they find washing machines of limited value because they feel that the clothes are poorly rinsed (in dirty water) and that clothes made of nonfast or delicate threads cannot be properly handled.

In any case, the goal is clean clothing, which goes beyond the articles themselves and reflects on the the wearer. Thus, for example, in a poem entitled "Ropa limpia" (Clean Clothing) by Guatemalan writer Rafael Arévalo Martínez Barrientos (Barrientos 1973: 31), "clean clothing" and a "clean/pure girl" (*muchacha limpia*) become poetically equivalent objects as laundry is washed and the young washerwoman smells of soap and clean clothes. Conversely, things that are *sucio* (dirty) are seen not only as physically soiled but morally tainted or lacking. For example, early in his life Miguel Ángel Asturias, a ladino, wrote on the condition of Indians in Guatemala and drew on the already-stereotyped parallels between dirt and racial deficiencies: "He [the Indian] represents the mental, moral and material dearth of the country: he is humble, he is dirty, he dresses differently and he suffers without flinching" (1977 [1923]: 66). Today, indigenous people still suffer from an enduring stereotype of "*indio sucio*" that equates the presence of dirt on one's clothing with lack of intelligence and morals. This results in the negative characterization of an entire ethnic group, as if dirty clothes always signaled more than an occupational hazard or a lack of economic resources.

Old Clothes

The cycle of washing and wearing clothes does have its limits when it comes to rejuvenating garments. Colors fade, threads fray, and seams rip out, leaving *ropa vieja* (old clothes) that are decidedly different from the original, newly finished ones. For an earlier era, Lilly de Jongh Osborne observes that "[Maya] clothing is not divided into 'everyday' and 'best' as with us" (1965: 142); rather, the norm was to own one complete outfit for a variety of occasions. Today, however, the "best clothes" of one year become the "everyday clothes" of the next; and, in the majority of cases, it is the age of a piece and not its tailoring or style that places it in one category or the other. Thus, for example, the blouse that a woman wore when she married half a decade ago is used around the house today, and a special fair outfit for one October becomes the woman's weekly market attire the next. Time, in the case of *traje*, is more often reflected in patterns of use and wear than it is in terms of fashion or style.

Ri'j po't signal the passage of time even less than other *huipiles*, in part because the style changes relatively little and also because they are used only on special occasions and receive special treatment in their storage and care. What is more, a slight patina of wear—usage that leaves pieces more supple, but not frayed or tattered—actually enhances the cultural value of overblouses because it means that they have a history of use, presumably within Maya ritual contexts. *Ri'j po't* are used repeatedly within a family as the blouse is passed from generation to generation; however, as far as I know, Tecpanecos are not interested in acquiring used *ri'j po't* from other families for their personal use.

Because of the special qualities of some articles of *traje* and the expense of all of them, efforts to prolong the functional life of a piece are more or less drastic, depending on such factors as the nature of the item or the financial situation of a family. For example, while virtually all women wash their *huipiles* inside out to prevent fraying and dry them inside out to prevent fading, only a certain portion of the female population will wear them inside out to protect them from the sun. In 1980, for example, I regularly saw market vendors selling produce in the open plaza with their *huipiles* worn inside out; however, when I returned ten years later, this was not the case. I attribute this change to increased wealth in Tecpán, which includes recovery from the 1976 earthquake.

A more extreme attempt at prolonging the life of *traje*, and one virtually unheard of among the relatively affluent residents of the center of Tecpán, is to make a "new" *huipil* by turning an old one upside down. This transformation is accomplished by slicing the tattered blouse along the shoulder line, hemming what is now a two-yard-long circumference, and then sewing up what was previously the bottom hem so as to leave a neckhole. The old armholes are also closed and new ones opened at what used to be the bottom sides of the garment. This procedure exposes the protected (hence newer-looking) cloth of the *ruxe' po't* (the base of the blouse) and hides the worn parts that originally fell over the shoulders and chest. A major drawback, however, is that the "new" *huipil* will have few

43. Woman wearing a *sobre huipil* inside out, 1980. The crowd is standing outside the
     new Catholic church.

visible woven designs since almost all of these now fall below the waistline. In addition, a blouse like this makes a clear and public statement
about the wearer's poverty, which few Tecpanecos would care to do.

Old pieces of Tecpán *traje* are more likely to be used in other ways.
Extremely tattered items (especially ones that were inexpensive to begin
with) are used as rags around the house, or they may be cut up into
patches and used to repair other articles of clothing. The better pieces can
also be resold. For example, a number of people from the center of town
have connections with rural communities where clothes may be taken
and sold. Likewise, people from these rural areas come into town for

44. One side of the tourist market surrounding Antigua's central plaza, 1990.

market day and sometimes inquire about secondhand clothing. Maya and non-Maya vendors who sell *típica* ("Indian" goods) in tourist centers like Chichicastenango, Panajachel, and Antigua also purchase used clothing to sell whole or reconstituted into tourist items. In 1980 I occasionally found used Tecpán *traje* for sale in these heavily frequented tourist centers (Tecpán itself had virtually no tourist market), but never in any great quantity. Ten years later, however, I saw pieces of the town *traje* everywhere being sold as whole or refashioned pieces, in market stalls and shops in Guatemala and the United States. I even found a piece whose "life history" included multiple assignments to the used-clothing category: a ladino-style vest made from used Tecpán *huipil* cloth that appeared for sale in a secondhand store in Brattleboro, Vermont.

Many of the used *huipiles*, *cortes*, and belts that make it to Guatemalan tourist markets are sold "as is" to people who want an authentic piece of highland life and who buy items because of aesthetic concerns (color, design, etc.), low prices (especially when compared with the cost of new pieces), and an interest in having something that was once worn by "a real Indian" (the patina of use). This enthusiasm for used *traje* sometimes leads foreigners to trade Maya vendors new articles of *vestido* (blue jeans or T-shirts, for example) for older and well-worn *traje* pieces. In these situations both sides can feel a certain satisfaction for getting the better deal by trading an object that has less value for one that has more.

At other times used *traje* (especially blouses and skirt material) is cut up and sewn into wallets, shirts, patchwork blankets, purses, duffle bags, pillowcases, and jackets, to name only a few from the vast sea of tourist products offered in Guatemalan markets. Dying *traje* cloth to give it a uniform hue is also fairly common, as it converts bright, multicolored pieces to shades that are popular with tourists. A deep purple dye, for example, is often used ("Tourists like purple," I was told by a woman who runs a weaving cooperative), as are rust brown and amber washes.

Dealers in "ethnic art" are also interested in locating old *traje* pieces, especially unique items that are well preserved. Objects with religious connections—*ri'j po't* or clothes used to dress the statues of saints, for example—are especially prized. However, as often happens in the world market system, it is not the original producers of the cloth who realize large profits for their pieces. Rather, the wealth goes to elite intermediaries, both Guatemalans and foreigners, who participate in and help to create a market of fine and antique "art objects" from around the world.

No matter who the buyers are, Maya women often sell used *traje* in order to purchase more thread with which to weave new garments. In this way, too, old clothes beget the new and provide a concrete link to subsequent creations.

SIX

TRANSFORMING THE TRADITIONAL
The Creative in *Traje*

> *Tecpán with its . . . young women who cook on the life-giving* comal *[tortilla griddle] and weave the threads of the future.*
>
> *TECPANIDAD*
> (AJOZAL XUYÁ 1977A: 3, MY TRANSLATION)

The production of *traje* is part of daily life in the central highlands. All Tecpanecos are at least minimally aware of the conventional steps by which thread and other raw materials are transformed by weaving and sewing. The final products of these processes are also something expected—new items of clothing, yes, but ones shaped by preexisting standards.

Because of these conventional processes and categories of objects, virtually all individual items can be "reduced" to instances of more general types. Of course, no single classification totally defines an "object" (be it a person, thing, or action), nor can an object be considered exceptional or rare by every person, on every single count. For example, one's nine-year-old child is like every other nine-year-old child only from a very particular perspective, and a weaver's newly completed *huipil* is much more likely to be considered "just another *huipil*" by some unappreciative third party than by the creator herself. Still, the relative uniqueness of most nine-year-olds and *huipiles* is at a level where *all* such objects are incomparable and hence, at the same time, not exceptional. This is what I call "stereotypical creation."

On the other hand, objects are candidates for the truly "creative" when they push beyond the expected at a level of classification where striking differences are *not* expected. Such objects are seen to differ from the objects with which they are normally associated more than they resemble them: they exhibit qualities in such a way that people who should know better are struck with differences instead of similarities. In sum, they defy the centripetal force of classificatory schemes so as to stand opposed to existing categories, and not merely as another element of one. However, at the same time that the creative is transformative, bringing to light the new and heretofore unthought of, it is inextricably bound with elements of the old. The old and the usual, in fact, provide the very stuff from which the new is constructed and with which it is compared: within the old and preexisting lie the elements—and the potential—for what can be perceived as manifestly new.[1]

What is creative or new in society, then, is essentially a judgment in the classification of things. But the strength of this judgment depends on such factors as who or what segment of society makes it, under what circumstances, and for what purposes. What is more, the conditions of these other factors might also be shifting in critical ways; hence the nature of their separate but related development also needs to be examined.

That said, I turn now to some examples of *traje* made or worn in Tecpán. I use as illustrations certain instances that do not immediately fit within existing categories of clothes, at least not for some people. In each of the cases, I examine the appearance of the pieces for the additional comments they provide on the social context of their production and use; and I argue that attempts at changes in *traje* are, in fact, attempts at or hopes for transformations in social relations.

Four Candidates for the New

In this section, I discuss four examples in which the manipulation of conventional components of highland clothing is thought to produce pieces hitherto unknown in some classificatory sense. As I hope to show, all of these items have roots in *lo tradicional* (the traditional), yet each is perceived by at least one person to fall outside existing categories at some significant level. That claim, of course, can be made for a number of innovations that weavers and handsewers see in their work. I have selected these particular examples because they demonstrate different degrees of recognition in the community, have gained expression through different classes of individuals, and were accompanied by significant amounts of local commentary on the creative process.

When I first wrote this chapter, I labeled these cases "candidates for the new" in order to express the tentativeness with which I made my claims. Time is needed to determine whether innovations will have imitators and whether the new sets themselves will become conventional and a standard against which yet newer creations are judged. Because more than a decade has passed since I first made these observations, I have a modest historical perspective and so can also comment on the fates of these four "inventions."

Case 1. Tecpanecos have a notion that when someone tries something new and it gets a favorable response, others will flock to copy it. I was told that this is how many people in the area came to grow strawberries: one person tried the crop and made a substantial profit, so everyone else immediately began devoting land to berries. The same is also said of people's interest in planting broccoli.

Referring to this phenomenon, a woman explained an innovation in blouse design that she considered her own and that she thought would appeal to Tecpán Maya. Instead of using the satin stitch to form flowers around the neck and sleeve edges, as is usual for the hand-embroidered Indian *blusas* (blouses), the woman created floral patterns using bullion knots—a sort of elongated French knot. While bullion knots are often part of the repertoire of local handsewers, they are rarely used to create entire flowers and their appearance as the body of the embroidered flowers on the *blusa* was the woman's creative twist.

While this project was underway, the woman sewed in the privacy of her own house. She said that she did not want other people to see what she was doing, as they are quick to copy any attractive innovations. However, when the blouse was finished and worn, it was admired and commented upon by others but, as far as I know, not imitated.

Case 2. On 23 February 1980 the first Maya priest native to Tecpán was ordained. To mark the special event and his unique membership in the category of people who are priests, Maya, and Tecpaneco, the young man enlisted a local weaver to make two *lienzos* of the handspun brown cotton cloth usually reserved for *sobre huipiles*. The young priest, however, had the specially loomed fabric, complete with traditional silk designs, sewn into ordination robes by nuns in the city of Quezaltenango. This unique combination of the Tecpán *huipil* cloth sewn into a traditional priest's chasuble paralleled the young man's unique status as an indigenous priest native to Tecpán. It also signaled his awareness of his Maya identity at a time when the indigenous population was taking a strong stand on political and social issues in the highlands and when the popular Catholic church was being charged by the church hierarchy and Protestant groups with taking too political a position on civil struggles. (Unfortunately I do not have a photograph of the chasuble, but Photo 45 illustrates *sobre huipil* cloth that was transformed into another sort of ritual garment, a cape for the 1980 fair's Princess Ixmucané.)

Case 3. Years before I began working in Tecpán, weavers started including bands of floral and fruit designs on their *huipiles de Tecpán*. In 1980 modestly sized strips of these naturalistic designs appeared in structurally

45. Indian fair princesses at the *traje* presentation, 28 September 1980. Princess Ixmucanè (right) wears a cape made from two *lienzos* of *sobre huipil* material; Princess Iximché (left) wears a length of backstrap-woven cloth draped across her chest and back, beauty-pageant style.

and visually important areas of the blouses—across the chest and shoulders—and on *huipiles* made for special events. By the time I returned to Tecpán in 1985, large and beautifully detailed *cruceta* designs had taken over the whole chest and shoulder areas of some particularly stunning blouses. On yet another visit five years later, I discovered the logical extension of the trend: Tecpán *huipiles* covered entirely in *cruceta* designs. Whether or not the expansion of the *cruceta* patterns proceeded as smoothly as it appeared to me from the perspective of my infrequent trips, the general trend seems quite apparent: to innovate, first, by introducing a particular technique and, then, by using it in more and more areas of the blouse.

Case 4. In general, Maya women have a keen interest in earlier styles of municipal dress. Some can give detailed descriptions of older forms of *huipiles, cortes,* and belts and can recall when they, their mothers, or their grandmothers wore such pieces. They are eager for additional information on Tecpán's material past. And they talk about making or commissioning new blouses in one of these older styles at some point in their lives.

In the previous chapter, I mentioned the case of the weaver who produced a contemporary example of an old style of municipal *huipil* from a description provided by her mother. When I showed the weaver a photograph of a similar blouse from a private textile collection, she carefully inspected the picture and regarded it as additional proof of the authenticity of the recollected style. At that time, I speculated that the new-old *huipil* would be reproduced by other weavers with a similar interest in styles of *traje* from the past.

As it turned out, when I returned to Guatemala in 1983, I did, in fact, see Tecpán women wearing a "new" traditional *huipil* style. However, instead of the one I had expected to find, it was an updated version of the white, striped *xilon* (or *kajin chij säq*) style. This *huipil* is said to have been common in the early part of the century—when today's oldest women in the community were young. This style is the one I had seen only once in 1980–1981 on a very old woman in a rural area of Tecpán. In September of 1983, however, an updated version—with larger design motifs woven on a field of white with dark (red, blue, black, etc.) vertical stripes—was being worn by a number of school girls in the Independence Day parade (Photo 46).

Exegeses of the Textiles

A closer look at the four cases will illuminate why each is and is not an example of the new as well as why it is and is not an example of the traditional.

The first case is an example of an individual innovative effort that never succeeded in having any collective voice. Like the vast majority of innovations, it did not gain anything close to the significance that its creator attributed to it once it was worn publicly. These kinds of innovations may have individual admirers, but they receive rather limited comment and, in general, do not have enough presence to be considered much more than a variation on one of the existing classes of objects. This is often the reac-

46. Maya students in *xilon* blouses marching in Tecpán's Independence Day parade, 15 September 1983.

tion when the creative aspect of *traje* is seen as "merely" a technical variation. It may be copied later on but not enough times *or* by the right people *or* in relation to key social issues, any one of which might mark it as special and essentially different.

But why did this particular blouse not receive greater attention? As I mentioned, a blouse with floral designs sewn exclusively in bullion knots is a variation on the more common *blusa* done in satin stitch. Embroidery techniques aside, *blusas* are not traditional Tecpán wear and, in fact, have no municipal associations with local *traje*. Because of this, they do not receive a great deal of attention, nor are they a prime object of local innovative efforts. Thus, while a creative variation in *blusas* might be widely admired, it is seldom widely imitated.

The ordination robe made of Tecpán *ri'j po't* material presents a different and rather exceptional case. While significant shifts in *huipil* styles generally do not occur in an instant and are not identified with individual weavers or wearers, both the creative force behind the new priest's ordination robes and the moment of its first appearance can be clearly assigned. Who was behind the changes, why, and during what point in

Guatemalan history are all important questions that help explain the uniqueness of the creation.

The ordination of the first indigenous Tecpán priest was a noteworthy event in that he was a member of two groups—Maya and Catholic priests—who had active roles in the sociopolitical life in the highlands in early 1980. By that time, much of the highland area to the north and west of the municipality was an arena for government or guerrilla actions. This situation was known to Tecpanecos, a number of whom privately favored one side or the other based on their perceptions of what the government was doing and how it was treating the local population. Among Tecpán Maya, opinions ranged from an extremely negative attitude toward the government to one of ostensible neutrality; indigenous Tecpanecos who were strongly pro-government were scarce.

Within this context, the young priest was something of a known quantity. He, like many young, educated Tecpanecos, had a definite opinion on the social situation in Guatemala and the state's link to local injustices. Tecpanecos who knew him well were aware of his opinions and recognized that these convictions could motivate his church work. His use of the special robe sent a clear public signal that not just any man was being ordained a priest or that the new priest happened to be an Indian. Indeed, it conveyed to the townspeople and church authorities that the man saw connections between his being Maya and a priest (notably a priest within the tradition of Catholic Action), and that he would combine the two individual identities so that their sum would equal more than they would separately. By using the most special—one might say "sacred"—*traje* cloth to make the ordination robes, the young priest combined two revered items into one. He also struck something of a balance between them: the indigenous aspect was not a mere adornment tacked on to the more usual Catholic robes. The Maya contribution to the garment was virtually the entire material aspect (one coded as "female," too), while the traditional Catholic contribution was the cut (though even here the loose, unfitted shape of the priest's chasuble resembles that of a *sobre huipil*).[2] Likewise, being Maya was not an "interesting" fact about the young priest but rather an integral and active aspect of his social identity; and being a priest allowed him to take a strong, institutionally supported moral stand on issues that arose from his essential identity as a Maya. In this way he embodied the joining of two powerful forces in the current highland struggle: the indigenous sector and the Catholic church.[3]

The inclusion of the third example—the *huipiles* with *cruceta* designs—is based as much on my own perceptions of innovation in *traje* as that of

Tecpanecos. According to my initial thinking, at least, something that looked so different had to be seen as new and distinct. Or so it seemed. To be sure, *cruceta* designs involve a weaving technique different from those used to produce the other design motifs in the Tecpán weaving repertoire. The subject matter and sources of these designs are also distinct. However, the *cruceta* flowers and fruits are woven into the "same" named bands of the municipal *huipil* and are placed according to the same general rules as for other woven *figuras*. In fact, when I referred to blouses with the *cruceta* designs as a new style of municipal *traje*, I was corrected: no, these were just "*huipiles de Tecpán*," members of the broadest, most general category for local Maya blouses.

Despite this reaction, I still believe that the appearance of *cruceta* designs on *huipiles de Tecpán* were conscious (though not easily verbalized) attempts to innovate and promote new cultural meanings via *traje* in the early 1980s. As I noted earlier, these innovations in weaving went along with women's efforts to signal new information about themselves—the weavers and wearers—and their status as preservers of *costumbre* and knowledgeable actors within a highly ladinoized world. As far as I am aware, however, the general appearance of *huipiles* with *cruceta* designs was never associated with a single, noteworthy event, as was the case with the ordination robes. A better example of a link between innovation in women's *traje* and a significant social situation is provided by the fourth candidate I described.

In this fourth case—the one involving the reappearance of the *xilon* blouse—different themes arising both within the indigenous experience and within the national arena are brought together in a powerful clothing statement. Tecpanecos immediately identify *xilon* blouses with those their grandmothers wore when they were young and, in doing so, acknowledge the historical significance of the style. Notwithstanding ties to the past and to elderly women, in September of 1983 *xilon* blouses were "new" to their youthful wearers—they stood out as significantly different from the other Tecpán *traje* worn at the time. While just a few years before such blouses were seen only in rural areas, and then rarely (primarily old, ragged pieces on elderly women), in 1983 they were relatively numerous in the center of Tecpán. Newly woven and made with the finest materials, they were worn by younger women for the most special occasions.

But what was the force behind this change in dress between early 1981, when I left Tecpán, and mid-1983, when I returned? Certainly there was no one individual, like the young priest, who had single-handedly precipitated this change. The production and wearing of *traje* in Tecpán, being collective acts with a range of skilled producers and wearers but no singular creative authorities, tends to eclipse the maker or wearer and render him or her virtually anonymous. While individual weavers take pride in their work and never think of themselves as slavishly copying "traditional patterns," it is not through associations with particular individuals that *traje* gains its presence and power. What is more, the *xilon*-style *huipil* appears to have gained (or regained) a critical mass that will assure its continued recognition as one of several styles common in Tecpán daily wear. No longer a mere curiosity piece on an individual or two, it has reemerged as a recognizable social actor with its own substantial force.

When I asked people what had brought about the sudden popularity of these *huipiles*, the most common response was "They're pretty" or the equivalent. On other occasions people talked about the respect that one pays to one's Maya heritage by such a display. And, speculating as to why the change occurred when it did, one woman suggested that it was a female expression of Maya pride at a time when other, more overt expressions could result in death. Indeed, between May 1981 and September 1983, a significant number of Tecpán's indigenous male leaders had been killed or driven into hiding for speaking out against the establishment, in the course of performing their jobs or working with Maya organizations. The indigenous men who remained in town were much more cautious and less outspoken on issues.

Maya women, though seen as less publicly active than males and tied to the domestic sphere, nonetheless had the means by which to express similar strong social sentiments. Taken in the context of the 1980s, the *xilon*-style *huipiles*, though "mere cloth" and incapable of any direct, referential statement, brought into sharp focus Tecpanecos' pride in their Maya heritage and the active role of *traje* in community life.

The strong showing of the *huipil* in the municipality-wide Independence Day parade is further evidence of this phenomenon. Worn by indigenous girls in the ranks of marching schoolchildren, the blouses were seen in the same context as the army troops from the town's military garrison and townsmen parading as members of the civil patrol. For the Maya audience, the troops were an unwelcome intrusion by the national government into town life, and the civil patrol but one example of how local citizens are coerced by the government. Thus, the revived *xilon* blouse highlighted the message that indigenous culture is a vital force that can adapt to difficult times and yet retain its strength and unique relation to the Maya past.

In conclusion, I want to note several general points on the nature of change and creativity in *traje*. First, to say that something is "*tradicional*" does not mean it has been slavishly copied from existing works. A piece is judged to be usual, innovative, or inappropriate for a category based on a perception of what is expected. Expectations, of course, differ depending on the category, but, in the case of *traje*, many of the classificatory boundaries of the traditional are sufficiently wide or flexible so as to allow for the production and use of what, to the untrained eye at least, looks like unrelated clothing pieces. The blouses with *cruceta* designs are an example of this.

Second, elements of the past are, in fact, often the raw materials from which the new is created. An embroidery stitch rarely seen on other *traje* pieces can be used to create the figures on a "new" blouse, one that still has a traditional cut and construction. Lengths of cloth woven in a time-honored, quintessentially Maya manner are cut and sewn to make a Catholic priest's robe. And patterns of colors recalled from the past form the warp threads that are then woven with currently popular design motifs.

Third, despite their innovative aspects, all the pieces discussed here are still considered traditional at some level of classification. In the first and fourth examples, the blouses are unquestionably Maya even if they are not exactly like any other *blusa* or *huipil* seen in recent history. The chasuble, while a vestment in the Catholic tradition, is immediately identified as a special garment related to indigenous culture by virtue of its *ri'j po't* material. And, as I said earlier, the blouses made with *cruceta* designs are firmly established as Tecpán *huipiles*, at least as long as I've been asking questions.

Fourth, the "new" cannot endure as such for a very long time. It quickly becomes part of the established classificatory scheme and, as such, part of the background for additional new works. This evolution is what I see as the progress—or life curve—of the *xilon* blouse. And this is why, I believe, the *cruceta* designs were probably seen as much more innovative in their scope at some point prior to my appearance in the central highlands.

Finally, the data suggest that, in Tecpán, the strongest creative statements—ones that are particularly striking to a wide range of people—combine innovations in technical aspects of weaving, handsewing, or wearing *traje* with "comments" on the broader social situation. Creativity is not just a text—or text(ile)—internal play on weaving techniques. The sociocultural commentary of *traje* is made possible through the manipulation of elements of dress that have widely understood meanings. In the most striking cases, the visual episodes are open to complex interpretations that can bring together themes from virtually every segment of life. The exact manner in which these themes come together creatively is, of course, unpredictable. However, the issues that at any given moment dominate community life—or even threaten it—are also likely to be the ones that receive people's creative attention. Indeed, in the most striking cases I recorded, cloth goes against its seemingly innocent and mute nature and functions as a highly insightful and critical social commentator.

But cloth and clothing can do more than simply reflect or "comment on" other aspects of the social situation. Manipulated creatively, *traje* itself can become the "event" that defines a particular social situation—a particular point in history. And *traje* does so by the seemingly impossible feat of being traditional and new simultaneously.

SEVEN

TO WEAR *TRAJE* IS TO SAY "WE ARE MAYA"

To wear Maya traje *is to say to ourselves and to others:
I am Maya, we are Maya, we continue and will continue
being Maya.*

CHOLB'ÄL SAMAJ
(EDITORIAL MAYA WUJ 1991, MY TRANSLATION)[1]

The people who wear *traje* or make it or know something about it are not all the same. Ladino vendors may be experts on *corte* craftsmanship and design, Maya men who encourage other Maya to wear *traje* may not do so themselves, a Maya woman's blouse may be bought and worn by a male tourist from the United States or Switzerland, and, at times of national celebration, a variety of Guatemalans—both Maya and ladino—may dress in the "national costume," *traje*. As I have illustrated in numerous ways throughout this study, in Tecpán—as, indeed, in the larger national "community" of Guatemala—*traje* provides a system of socialized objects through which a body of knowledge is expressed, issues are contested, and new meanings are created. The knowledge, issues, and meanings emerge and take on active, public roles when particular pieces of *traje* are worn on particular social occasions and are recognized by at least some of those present as being meaningful within a particular context.

But some members of the Tecpán community have an association with *traje*—better, a feeling for *traje*—that goes beyond wearing indigenous dress or commenting on its social context of production and use. For many, there is an ideological and emotional identification with *traje* such that dress is inextricably associated with the person's very being.[2] It is the felt truth of this equivalence between dress and cultural heart that causes an indigenous man in blue jeans and a plaid flannel shirt to address a group of people and utter the seemingly contradictory statement that all Maya should wear *traje*. It is this same felt truth that also inspires indigenous people to voice the criticism that, in dressing a ladino Miss Guatemala in *traje*, the government is abusing its indigenous population: to violate the relationship between "Maya" and "*traje*" is to abuse Maya people themselves.

There are other nationalistic efforts beyond the Miss Guatemala competition that attempt to make *traje* synonymous with something more than the Maya segment of the Guatemalan population. However, these equations between *traje* and Guatemala are useful only in particular contexts—for example, where Guatemala is compared with other national units in terms of "heritage" or "national spirit." In these cases, the equivalences are so context-specific and dependent on assumptions that are open to debate that the validity of the equation is regularly questioned. The equation between "*traje*" and "Maya," on the other hand, is accepted without debate throughout Guatemala, even though not all Maya necessarily wear *traje* or are able to make, buy, or explain it. In municipalities like Tecpán, it finds active expression in virtually every aspect of community life, including key social spheres such as the home, church, school, and market.

But what is the nature of this strong ideological and emotional identification between Maya identity and dress? Does it spring first and foremost from contrasts with ladinos and *vestido*, such as those discussed in Chapters 2 and 3? I think not. It seems to me that this particular link between Maya identity and *traje* is strongly exclusionary and built from systems of meaning that are perceived to arise within a strictly bounded Maya context (and here I am thinking of situations in which who or what is Maya is obvious). *Traje*, seen in this light, is not dependent on the Indian-ladino opposition with its colonial roots;[3] rather, it represents the image of Maya as an autonomous people with a history and culture all to themselves.

Bogatyrev's Contribution to the Analysis of Dress

In his early study of clothing (1971 [1937]), Petr Bogatyrev discusses the "general function" of folk costume in Moravian Slovakia, an idea that I see related to the ideological equivalence of "Maya" and "*traje*." Bogatyrev spends considerable time detailing the various functional aspects of dress (e.g., its magical, religious, erotic, practical, and nationalistic functions). However, in the end, he concludes that "structurally-linked facts represent something quite different from the sum of those facts. Structurally-linked facts A, B, and C represent something distinct which is not to be found in A, B, or C alone" (95). For Bogatyrev, the function of these structurally linked facts—the "general function" or the "function of the structure of functions"—is felt in the term "our costume," which, like the notion of "our mother tongue," "indicates not only the regionalistic function, but some kind of special function which cannot be derived from all the other functions which make up the structural whole" (96). To make his concepts more precise, Bogatyrev explains that both "our mother tongue" and "our costume" are "*closest*" to the people involved, and that this proximity results in their having an "emotional coloring" that distinguishes them from other cultural objects. As partial evidence of this theory, he notes that "it is sufficient to ridicule that community's *signs*, such as its costume, dialect, etc., which in turn incenses the insulted group to defend these signs" (97). Finally, he states that "only a garment of the type which has a tendency at least in certain of its parts to remain unchanged . . . acquires that emotional coloring [associated with the general function]" (97).

Although the world reflected through dress as I portray it is much more active and argued than the bounded, static, structured/structural domain of Bogatyrev's folk costumes, his ideas still illuminate important aspects of the Guatemalan material. Consider again the example of the 1980 *traje* presentation in Tecpán. Arguably, the spirit of the "general function," as something that is dear to people and summarizes their identity in a heartfelt manner, was the principal message that indigenous organizers of the *traje* presentation wanted to convey to their audience, more so than the "municipal" or "regionalistic function" of the dress on the young Tecpán models or the "historical function" of elders in "traditional" attire or the "ethnic function" of Maya versus ladino clothing. The presentation was loaded to create a visually, conceptually, and emotionally dense environment, saturated with the message "We are Maya." The central role of *traje* was supported during the event by the participation of young and old, the silent and the outspoken, people watching and being watched, Tecpanecos who lived in Tecpán as well as those who had moved away. It was also supported by Maya music (the marimba), the use of the Kaqchikel language, and the painted images of preconquest Maya and a hieroglyphic text on the back wall of the stage. The audience, too, had its part in creating this total atmosphere. It was large, which signaled the strength of Maya presence in Tecpán and Tecpanecos' interest in Maya culture. It more than filled the amphitheater-like space, so the audience could see the stage and each other as well. This arrangment, in effect, muted the distinction between spectators and presenters, as did the presence of children running from the stage to the audience and back. Likewise, the placement of the elders wearing "traditional *traje*" at the front—as part of the spectators looking at the stage but also part of the organized presentation—blurred the line between the "actors" and all those who came to watch. Finally, the appearance of the older forms of dress—the ones thought to have changed the least and hence, according to Bogatyrev, the ones with the "emotional coloring" associated with "our costume"—was balanced and reenforced by the more "modern" dress of the fair princesses and their attendants, clothing that both reflected the latest trends in *traje* fashion and demonstrated the continuous presence of the past in indigenous weaving.

While the fair presentation is a good illustration of *traje* seen in terms of Bogatyrev's "general function," it is far from unique. On a number of occasions Maya explicitly argue for the worth of indigenous dress as a symbol for all things Maya. What is more, *traje* does not need to be consciously displayed or explicitly discussed in order to summarize all that it means to be Indian. In small ways and every day—at church or in the marketplace, in the home or at school—the meaningfulness of indigenous dress saturates highland life and represents the heart of the Maya.

This said, I need to complicate matters by reminding the reader that this summary attitude toward *traje* is but one of many ways that people experience and interpret indigenous dress. Although the emotion of an event like the fair presentation might work to overwhelm or erase other possibilities—might create, at least momentarily, a complete Maya world—in fact these other attitudes toward and associations with dress remain latent in the situation. *Traje*, in fact, is *always* surrounded by a complex of overlapping, sometimes complementary, and sometimes contradictory meanings. These meanings become more or less important, more or less evident, in the interpretation of an event depending on the people involved, what is said, who is wearing the clothes, what events have preceded the moment, and other factors. For example, I could also argue that while *traje*, understood as the embodiment of "Maya," did not depend on any sort of comparison at the 1980 fair presentation, it was also, ironically, best able to function as a monumental "refusal" of the ladino world (cf. Hebdige 1983: 3). The circumstances surrounding the event also support this interpretation in that the Indigenous Fair Committee had recently split from a joint ladino and Indian group because of perceived injustices by ladinos toward Maya committee members. Moreover, this was an era of violence, with murders, disappearances, searches, and attacks drawing closer and closer to Tecpanecos. In light of events such as these and the active politico-cultural nature of the indigenous community, the presentation of *traje* functioned as an instance of pride in Maya identity, a distancing from "the other," and a presentation of a viable alternative to the ladino order of things. That this alternative—this refusal or resistance—was expressed in dress can also be interpreted in various ways. With "mere clothes" as weapons (cf. Scott 1985), the Indigenous Fair Committee suggested both an "impotence and a kind of power" (Hebdige 1983: 3), both a weakness (manifested by their use of such "trivial" objects as clothing) and a potential (for a very different sort of confrontation and society).

Interweavings

I want to address the idea of "the general" another way, this time by summarizing some of the major themes and issues that have threaded their way in and out of this study. My intention is to present these briefly, to detach them from the tangle of ethnographic detail (the very detail that brought them to life in the first place) and leave them as links to similar concerns in other studies.

The first of these has to do with connections between the past and the present, the traditional and the new, the enduring and the changing. As I have tried to make clear throughout, persistence and change are integrally related. What endures needs to be recreated daily, in different ways, for people to be aware of it as "always there." Indigenous activists who urge people to be conscious of their Maya heritage, to wear *traje*, to speak *lengua*, and to practice *costumbre* recognize this if only implicitly. The persistent is also hard to shake, as it keeps reappearing—sometimes in very changed and "invisible" forms—even if a people desperately want it to change. The enduring negative image of "*indios*" dressed in *traje* is but one such example. What endures, however, is not necessarily static: change itself can be a predictable, enduring quality of life, whether in the production and use of *traje* or the reproduction and raising of children. And, finally, even the most creative acts do not appear out of thin air. As suggested by the examples in the preceding chapter, the "new" and the "different" are built from and explained by established, traditional "facts" of social life. Thus, the past is seen as "the past" only insofar as it lives at the moment, and the new makes sense only insofar as it relates to, builds on, or contrasts with the old or traditional. In a similar vein, a study does not have to be "historical" to be concerned with history. I think of this ethnography as a case in point. Tecpanecos use history to make history, and in my analysis I have tried to show how history appears to them and how they use it to weave and wear clothes.

Another complex of issues central to this book concerns the formation of groups, boundaries, and identities. To say that boundaries and group membership are fluid or changeable should not imply that they are arbitrary. As I discussed in Chapter 3 in connection with the enduring images of Indians, very specific constructions of "the Maya" can be manipulated and used (consciously or unconsciously) for very specific social goals, to the benefit or detriment of the persons involved. Likewise, the "same" construction may be interpreted very differently, depending on who is passing judgment, for what purposes, and under what circumstances. In addition, while individuals attempting to promote a particular image of a group might intend it to have a solidifying effect, the result may be quite different. For example, revitalization efforts meant to raise people's ethnic consciousness and unite them as Maya can move people to reject a particular set of activities and public construction of identity, even as they continue to embrace the label "Maya." Finally, group and individual identities are so multifaceted—and the social context so thick with meanings that don't quite mesh—that it is virtually impossible for a person to escape being ironic and contradictory. Thus, Maya men who promote *traje* may not wear it; Maya women who pride themselves in preserving the use of *traje* may wear sunglasses and high-heeled shoes, too; and those who express ethnic pride by wearing beautiful and expensive *traje* may be accused of materialistic desires and disregard for the welfare of their families.

The last set of issues has to do with the power and influence of indigenous cloth and clothing in Tecpán specifically and in Guatemala (and beyond) more generally. As the examples in this study illustrate, *traje* is seen very differently by different people: as beautiful, silent, and expensive; as mere clothing, a craft that is largely women's work; or as ugly, primitive, and representative of an ignorance of the modern world. It is part of Maya "culture"—the kind glorified in tourist brochures or described in terms of lists in older anthropological writings—but it is also part of a larger "cultural politics," manifested locally with strategic uses of dress in schools, parades, and queen contests and globally through export businesses and aid to those widowed by the violence.[4] Relegated to the decontextualized realm of "Culture" (in art museums and galleries, for example) or to the folkloristic world of "vanishing peoples" (the often ahistorical world of natural history museum exhibits and guided tours), *traje* is a safe, palatable subject, culture without teeth. It is assumed to represent Maya as a whole and to do so with great beauty. Recognizing this consciously or unconsciously (it is especially hard to tell if there is no verbal element), Maya have used this gentle image of *traje* to their advantage, promoting indigenous identity through dress when other modes of expression might be inappropriate or too dangerous. But a consistent and pervasive view of *traje* as "soft"—as well as the stigma attached to the idea of craft, clothing, and "women's work"—also means that some of its power cannot be realized.[5] This is why *traje* presents such a challenge to indigenous Guatemalans as they work to bring to consciousness Maya issues and Maya identity.[6]

Whither Traje?

I conclude this chapter knowing full well that this is not the end of my relationship with the subject, the people, or the place. I take it as a sign of a topic well chosen that now, years after starting this project, I am still profoundly interested in the issues and have more questions to ask than when I began. So to end this chapter in what I see as an ongoing project, I want to offer a series of questions related to my own interests, to anthropology, and to the Guatemalan context.

As the people of the highlands continue to repair their lives after years of natural and human violence, what sorts of wealth-based issues will develop in relation to *traje*? How will people's level of education relate to what they wear? Will the split between those who weave and those who go on in school continue? In what new ways will *traje* be linked to Maya in different economic classes?

The road to Iximche' is being paved, and INGUAT has prepared a tourist brochure featuring Tecpán. What will these initiatives mean for the town and for *traje*? How will *traje* be marketed in the future? What will be sold, where will it be sold, how will it be sold, and who will sell it? As more people come to Tecpán and buy, what new categories of textiles will emerge?

As revitalization efforts move from special events to activities that are more a part of daily life, how will weaving and *traje* fit in? What will happen with men's *traje*? What new dimensions of the past will be mined as raw materials for future dress? What will happen as the young activists of today become the elders of the next century?[7]

As Tecpanecos become more educated and more established in academic fields, what scholarly projects focused on *traje* will occupy their attention? How will the work of foreign scholars such as myself comple-ment or work at odds with the efforts of local scholars?

In this book I have focused on a largely visual aspect of Tecpán society and turned it into a largely verbal endeavor. Whereas at times I might have wished that Guatemalans had said more on the subject, I worry now that I say too much and, in doing so, bury in words and analysis the very object I wish to illuminate. Still the word–image link exists in Maya think-ing, and "silent" *traje* speaks volumes to those for whom it is dear. That precise link is expressed cogently in the inspirational message that pro-vided the epigraph for this chapter, for, indeed, to wear *traje* is to say "I am Maya, we are Maya, and we will continue being Maya."

1. *Introduction*

1. I use the words "dress," "clothes," and "clothing" to refer to *traje*, but I use "costume" only under very specific circumstances. While the primary meanings of the term "costume," as given in dictionaries and museum studies, for example, relate well to *traje* (e.g., see Schevill 1986: 1), it connotes clothing that is slightly alien, worn for special occasions or in "exotic" contexts (at a Halloween party, on stage in the theater, in Elizabethan England, at a "tribal dance"): in other words, "we" wear clothing; "they" wear costume. In this work I want to stress that in most cases *traje* is clothing that Maya wear every day and it bears special meaning because of this habitual use.

2. Iximche' is from the Kaqchikel word *ixim-che'* (corn-tree or tree of corn).

3. See Polo Sifontes (1986: 80–83) for a discussion of the founding of the capital. Because of its early colonial status, Tecpán was bestowed the rank of *ciudad* (city) by the national government on 28 May 1924. However, in everyday speech residents of the central highlands almost always refer to Tecpán as a *pueblo*; in keeping with this custom, I use the term "town."

4. That situation has not changed a great deal in the 1990s. In 1991 the museum at the archaeological site expanded to include a small exhibit of local arts and a notice about a shop in Tecpán where weavings and other items are sold. This shop is modest in scale and not well situated to attract tourists. A relatively new hotel, on the other hand, is large and prominently placed at the corner of the plaza, but it seems to cater much more to a local Guatemalan clientele (participants in a local bike race, for example) rather than the foreign tourist market.

5. The disproportionate number of deaths in the urban area can be substantiated somewhat by comparing census figures for 1973 and 1981. For 1973, the national census lists the total population of Tecpán as 24,181, with 5,843 people (24 percent) living in the urban area and 18,338 (76 percent) living in the rural area (Dirección General de Estadística

1975: 7). By 1981, the total population had risen to 29,564, but the urban population had remained nearly the same—5,977 (20 percent). The rural population, at 23,587 (or 80 percent), accounted for nearly all of the growth (Dirección General de Estadística 1984: 121).

6. In November 1981, when the municipal building was blown up by a truckload of dynamite (reports differ as to whether the ladino mayor was killed by the blast or, beforehand, by gunshot), the "unknowns" also turned their weapons on people as well as the health clinic, police station, and post office around the plaza.

7. Hill (1992: 158–160) discusses the decline of the system of *parcialidades* in late-eighteenth-century Tecpán, with the only memory of their existence arguably being the four *barrios* in the *cabecera* today. A *parcialidad* was the Spanish label for a unit of the indigenous community that had territorial, political, social, and economic functions (39). In Tecpán these *parcialidades* extended from the center of town into the countryside (160).

8. David Stoll (1982: 37) cites writings from 1924–1925 by Cameron Townsend, the founder of the Summer Institute of Linguistics and the Wycliffe Bible Translators, that note the presence of Maya evangelists in Tecpán, Chimaltenango, and Acatenango some two decades before the earliest estimated date I was given.

9. Estimating what backstrap weavers earn is difficult, largely because their working hours and days are not regular. Nonetheless, in 1980 a good-quality Tecpán *huipil* cost between Q30.00 and Q50.00, with the materials amounting to approximately Q10.00 or Q15.00; the time to complete the garment was two or three months of more or less regular work (i.e., most days of the week, except possibly Sunday, for four to eight hours per day). Thus the weaver earned roughly Q20.00 to Q35.00 for her labor.

10. The use of the ethnographic present to stand for 1980–1981 means that the market I describe is somewhat different from the one that exists now. In particular, there are a number of stalls in the plaza that are more or less permanent. Their construction is basically the same as the impermanent ones, but at night they are wrapped or otherwise secured and left in place until morning.

11. Briggs (1989: 44) and Feld (1982: 230–232) mention their attempts and talents in woodcarving and music, respectively, and how a focus on these activities in the field enabled them to tap into, in Briggs's words, the "artistic metacommunication [that] was encompassed by a more comprehensive semiotic" (44).

12. In Tecpán, the two terms *natural* and *indígena* are widely used in everyday Spanish speech. My impression is that the term *Maya* is used most often in Spanish contexts when speakers want to give a sense that they are talking about or affiliating themselves with a large, more abstractly conceived group: the ancient Maya or the Maya people of Guatemala. (Note that the latter is a unit that generally has national boundaries; the Maya of Mexico are less commonly implied.) Thus the term is used in situations of Maya solidarity and Maya revitalization efforts—as in Carol Smith's "Maya nationalist movement" (1991: 29). The term *indio* (Indian) and, worse yet, the diminutive *indito* have derogatory connotations and are rarely used by Maya, except perhaps in quoted speech. The Maya scholar Demetrio Cojtí Cuxil is an exception in his use of *indio* in academic writings and talks. His action has the effect of appropriating a term whose meanings have been foisted on the Maya, bringing into question its power, and highlighting its use in situations of unequal social status, as in "*con el actual modelo colonial en el cual los ladinos gobiernan a los indios, y los gobiernan en Castellano*" (with the current colonial model in which ladinos govern *indios*, and govern them in Spanish; Cojtí Cuxil 1990: 9, my translation). The Spanish adjectives *típico* (typical) and, somewhat less consistently, *tradicional* (traditional) also carry the meaning of *indígena*, especially when used in reference to dress, ceramics, music, and dance.

In Kaqchikel, the common terms are *qawinaqi'* and, more recently, *Mayab'*, which has been taken from colonial documents. Both are used primarily in solidarity and revitalization contexts (Maxwell 1991, 1992). I generally use the English terms "indigenous" and "Indian" as well as "Maya." I have chosen to include "Indian" here *not* as a translation of *indio* but because it is commonly used in contemporary anthropological literature on the highlands and because it has a public or popular ring to it that fits well with the local use of Spanish and Kaqchikel terms. I use "Maya," instead of "Mayan," in accord with the local (Spanish) use of the term rather than the convention articulated by Schele and Miller (1986: 7). They use the word "Mayan" to describe language and linguistics, while "Maya" is reserved for the people and for all other terms.

13. Similar attitudes about giving up the use of *traje* arise in the extreme and very real situations of refugee camps, in which Maya women often find themselves. As one Guatemalan women said, "When we were in Chiapas, people told me I had to stop wearing *traje*. I cried when I put away my *traje*. When I put on a dress I felt as though I was naked. It wasn't like wearing things you make yourself, that are so comfortable. I didn't

want to show myself to my children in a dress. But out of necessity I did it" (Anderson and Garlock 1988: 103).

14. In English, the terms "highland" and "highlands" have become more or less synonymous with areas of Guatemala that have a large Maya population. This shorthand is not altogether accurate, but it works well for the Tecpán area. While it is true that the high mountain ranges to the west and north of Guatemala City are home to millions of Maya, these mountains continue south and east through largely ladino areas. At the same time, there are communities of Indians living in the large Department of Petén, a low-lying region in the very northernmost part of the country.

The terms used in Guatemalan Spanish that have both geographic and ethnic dimensions are *oriente*, referring to the ladino eastern part of the country, and *occidente,* referring to the indigenous west. Again, Guatemala's northern lowlands, the site of numerous Classic Era Maya sites and home to a small Indian population today, fall outside this broad equation.

15. Kaqchikel terms used to refer to ladinos include *q'eq* (also meaning "wicked," "black") or *q'eqa'*; and *mo's* (for men) and *sanyora* (for women, from the Spanish "*señora*").

16. I was somewhat surprised by the lack of women claiming to be in the "*no aplica*" category. Initially I suggested that women, being sheltered at home by parents and spouses, are less likely to get the spatial distance from families and family ethnic associations that would prompt them to change their self-definition. For those who leave, residency patterns after marriage make it less likely that a woman who drops the public signs of being Indian would return to her hometown and be judged by (or judge herself in terms of) people acquainted with her roots, upbringing, social relations, and the like. While that idea still makes some sense to me, the statistics that it seeks to explain may not be supported by those of the 1981 national census (Dirección General de Estadística 1984: 121). Of a total population of 29,564 Tecpanecos, 9 people claim "*ignorado*" (do not know), as opposed to "*indígena*" and "*no indígena*" (note that this latter category is simply the negation of "*indígena*"), and all but one of these were women. While it is not clear what these terms meant to the respondents—or who the respondents were—the figures nonetheless show that the auto-classification of the population into groups is not simple.

17. The word *traje* is a Spanish one that, in most places where the language is spoken, has nothing to do with Maya clothing; it can mean "dress" in general or "suit" more particularly. In Guatemala, but outside of Maya contexts, one hears the word used most often with reference to

"formal dress" for business or social occasions or in a phrase like "*traje de baño*" (bathing suit). In such instances, any reference to Maya clothing would have to be specified. However, within the context of the Guatemalan highlands, "Maya dress" is the most general or unmarked sense of the word and the assumed referent of the term *traje*.

18. In the text I use both the Spanish and Kaqchikel words for such articles of clothing as *po't* / *huipil* and *uq* / *corte* as the two forms are used regularly by indigenous Tecpanecos. In the literature on Maya dress, the Spanish version is more prevalent, though the Kaqchikel forms are appearing more as writers become aware of their role in representing and perpetuating important aspects of Maya culture.

19. A *vara* is a Spanish measure of length and equals 0.84 meter or almost exactly 33 inches.

20. While *ri'j* means "old" or "ancient," *rij* means "its-back" or "covering"; both *ri'j po't* and *rij po't* have been given to me as the Kaqchikel term for *sobre huipil*. Each in its own way makes sense; however, I have decided to use the former term in this work because it is more frequently used. Note, however, that Linda Asturias de Barrios (1985: 39) uses *rij po't* (its-behind *huipil*) in her book on Comalapa *traje*.

21. Anawalt's research focuses exclusively on the preconquest era and, for the Maya, on the Yucatan lowlands. However, because she is aiming at broad, pan-Mesoamerican characterizations of dress, I have included her in this listing.

22. Otzoy (1992a) writes a broad survey article on issues associated with *traje*; however, within a few pages she is able to synthesize resources and link the subject to important current debates on gender, identity, colonialism and postcolonialism, politics, and change.

23. Braudel expresses this in similar terms when he states: "This second book has, in fact, to meet two contradictory purposes. It is concerned with social structures, that is with mechanisms that withstand the march of time; it is also concerned with the development of those structures. It combines, therefore, what have come to be known as *structure* and *conjuncture* the permanent and the ephemeral, the slow-moving and the fast. These two aspects of reality . . . are always present in everyday life, which is a constant blend of what changes and what endures" (1976, 1:353).

24. This term is used by Bogatyrev (1971 [1937]) to explain the idea of the "function of the structure of functions," which is discussed in more detail in Chapter 7.

2. *The Geography of Clothing*

1. Cantel, a town in the Department of Quezaltenango, is the site of the large-scale production of a basic cotton cloth sold throughout the highlands. German velvet is a thick, 100 percent cotton cloth, whereas American velvet is a slightly cheaper polyester blend.

2. While this division of labor—men on treadle looms and women on backstrap looms—is usual in many municipalities (Tecpán included), there are variations by town, industry, and family. Ehlers, for example, discusses female treadle-loom weavers in San Pedro Sacatepéquez, San Marcos (1990: 42). Reflecting changes in industry, economics, and fashion, San Pedro women moved from using backstrap looms to treadle looms around the mid-twentieth century. More recently, better-capitalized weaving factories in neighboring communities, shifts in male work patterns in San Pedro, changes in gender roles, and further changes in clothing fashion mean that women in this community no longer produce much cloth on treadle looms or retain the economic autonomy they once had (ibid.). I discuss the Tecpán case in chapter 5.

3. The unit of Guatemalan currency is the quetzal (Q), with Q1.00 equal to US$1.00 in 1980. Since 1985 the quetzal has lost value against the dollar and was worth close to US$0.20 by the summer of 1991. Any unqualified mention of prices are in 1980 quetzals. Occasionally I will cite a more recent figure, but I will make clear how it relates to the earlier value.

4. This particular village lies at the northern tip of Tecpán relatively near the boundaries of San Martín Jilotepeque, a municipality where Tani Adams (1978) reports that a number of local people participate in seasonal labor on the coast.

5. The perception, at least, is that *k'aqo'j* grows only in the lowlands. In 1991 the Ixchel Museum of Indigenous Traje in Guatemala City was growing the brown cotton in front of the museum and encouraging people to try growing it in their highland communities.

6. Note that *ancla* is Spanish for "anchor" and that the same picture of an anchor appears on both the Colombian Ancla and British Anchor labels. I would guess that the Colombian brand name is in imitation of the British one. My reasoning is based on the fact that the Coats Company first registered its trademarks in Guatemala in 1895 and 1899 (Lathbury 1974: 55), though I do not know whether the registration included the Anchor brand name or how these dates compare with the founding of the Colombian company. However, the tendency for Latin

American companies to capitalize on well-known and respected European and U.S. brand names is widespread.

7. The Totonicapán *huipil* is favored in Tecpán, possibly because it is "finished" when it comes off the loom: it is not generally embellished further aside from the usual addition of velvet at the neck and arms. The Quezaltenango *huipil*, on the other hand, is considered more finished with hand- or machine-embroidered flowers on its woven base, and these additional elements add greatly to the original cost of the piece.

8. The names used in these examples are pseudonyms, but ones chosen from a list of women's names that, in 1980, were considered to be "more Indian" than such "ladino" names as Claudia, Irasema, Janet, Orfa, and Gladis. In the 1990s, with the spirit of Maya revitalization carrying over into naming practices, some children are being given Maya names with precontact roots—for example, Nik'te' or Ixmukane for girls, Pakal or Tojil for boys.

9. That is, if they have not given up *traje* altogether. Though most do not take this extreme route, some girls wear common clothes—dresses and skirts, even slacks—while in the city, but switch back to *traje* before returning to their hometowns for Sunday visits or for good. Parents are generally against such changes and will discipline their daughters soundly if the matter is brought to light.

10. Along with being made from "Indian cloth," the shirt was cut in the style of "cowboy" or "western" shirts (i.e., with a "western yoke"). In fact, this link between "Indian" and the U.S. West or Southwest is not uncommon: a number of Guatemalan textile goods sold in U.S. mail-order catalogs make this link explicit in the catalog blurb (see Hendrickson 1993).

11. Historically, Santa Apolonia has been subordinate to Tecpán. Cortés y Larraz (1958 [1769–1770]: 171) notes that Santa Apolonia was an *anexo* of Tecpán, and Hill (1992: 80) writes that "the town of Santa Apolonia developed as a dependency of Tecpán and supplied the entire region of the former Iximche' polity with pottery."

12. The advertisement has the additional touches of an Anglicized name, Lorenzo's, for the pizzeria and the English-language slogan "Lorenzo's pizza is for lovers" written under a sketch of a city (New York?) skyline.

13. In this game, a group of children (*B*) approach *A*, who is "it" and yell *"Aqui venimos"* (Here we come). *A* then asks:

A: *¿De donde viene?*   A: *¿Que cosa traía?*
B: *De Nueva York.*   B: *Mi cosa tan mejor.*

A: *¿Con que letra comienza?*   B: *Con* _____.

A proceeds to guess and, when he or she succeeds in naming the object, runs after the others. When *A* tags someone, that person becomes "it" for the next round.

14. People from the United States who buy Guatemalan goods also want high quality at low prices. In this case, however, the desired items are characteristically "low-technology" pieces such as weaving and pottery. Given this difference, the buying patterns of Guatemalan and U.S. tourists make an interesting statement about the relation between the two countries, one specializing in and renowned for its cheap, high-technology goods and the other for its cheap, low-technology items.

15. Interest in a more "*civilizado*" existence and the discrepancies between that dream and actual life in Tecpán are reflected in joking routines among Tecpanecos. For example, they often refer to local places in terms that reflect wealth, technological sophistication, or foreign status. A teacher in Tecpán, getting ready to board a bus to visit his family in a more cosmopolitan area, says that he will be "leaving in five minutes from the Great Airport of Tecpán" (his exaggerated speech suggests capital letters). Another worker, a low-paid secretary, refers to his modest home as his "palace." And Tecpán itself has the nickname "Texas." The parallel between the two names becomes more obvious when the accent is shifted to the first syllable of Tecpán, which happens in the word play of bus attendants as they cry out the destination of their vehicle. Thus, So-lo-lá becomes So-ló-la and Tec-pán becomes Téc-pan and then Téc-sas. When I asked about the roots of the Tecpán-Texas link, I was told that it had originated with the bus attendants' cries, but I think it has stuck because it also fits, in a playful way, with how Tecpanecos like to see themselves (see Photo 13).

16. The year before, Editorial Maya Wuj (1990) published a similar calendar-booklet with inspirational slogans, this time with messages promoting the use of Maya names and languages. Many of these differed from the ones of the following year only in terms of key nouns. For example, "*Al renunciar a nuestros idiomas* [languages] *estamos renunciando a ser nosotros mismos.*"

3. *The Enduring Indian: Images of the Maya*

1. See also Otzoy (1992b) for another treatment of the multiple ways in which Maya are portrayed: as "colonial Indian," "heroic Indian," "backward Indian," "true Indian," and "ideal Indian."

2. From what I have read about the founders of and principal forces behind this celebration, they appear similar to those in the Mexican Movimiento described by Judith Friedlander in the introduction of her book *Being Indian in Hueyapan* (1975).

3. In this piece, Rafael Téllez García, the head of the present-day Tecún Umán Association and one of the founding members, goes on to explain that, in Guatemala,

> we are reticent to praise our own and even [go so far as] to deny his proper existence, the answer I have given is that: if there was a conquest of Guatemala, there necessarily had to be some leader who confronted the conqueror. It is logical.
>
> Unfortunately, . . . in those times there were not, there did not exist the global means of communication that exist in the world today, that might take note of who were the leaders of that epic event; but the truth is that if at this time there were to be an invasion of the territory of Guatemala, logically you would have to appoint a military leader who would defend your territory, your land.
>
> So you can assure yourself that Tecún Umán physically existed; and, sincerely, to deny him is to deny our own national essence.
>
> (EL GRÁFICO 1980D: 5, MY TRANSLATION)

4. Recent literature on nationalism and the nation-state addresses some of the issues brought out in this example, including tensions within the state over the use of military force versus peaceful assimilative activities and the appropriation by the state of emblems belonging to distinct, historically autonomous groups. See, for example, Smith (1990b) on Guatemala and Urban and Sherzer (1991) on Latin America more generally.

5. I also felt the tension between ethnic groups in the 1980 *traje* presentation in the use of Kaqchikel by the emcees, which symbolically (if not actually) barred the participation of non-Maya.

6. The god/ancestor Ixmucané was described to me as "*la abuela de los antepasados*" (the grandmother of the ancestors). She and her male partner appear in the creation account in the *Popol Vuh.* A second Tecpán Indian fair queen bears her name. (Note that by the early 1990s the queen's name was written as Ixmukane and the creation account *Popul wuj* because of the shift to the unified alphabet.)

7. Note how the issue of markedness of ethnic terms plays into the subject of queen titles and the population represented by each winner. On another occasion, a young ladino woman is crowned Madrina del

Deporte (Godmother of Sports) for the fair. In 1980 she was chosen from candidates representing local soccer players, basketball players, and cyclists. The winner that year was a somewhat controversial choice because she and her family did not reside in Tecpán but rather had ties to the town through relatives.

8. Later, when the ladino women appeared in evening dress, the Maya contestants each put on a short skit illustrating some aspect of *costumbre* (e.g., two contestants enacted aspects of local Maya courting and wedding traditions). The skit usually called for the contestant and her fellow actors to wear older forms of dress. At the very end of the competition, the same Indian women appeared on stage in particularly fine, contemporary styles of Tecpán *traje*.

9. I use the term "primitive" in the sense discussed by Marianna Torgovnick in *Gone Primitive* (1990) and point especially to her comments on "Western lust for things primitive" (38). I take the term "glamour" from John Berger's discussion of publicity and his claim that "the state of being envied is what constitutes glamour" (1983: 131).

10. The notion that wearing *traje* makes non-Indians more like Indians is one theory, at least. The following riddle, related by Robert McKenna Brown in the context of an academic presentation to a Maya and foreign audience, presents another reading:

Q: What is a *huipil*?
A: An indigenous garment that a ladina wears in order to be a gringa.

11. Dumont (1988), in his article on the concept of the Tasaday (Tasadayity, as he puts it), makes a similar distinction between the temporal and spatial gap that separates the western "Self" and the distant "Other," and the appeal (aesthetic, moral, etc.) of the same Other to the Self.

12. Use of these themes is found outside the realm of tourist literature. For example, in 1980 INGUAT ran a series of antilittering advertisements in the national newspapers. In one of these, a close-up of an Indian man (with enough *traje* in view to fix his ethnic identity) shows him weeping while, in an inset, litter is being tossed from a car. The message reads: "Don't attack the land that gives you shelter. Don't attack through carelessness the land that gives you shelter. Don't offend that land or the people who love it, as you love it. Don't litter it or let it be littered" (*El Gráfico* 31 January 1980, my translation). Like the U.S. anti-

littering campaign that featured "The Indian with the Tear," this one also features a weeping Indian man, something that further distances him from his nonindigenous countrymen. Public displays of tears are not acceptable for males in Guatemala, though women, because of their "delicate nature," are excused. Rather, Indians are put in a special category where their actions are permissible or at least understandable. Like the young girl in a school uniform who appears in a similar antilittering ad, the Indian man is seen as having a "natural" sensitivity toward the earth.

13. Tani Adams (1978), for example, writes on neighboring San Martín Jilotepeque and offers numerous direct statements by ladinos slurring Indian character.

14. I also encountered more public expressions of negative sentiments toward the Maya population when I visited largely ladino areas of Guatemala. For example, when I traveled to eastern Guatemala, I took along my backstrap loom. I wanted to weave during my stay and elicit comments from people who stopped to talk. At one point, after I had explained the loom and shown my partially completed weaving, one person had this comment about Indians: "Doing that [weaving], they're intelligent, but that's their work; but with other things they're stupid [*brutos*]."

15. In an interview with the ladino fair queen (Q), another side was heard:

T: Do you believe that there's racial discrimination in the different social groups of our town?
Q: Yes, of course, and it's obvious enough since these fair celebrations are town-wide festivities and it doesn't seem to me that the Indians [*la raza indígena*] see it like that. They're celebrating the fair apart from the ladinos [*la raza ladina*]. Since they're town festivities we ought to celebrate them together.

(AJOZAL XUYÁ 1979–1980: 22)

16. The depiction of clothing in drawings found in "guerrilla" publications like flyers and petitions is telling since the key social groups that are presented as being involved in antigovernment activities are easily identified by what the people are wearing: *traje* for Indians, university sweaters for students, hard hats and work clothes for urban laborers, clerical collars for clergy and other religious leaders, and loose-fitting white shirts and pants with cinched-in belts (as well as machetes) for Indian and ladino (male) peasants. Kay Warren (personal communication, 1992) has

suggested that the popular left, like the government and ladino capitalists in the tourist industry, is also using indigenous imagery for its own purposes.

17. The debates and discussions surrounding the second gathering of the Continental Campaign of 500 Years of Indigenous and Popular Resistance, held 7–12 October 1991 in Quezaltenango, provide a good example of what can happen when indigenous activists and nonindigenous activists (in this case, from all over the Americas) meet and attempt to collaborate. While some Indians (including Maya) saw hope in the meeting—hope for progressive work that spans ethnic lines—others saw the reproduction of structures of domination, with indigenous participants needing to bow to non-Indian initiatives and power (Willis 1991).

18. Maya businesses—and here I am thinking particularly of Maya efforts in publishing—are examples from the late 1980s and early 1990s of groups intent on strengthening ethnic pride and disseminating Maya information and inspiration. The visual imagery that predominates in the materials produced by these groups includes preconquest images (glyphs, figures from ceramics, and so on) or contemporary renditions that have the feel of the conventional glyph drawing style. Designs from weavings are also used in their publications, as are line drawings of local life (often showing customs from decades past) done in a style that art historians would label "folk" or "primitive."

19. Lack of local sanction does not stop individuals from entering this contest. When I returned to Tecpán in 1983, I learned that a local woman was the Rabín Ajau: she had entered the contest on her own initiative and won the crown.

4. *Between Birth and Death:* Traje *and the Human Life Cycle*

1. Compare this idea to that of "Chimalteco-ness" that John Watanabe (1992) uses to describe a sense of community and belonging in the western highland municipality of Santiago Chimaltenango.

2. While the home is the traditional birthing place, hospital deliveries in Chimaltenango or Guatemala City are not uncommon for Tecpán women. Many women have children in both settings, weighing the hospital or home option according to expense, safety, and other factors that may be relevant for a particular birth.

3. *Temescales* were much more widespread before the 1976 earthquake. In 1980 many families had not rebuilt the baths (or were slow to do so), preferring showers or baths in a tub of hot water.

4. Beliefs about *ojo, malhechos,* and the strength of red are not confined to indigenous Guatemalans; they are common throughout Latin America.

5. This custom has changed little despite the growth in Maya revitalization efforts and the prevalence of gender-neutral slogans in Maya publications urging, "Papa, Mama, please! Dress me in Maya *traje*" (Editorial Maya Wuj 1991, my translation). At best, little Maya boys are dressed in *traje* for special occasions. For instance, one Tecpán couple claims that they are dressing their young son in *traje* for special family events so that the boy will grow used to wearing these clothes.

6. This segregation is not absolutely rigid. A small number of girls go to the boys' school.

7. Kay Warren (personal communication, 1992) has suggested that the positive attribute of "height" can be interpreted as somewhat ladinoized, as, I would add, could "body" if not also "beauty." If so, in the view of this particular queen, her personal qualities fulfilled beauty contest standards from not only an indigenous perspective (e.g., by adhering to and promoting the use of *traje*) but from a nonindigenous one as well.

8. The Spanish term *novio/novia* has various meanings depending on context. It means "boyfriend" or "girlfriend" in school situations; "fiancé" or "fiancée" for older, more serious couples (such as those in this example); and "groom" and "bride" on the wedding day.

9. All of the cases I know involve families in which the parents do not hold salaried jobs. The financial arrangements for a wedding might change if the parents, as well as the *novios,* have a substantial cash income.

10. This point was reenforced for me during a three-day field trip that I made with a group of young Maya and ladino women (married and unmarried, in their mid- to late teens and early twenties). One warm afternoon the group of us stopped at a recreational area surrounding a small lake. A number of the ladino women quickly stripped to their underwear and bathed, washed their hair, and washed a few clothes. At the same time, the indigenous women, who were in a separate group and absorbed in their own activities, were inching their way into the water. All laughed, partly from amusement and partly from embarrassment it seemed, as they hiked up their *cortes* inch by inch to keep them from getting too wet. Standing in knee-deep water, the most daring held their skirts a few inches above the knees while the most modest had theirs right at water level or slightly below.

11. Rigoberta Menchú (1984: 210) relates how her mother told her

about the facts of life when Menchú was ten, but her mother referred to experiences of the mother's grandmother in order to avoid the discomfort of talking about her own.

12. Because *ri'j po't* are associated with both the Catholic church and strictly Maya contexts (apart from an institutionalized church), most of the women who wear them are at least nominally Catholic.

13. I would like to thank Edward Fischer and Mareike Sattler for insights on *tuj ya'* from their 1993–1994 fieldwork.

5. *The Cultural Biography of* Traje

1. The *S* or *Z* spin of a thread is important in instances when a weaver wants to respin it (e.g., brown acrylic thread is respun and used to imitate *k'aqo'j* in *sobre huipiles*). Likewise, weavers pay attention to the spin of threads when they twist two different colors together and use the diagonal stripes that this process creates for special effects on some weavings. (Weavers in Comalapa make use of this technique much more, but it is not unknown in Tecpán.)

2. Threads that bleed are not always considered undesirable. In Nahualá, a town in the Department of Sololá, weavers often use a particular red thread for the supplementary weft designs of *huipiles*; they know the thread will run when washed and tint the white foundation cloth a cherry pink.

3. This situation has changed a great deal in the past decade. By 1990, a number of Patzicía *huipiles* could be seen in the marketplace, most of these on younger women. Far more lavishly decorated with supplementary weft weavings than the ones I saw in 1980, the most elaborate of these dazzled the eyes with their bright and shiny designs woven in synthetic threads imitative of silk and with their rich, red base cloth made from expensive mercerized cotton thread.

4. One woman said that, when she was learning to weave, her mother had her drink the masa water after sizing the thread, saying that it would help the girl learn faster. Other women to whom I mentioned this custom had not heard of such a thing and some, in fact, were quite put off by the thought.

5. When I returned to Tecpán in the 1990s, I found more people using acrylic threads for the basic warp and weft threads. Some new types of acrylic fibers appear to have a tighter, smoother finish. Women also respin acrylic threads so that the resulting product is extremely hard and durable and allegedly shinier than many cottons. As mentioned

earlier, respun brown acrylic threads are used as a cheaper substitute for *k'aqo'j*.

6. I feel confident making this claim for 1980 but not for 1990. During the 1980s the value of the quetzal ceased being tied to the U.S. dollar. Tough economic times saw prices rise, especially for imported goods such as pearl cotton. Meanwhile, new thread products came on the market, both from national and international sources. Thus, while the threads that were common in 1980 still remain in use, they have been joined by other products, each with its own cultural value.

7. Compare this attitude to the comments made by Lois Paul (1974) based on her 1941 fieldwork in San Pedro la Laguna.

8. Guatemala is a country where accomplishments (completion of typing lessons, secretarial school, high school, or university; community service; or attendance at meetings) are regularly certified and acknowledged by an elaborate document. These official papers, with seals and quantities of signatures, are then framed and displayed in the home. See also Hendrickson (1992, 1994).

9. See Sperlich and Sperlich (1980: 16, 22) for diagrams of warping boards and thread configurations for warping. The Tecpán method is similar to that labeled as being from Zunil. Chapters 7 and 8 of their book contain information on loom parts and the backstrap loom setup. The diagram in *Comalapa: Native Dress and Its Significance* (Asturias de Barrios 1985: IV) also shows a backstrap loom and the Kaqchikel terms for the loom parts, which are nearly identical to those used in Tecpán.

10. *Lienzos* with four selvages (rather than three or two) are the most difficult to make because no warp threads are cut. As the cloth nears completion and the space for the remainder of the weaving gets smaller and smaller, there is very little room in which to manipulate the weft thread. The easiest thing to do at this point would be to cut the warp threads and make a fringe or sew the raw edge under. Instead, for a *lienzo* with four selvages, a weaver needs to keep working, sometimes with the help of a needle, to fill in as many weft threads as possible. Sometimes a small strip of very loose weaving can be located about one or two inches up from a bottom edge of a *lienzo*, indicating that the weaver completed an inch or so of weaving when she first started the piece, turned the whole loom around, and started weaving again until she reached the small band of finished cloth at what is now the top of the loom.

11. See Tedlock and Tedlock (1985: 129–132) for an insightful discussion of sequencing patterns and intertextuality in the weaving and poetry of the K'iche' Maya.

12. The *ruxe' po't* is also the space where weavers hide certain sorts of errors and experiment with different threads and designs. Warping errors (e.g., a difference in length between the two warp selvage edges) can be compensated for in the *ruxe' po't*; when the blouse is worn, no one will be the wiser. A weaver might also use up old threads, try out a different design, or situate knots in this unseen area.

On the subject of center-periphery organization of weavings, see Adams's discussion of Sumba cloth (1980) and its structural relations to the organization of villages, the local marriage system, and so forth.

13. The designs found on Comalapa *huipiles* can likewise be divided into "old" and "modern" varieties (the latter including *marcador* designs). See Asturias de Barrios (1985: 32–33) for a discussion of these designs.

14. In 1980 I collected information on thirty-four everyday *huipiles*, all of which had at least some geometric figures (ones woven in the *jun ruwa kem* technique that I discuss shortly). I was interested in seeing what design motifs fell in what areas of the *huipiles*. Of these thirty-four, twenty-eight blouses had an *arco* in the central chest band, one had *arcos* symmetrically placed in the *pa ruwi' k'u'x* and *ruxe' ruk'u'x* positions, and five had no *arcos*. In the 1990s, it seems that the percentage of *arcos* has decreased slightly and that more *cruceta* designs occupy that central position.

15. I have heard the dove design associated with liberty on other occasions. I can only surmise that the *paloma* design somehow became associated with the quetzal, the national bird of Guatemala and an animal that so loves its freedom that it dies in captivity (or so goes the legend). This connection makes sense in terms of other contestants' interpretations of design motifs, some of which were likewise linked to symbols of the nation-state.

16. Note that this description does not accurately reflect the process of pattern innovation in Tecpán today.

17. In her book on Comalapa *traje*, Linda Asturias de Barrios (1985) describes a similar taxonomy of weaving techniques.

18. People's attitudes toward clothing and public display of their bodies change with time. For example, some of the women I met in 1980 who would not remove *traje* to go swimming now dress in *vestido* for a day at the beach. Others who do not themselves go swimming provide *vestido* for their children who do. Because bathing suits are expensive and trips to the beach rare, these people often make do with items like T-shirts and gym shorts.

19. I was first introduced to the idea of combining swimming and washing when I lived in Jutiapa and the water system in the village broke down. I was part of a group of females (aged ten to twenty-five) plus some very young male "guides" who ventured to a pool in the local river where we swam, did laundry, and bathed. (Note the thin, often artificial line between swimming [recreation] and bathing ["work"].) While I was the only person in an "official" bathing suit, I was definitely not the envy of the crowd. That honor rested with the young women who appeared in thin white and pastel-colored negligees. No doubt they had few other opportunities to model the pieces in such a public arena.

20. Diane Nelson's paper (1993) on Rigoberta Menchú jokes deals with some of these clothing issues.

21. When I returned to Guatemala in 1990, the worsening economy was seen as responsible for a wave of assaults and robberies, especially in the capital. One report that shocked everyone was the theft of an expensive *corte*, stolen right off a woman attacked by a group of Indian women in the large, bustling central bus station.

22. The erotic power of thighs comes out in several nonindigenous sources. In *fotonovelas* women and men endlessly contemplate their own and each other's bodies (although women are the ones most commonly shown being observed by themselves, by other women, and by men [cf. Berger 1983: 36–64]). One woman, for example, considering the seductive power of her body, gazes at her thighs and says, "And my flesh, it's still solid and firm! My thighs are still splendid!" (*Fiebre de pasiones* 1980a: 14, my translation). And, in another, a recently widowed man lusts after his dead wife, exclaiming, "On the whole, she had formidable thighs ..." (*Fiebre de pasiones* 1980b: 18, my translation). In many cases, the photographs accompanying the texts are shot from hip or bed level. As a result, the thighs and buttocks loom large while the head and upper body appear disproportionately small.

23. Rigoberta Menchú (1984: 211) also mentions the importance of aprons for Maya women. For example, she quotes her mother as saying, "Never forget to wear your apron, my child," and claims that her mother "often used to scold us [Menchú and her sisters] when we'd run off without our aprons." She adds: "Our aprons are also something very important: women use them all the time, in the market, in the street, in all her work. It's something sacred for a woman and she must always have it with her."

In my own experience I noted women putting on and taking off aprons at very specific points in the day. They put on aprons in the morning as soon as they rose; they took them off for photographs, for salaried work outside the home, and—among some—for trips to the market; they quickly put them on again after completing activities that did not call for aprons.

24. The revitalization movement is changing this attitude, too. More women now purposely choose to wear "Maya" jewelry as yet another way of preserving *costumbre*.

6. *Transforming the Traditional: The Creative in* Traje

1. This chapter does not address the situation of Maya living in the war-torn northwestern highlands or as refugees in Mexico or the United States. In these extreme cases the destruction of communities has been so great that the "evolution" of *traje* is not regular in any sense of the word. See Anderson and Garlock (1988: 96–111) for brief comments on this subject.

2. Recall that the jacket worn by Maya men involved in the revitalization movement in the early 1990s was made from an indigo blue cloth associated with women's *cortes* and adorned with figures from *huipiles*.

3. The public statement made through dress at the ordination ceremonies (at least as I have interpreted it) was true to the man's subsequent actions. As a priest, he devoted his early days to working in local parishes, including activities with Catholic Action groups. When violence struck the Tecpán area in 1981 and he received death threats, he moved to the capital where he felt he could work more anonymously. Even there, however, it was impossible to do the work he wanted and feel safe. Sometime in 1981 he left the country and took up residence in Mexico to begin work with the Guatemalan Church in Exile.

7. *To Wear* Traje *Is to Say "We Are Maya"*

1. *"Llevar un traje maya es decirnos a nosotros mismos y a los demás: soy maya, somos mayas, seguimos y seguiremos siendo mayas."*

2. When I first formulated these ideas, they related broadly to the concepts of "speech community," "linguistic community," and, in particular, my understanding of these terms as they emerged from ongoing discussions with Bonnie Urciuoli during the throes of dissertation writing in the early 1980s.

3. The image of the Indian created by this framing of *traje* stands in

contrast to what Irma Otzoy (1992b) labels the "colonial Indian." Referring to the arguments of author Severo Martínez Peláez, Otzoy writes that, according to this model, "the 'Indian' [*indio*], like 'his/her world,' was born from the historic cruelty of 'the conquest'" (2, my translation) and that, since then, Indians and all with which they are associated exist in contrast with and subordinate to non-Indians. According to this model, indigenous clothing from postconquest times onward developed in accordance with the desires and interests of non-Maya, who used *traje* for their own social and political ends.

4. These thoughts were inspired, in part, by *The Violence Within*, edited by Kay Warren (1993b). In particular, I have benefited from the ideas presented in the article by Michael Hanchard (1993) as well as in his informal talk during the 1992 NEH Institute's "The Encounter of Cultures in Brazil," where he discusses the idea of culturalism versus cultural politics in the context of Afro-Brazilian racial politics. According to Hanchard, culturalism "refers to the abstraction, reification, and commodification of artifacts and expressions of a particular social collectivity for the purpose of projecting the image of that collectivity as a whole" (1993: 61). Cultural politics, on the other hand, entails using culture for the transformation of social policy.

5. People who write about clothing and related subjects are also stigmatized. For example, in a recent issue of the *Times Literary Supplement*, Nicola Shulman, writing on Farid Chenoune's book *A History of Men's Fashion*, opens with this statement: "Writings about fashion have lately been infected by a suspicion that the study of clothes is insufficient occupation for a person of mind" (1993: 32). Ironically, in the same issue Terry Eagleton begins a piece with the statement "If you want to make it as a radical critic these days, slip the word 'body' into your book title" (1993: 10).

6. My recent work focuses on women, education, and the role of *traje* in revitalization activities (Hendrickson 1992, 1994).

7. In 1993–1994 Edward Fischer and Mareike Sattler conducted fieldwork in Tecpán on local dimensions of the pan-Maya movement. They note that linguist José Obispo Rodríguez Guaján (Pakal B'alam), a Tecpaneco, has opened a school of Kaqchikel language and culture in his hometown and that weaving is incorporated in certain programs of study (Fischer, personal communication, 1994). Rodríguez Guaján, along with several other Tecpán scholars (e.g., Demetrio Cojtí Cuxil, Narciso Cojtí Macario, and Paula López), are doing much to inject Maya voices into the literature.

GLOSSARY

Additional terms for articles of *traje* are discussed in Chapter 1, and additional terms related to weaving are discussed in Chapter 5.

abandonado abandoned; located in an isolated (often rural) area without access to modern conveniences, material goods, and ideas; said of people and the places they live (cf. *civilizado*)

aj q'ij diviner for traditional Maya religious practices

aldea village; a small residential unit within a municipality

a mano by hand; said of weaving done on a backstrap loom

a maquina by machine; said of weaving done on a treadle or foot loom

anciano old person, elder

barrio neighborhood; used to refer to each of Tecpán's four major divisions

básico the first three years of secondary education following six years of primary school

blusa Maya blouse made of factory-produced cloth with hand or machine-embroidered designs around the neck and armholes

brujería witchcraft

cabecera municipal or town center

caites sandals identified as being Indian

campesino rural farmer

carrera career; also used to refer to a course of study that leads to a specialized degree and certification for work in areas such as primary education, agricultural education, or accounting/bookkeeping

carriso a relatively thick and hard three-ply cotton thread, preferred by many for the warp threads of *huipiles*

caserío hamlet; residential unit of a municipality, smaller than an *aldea* (village)

chaket jacket made of dark blue or black wool; part of a Tecpán man's *traje*

civilizado civilized; located in a populated (and more urban) area with access to modern conveniences, material goods, and ideas; said of people and the places they live (cf. *abandonado*)

cofradía religious brotherhood or cofraternity whose activities include caring for a particular saint or saints of the Catholic church; sometimes associated with more conservative Catholic church practices

Colonia Iximché residential area in the northwest corner of Tecpán that was created with relief funds after the 1976 earthquake

corte Maya woman's skirt; *uq*

costumbre indigenous custom or tradition; often used to refer specifically to Maya ritual practices, but also more broadly to refer to such activities as wearing indigenous dress and speaking a Maya language

criollo native-born descendant of Spaniards with upper-class socioeconomic ties; used in colonial times

cruceta cross-stitch; a weaving technique achieved by wrapping small groups of warp threads with supplementary weft threads; used for the realistic depiction of flowers and fruit; also called *marcador*

departamento department or province; one of twenty-two administrative and territorial divisions in Guatemala

faja belt

figura design motif

finca large farm; administrative unit of a municipality

fotonovela romance comic book with photographs instead of cartoon drawings

fuerte strong; said of colors and blood (see *sangre fuerte*)

gringo foreigner; specifically, a white foreigner; used to refer to a North American or European

huipil Maya woman's woven blouse; *po't*

indígena Indian, Maya; one of the preferred terms for self-identification in Tecpán

indio Indian; a term with derogatory connotations

INGUAT Instituto Guatemalteco de Turismo, the Guatemalan government's Institute of Tourism

jaspe (adj., *jaspeado*) designs produced by weaving tie-dyed or ikat threads into cloth; also used to refer to the threads and dyeing process

jun ruwa kem single-faced supplementary weft patterning

ka'i' ruwa kem two-faced supplementary weft patterning

k'aqo'j brown; natural brown cotton

ladino mestizo or non-Maya; a Guatemalan defined by certain overt markers (the use of *vestido*, the Spanish language, etc.), blood or historical roots, and an association with the dominant national society

lana wool; acrylic thread or yarn

lengua language, tongue; in highland contexts, a Maya language *lienzo* length of woven cloth; two backstrap-woven lengths are used to make most Tecpán *huipiles*

marcador see *cruceta*

maxi faldas calf- or ankle-length skirts

Mayab' Maya; Kaqchikel term used primarily in solidarity and revitalization contexts

mero traje "real" Maya dress; used to emphasize the authenticity of an outfit from a particular municipality or earlier era

milpa cornfield

mish mercerized cotton thread produced in Guatemala

morga older style of *corte* made on the treadle loom with indigo-colored threads, often with white threads forming stripes and rectangular patterns distinctive of a municipality

el movimiento the movement, specifically the Maya revitalization movement

municipio municipality; administrative and geographic division of a department consisting of a town center and outlying residential units; seen as an ethnically distinct region characterized by different indigenous customs, dress, and speech

municipalidad municipal building, town hall

natural native, Indian; one of the preferred terms for self-identification in Tecpán

novia girlfriend, fiancée, or bride

novio boyfriend, fiancé, or groom

ombliguera cloth belt wrapped around the stomach and over the navel (*ombligo*) of a newborn infant

padrino godparent

penecita style of *morga* particular to Tecpán

pila large, waist-high sink with a basin to hold water and sections for washing dishes and clothes; often located outside in the patio

po't Maya woman's woven blouse; *huipil*

PRONEBI Programa Nacional de Educación Bilingüe (National Bilingual Education Program)

qawinaqi' Maya; literally, "our people"

Rabín Ajau national Indian queen selected each year at the Folkloric Festival sponsored by INGUAT

raza race; often used interchangeably with *grupo étnico* (ethnic group); in certain contexts understood to refer only to Indians (e.g., Día de la Raza)

ri'j po't handwoven overblouse, worn by Maya women on ceremonial occasions; *sobre huipil*

rodillera rectangle of black and white wool cloth secured at the waist by a belt and covering the front part of the lower torso and upper legs; part of a Tecpán man's *traje*

ropa corriente ladino clothing, literally "common clothes"

ropa ya hecho readymade clothes with factory labels

sangre fuerte strong blood; said of a person regarded as powerful, domineering, rigid, and able to do harm

sedalina pearl cotton thread

servilleta general-purpose cloth used around the home to cover baskets of food or clean dishes, wrap hot tortillas, protect televisions and radios from dust; also worn folded on the head as part of a Tecpán woman's *traje*

la situación euphemism for the violence of the 1980s

sobre huipil handwoven overblouse worn by Maya women on ceremonial occasions; *ri'j po't*

sucio soiled (with dirt, excrement, etc.); also said of a person reagarded as morally or socially tainted

Tecpaneco a person from Tecpán

tela típica cloth identified as Maya in origin or used by Maya

telar treadle loom

típico typical; in highland contexts, Maya or indigenous; used as a noun to refer to tourist items marked as Maya (cf. *tradicional*)

toga graduation gown

tradicional traditional; in highland contexts, Maya or indigenous (cf. *típico*)

los tradicionales the traditionals; traditional members of the Catholic church, those who support the *cofradía* system

traje dress or suit (of clothes); in highland contexts, used to refer to Maya clothing (e.g., *traje típico* and *traje tradicional*)

uq Maya woman's skirt; *corte*

vara Spanish measure of length equal to 0.84 meter (approximately 33 inches)

vestido clothing; specifically, ladino clothing (in contrast to *traje*)

xilon striped; used to refer to an old style of Tecpán *huipil*

BIBLIOGRAPHY

Adams, Marie Jeanne. 1969. *System and Meaning in East Sumba Textile Design: A Study in Traditional Indonesian Art.* Southeast Asia Studies Cultural Report Series, no. 16. New Haven: Yale University.

————. 1971. Work Patterns in a Village Culture, East Sumba, Indonesia. *Southeast Asia International Quarterly* 1 (4): 320–334.

————. 1980. Structural Aspects of East Sumbanese Art. In *The Flow of Life,* edited by James J. Fox, 208–220. Cambridge: Harvard University Press.

Adams, Tani Marielena. 1978. San Martín Jilotepequez: Aspects of the Political and Socioeconomic Structure of a Guatemalan Peasant Community. CIRMA, Antigua Guatemala. Photocopy.

Ajozal Xuyá, José Francisco. 1977a. Editorial. *Tecpanidad* 1: 3.

————. 1977b. La casa de cultura Tecpaneca sería una realidad. *Tecpanidad* 1: 13.

————. 1979–1980. Lo que piensan las reinas. *Tecpanidad* 3: 22.

Albers, Patricia C., and William R. James. 1983. Tourism and the Changing Photographic Image of the Great Lakes Indians. *Annals of Tourism Research* 10 (1): 123–148.

Anawalt, Patricia Rieff. 1981. *Indian Clothing before Cortes: Mesoamerican Costumes from the Codices.* Norman: University of Oklahoma Press.

Anderson, Marilyn. 1978. *Guatemalan Textiles Today.* New York: Watson-Guptill Publications.

Anderson, Marilyn, and Jonathan Garlock. 1988. *Granddaughters of Corn: Portraits of Guatemalan Women.* Willimantic, Conn.: Curbstone Press.

Annis, Sheldon. 1987. *God and Production in a Guatemalan Town.* Austin: University of Texas Press.

Anthony, Angela B. 1974. The Minority That Is a Majority: Guatemala's Indians. In *Guatemala,* edited by Susanne Jonas and David Tobias, 28–38. Berkeley, Calif.: North American Congress on Latin America.

Asturias, Miguel Angel. 1977 [1923]. *Sociología Guatemalteca: El problema social del Indio.* Original Spanish text with English. Translated by Maureen Ahern. Tempe: Arizona State University.

Asturias de Barrios, Linda. 1985. *Comalapa: Native Dress and Its Significance*. Guatemala City: Museo Ixchel.

Asturias de Barrios, Linda, Idalma Mejía de Rodas, and Rosario Miralbés de Polanco. 1989. *Santa María de Jesús: Traje y cofradía*. Guatemala City: Museo Ixchel.

Atwater, Mary M. 1965. *Guatemala Visited*. Monograph 15. Lansing, Mich.: Shuttle Craft Guild.

Banco de Guatemala. 1980. *Statistics*. September. Guatemala City.

Barrientos, Alfonso Enrique. 1973. *Poesía guatemalteca*. Guatemala City: Piedra Santa.

Barry, Tom. 1990. *Guatemala: A Country Guide*. Albuquerque, N.M.: Inter-Hemispheric Education Resource Center.

Basso, Keith. 1979. *Portraits of "the Whiteman": Linguistic Play and Cultural Symbols among the Western Apache*. Cambridge: Cambridge University Press.

Berger, John. 1983. *Ways of Seeing*. London: British Broadcasting Corporation.

Bjerregaard, Lena. 1977. *The Technique of Guatemalan Weaving*. New York: Van Nostrand Reinhold.

Bogatyrev, Petr. 1971 [1937]. *The Functions of Folk Costume in Moravian Slovakia*. The Hague: Mouton.

Bourdieu, Pierre. 1977. *Outline of a Theory of Practice*. Translated by Richard Nice. Cambridge: Cambridge University Press.

Braudel, Fernand. 1973. *Capitalism and Material Life: 1400–1800*. Translated by Miriam Kochan. New York: Harper and Row.

———. 1976. *The Mediterranean World in the Age of Philip II*. 2 vols. Translated by Siân Reynolds. New York: Harper and Row.

———. 1980 [1958]. History and the Social Sciences: The *Longue Durée*. In *On History*, translated by Sarah Matthews, 25–54. Chicago: University of Chicago Press.

Briggs, Charles L. 1989. *Learning How to Ask*. Cambridge: Cambridge University Press.

Brintnall, Douglas E. 1979. *Revolt against the Dead: The Modernization of a Mayan Community in the Highlands of Guatemala*. New York: Gordon and Breach.

Bunch, Roland, and Roger Bunch. 1977. *The Highland Maya: Patterns of Life and Clothing in Indian Guatemala*. Visalia, Calif.: Indigenous Publications.

Castillo, Oscar Romeo, ed. 1980. *Himnos y coros escogidos*. Guatemala City: Iglesia de Dios.

Chacach Cutzal, Martín. 1990. Una descripción fonológica y morfológica del Kaqchikel. In *Lecturas sobre la lingüística Maya*, edited by Nora C. England and Stephen R. Elliott, 145–191. Antigua Guatemala: Centro de Investigaciones Regionales de Mesoamérica.

Cojtí Cuxil, Demetrio. 1990. Lingüística e idiomas Maya en Guatemala. In *Lecturas sobre la lingüística Maya*, edited by Nora C. England and Stephen R. Elliott, 1–25. Antigua Guatemala: Centro de Investigaciones Regionales de Mesoamérica.

Comaroff, Jean, and John Comaroff. 1991. *Of Revelation and Revolution: Christianity, Colonialism, and Consciousness in South Africa*. Chicago: University of Chicago Press.

Conte, Christine. 1984. Maya Culture and Costume: A Catalogue of the Taylor Museum's E. B. Ricketson Collection of Guatemalan Textiles. Colorado Springs: Taylor Museum of the Colorado Fine Arts Center.

Cortés y Larraz, Pedro. 1958 [1769–1770]. *Descripción geográfico-moral de la diócesis de Goathemala*. 2 vols. Vol. 20 of Biblioteca "Goathemala." Guatemala City: Sociedad de Geografía e Historia.

Cultural Survival. 1981. Some Pesticides in Use around the World. *Newsletter* 5 (3): 6–7.

Danforth, Loring. 1989. *Firewalking and Religious Healing: The Anasternaria of Greece and the American Firewalking Movement*. Princeton: Princeton University Press.

Delgado, Hildegard Schmidt de. 1963. Aboriginal Guatemalan Handweaving and Costume. Ph.D. diss., Department of Anthropology, Indiana University.

Diagnóstico de salud y nutrición, Cuidad Tecpán, Chimaltenango, Guatemala. June 1979. Typescript.

Dieterich, Mary G., Jon T. Erickson, and Erin Younger. 1979. *Guatemalan Costumes: The Heard Museum Collection*. Phoenix, Ariz.: Heard Museum.

Dirección General de Estadística. 1975. *VIII Censo de población, 1973*. Guatemala City: Ministerio de Economía.

———. 1984. *Censos nacionales: IV habitación—IX población 1981*. Guatemala City: Ministerio de Economía.

Dumont, Jean-Paul. 1988. The Tasaday, Which and Whose?: Toward the Political Economy of an Ethnographic Sign. *Cultural Anthropology* 3 (3): 261–275.

Eagleton, Terry. 1993. International Books of the Year. *Times Literary Supplement*. 3 December, 10.

Editorial Maya Wuj. 1990. *Cholb'äl Samaj* (Agenda Kaqchikel). Guatemala City.

———. 1991. *Cholb'äl Samaj* (Agenda con el calendario Maya). Guatemala City.

Ehlers, Tracy Bachrach. 1990. *Silent Looms: Women and Production in a Guatemalan Town*. Boulder, Colo.: Westview Press.

Evans-Pritchard, E. E. 1969. *The Nuer*. New York: Oxford University Press.

Feld, Steven. 1982. *Sound and Sentiment: Birds, Weeping, Poetics, and Song in Kaluli Expression*. Philadelphia: University of Pennsylvania Press.

Fiebre de pasiones. 1980a. Así empiezan los destrampes. No. 35. Mexico City.

———. 1980b. La que volvió por lo suyo. No. 24. Mexico City.

Firth, Raymond. 1973. *Symbols: Public and Private*. Symbol, Myth, and Ritual Series. Edited by Victor Turner. Ithaca: Cornell University Press.

Forge, Anthony. 1973. Style and Meaning in Sepik Art. In *Primitive Art and Society*, edited by Anthony Forge, 169–192. London: Oxford University Press.

Friedlander, Judith. 1975. *Being Indian in Hueyapan: A Study of Forced Identity in Contemporary Mexico*. New York: St. Martin's Press.

Friedrich, Paul. 1986. *The Princes of Naranjo: An Essay in Anthrohistorical Method*. Austin: University of Texas Press.

Geertz, Clifford. 1973. *The Interpretation of Cultures*. New York: Basic Books.

Goldin, Liliana R. 1987. The 'Peace of the Market' in the Midst of Violence: A Symbolic Analysis of Markets and Exchanges in Western Guatemala. *Ethnos* 52 (3–4): 368–383.

Goldman, Robert. 1992. *Reading Ads Socially*. New York: Routledge.

Gombrich, E. H. 1972. Truth and Stereotype. In *Art and Illusion: A Study in the Psychology of Pictorial Representation*, 63–90. Princeton: Princeton University Press.

Good News Bible. 1976. New York: American Bible Society.

El Gráfico. 1980a. Editorial. 20 October, 6.

———. 1980b. Lo que simboliza cada color. 11 December, 20.

———. 1980c. Tecún Umán: Símbolo de la nacionalidad. 20 February, 6.

———. 1980d. Téllez García: Negar a Tecún Umán es negar nuestra esencia nacional. 20 February, 5.

Greenberg, Linda. 1984. Illness and Curing among Mam Indians in Highland Guatemala: Cosmological Balance and Cultural Transformation. Ph.D. diss., Department of Anthropology, University of Chicago.

Guatemala Information Center. 1981. *Iximché: The Indigenous People Declare Unity*. Popular Histories, no. 5. Long Beach, Calif.

Guzmán Böckler, Carlos. 1975. El ladino: Un ser ficticio. In *Guatemala: Una interpretación histórico-social*, edited by Carlos Guzmán Böckler and Jean-Loup Herbert, 101–121. Mexico City: Siglo XXI Editores.

Hagan, Alfred John. 1970. An Analysis of the Hand Weaving Sector of the Guatemalan Economy. Ph.D. diss., School of Business Administration, University of Texas at Austin.

Hanchard, Michael. 1993. Culturalism versus Cultural Politics: *Movimento Negro* in Rio de Janeiro and Sao Paulo, Brazil. In *The Violence Within: Cultural and Political Oppositions in Divided Nations*, edited by Kay B. Warren, 57–85. Boulder, Colo.: Westview Press.

Hawkins, John. 1984. *Inverse Images: The Meaning of Culture, Ethnicity, and Family in Postcolonial Guatemala*. Albuquerque: University of New Mexico Press.

Hebdige, Dick. 1983. *Subculture: The Meaning of Style*. New York: Methuen.

Hendrickson, Carol. 1992. Maya Revitalization: Women and Weaving. Paper presented at the Latin American Studies Association meeting, Los Angeles, September 24–27.

———. 1993. Selling Guatemala: Maya Products in U.S. Mail-Order Catalogs. Paper presented at the annual meeting of the American Ethnological Society, Santa Fe, April 15–18.

———. 1994. Maya Revitalization: Weaving and Education. Paper presented at the Latin American Studies Association meeting, Atlanta, March 10–12.

Hill, Robert M., II. 1992. *Colonial Cakchiquels: Highland Maya Adaptation to Spanish Rule, 1600–1700*. Fort Worth, Tex.: Harcourt Brace Jovanovich.

Instituto Guatemalteco de Turismo (INGUAT). 1980a. *Guatemala en Centro América*. Tourist brochure.

———. 1980b. *Olmeca: La Democracia*. Tourist brochure.

Jonas, Susanne. 1991. *The Battle for Guatemala: Rebels, Death Squads, and U.S. Power*. Boulder, Colo.: Westview Press.

Jonas, Susanne, and David Tobis, eds. 1974. *Guatemala*. Berkeley, Calif.: North American Congress on Latin America.

Kopytoff, Igor. 1988. The Cultural Biography of Things: Commoditization as Process. In *The Social Life of Things: Commodities in Cultural Perspective*, edited by Arjun Appadurai, 64–91. Cambridge: Cambridge University Press.

Lathbury, Virginia Locke. 1974. Textiles as the Expression of World View: San Antonio Aguas Calientes, Guatemala. Master's thesis, Department of Anthropology, University of Pennsylvania.

LeCount, Cynthia Gravelle. 1990. *Andean Folk Knitting: Traditions and Techniques from Peru and Bolivia*. St. Paul, Minn.: Dos Tejedoras.

Lutz, Christopher H. 1994. Santiago de Guatemala, 1541–1773: City, Caste, and the Colonial Experience. Norman: University of Oklahoma Press.

Martínez Peláez, Severo. 1979. *La patria del criollo: Ensayo de interpretación de la realidad colonial guatemalteca*. San José, Costa Rica: Editorial Universitaria Centroamericana.

Maxwell, Judith. 1991. "Rat" ncha / "You," he said: Language of Solidarity among the Kaqchikel (Maya). Handout at the annual meeting of the American Anthropological Association, Chicago, November 20–24.

———. 1992. Language of Solidarity among the Kaqchikel (Maya). Paper presented at the annual meeting of the Latin American Studies Association, Los Angeles, September 24–27.

Maxwell Museum of Anthropology. 1976. *Weavers of the Jade Needle: Textiles of Highland Guatemala*. Publication no. 1. Albuquerque: University of New Mexico.

Mayén de Castellanos, Guisela. 1986. *Tzute y jerarquía en Sololá*. Guatemala City: Museo Ixchel.

Mejía de Rodas, Idalma, and Rosario Miralbés de Polanco. 1987. *Cambio en Colotenango: Traje, migración, y jerarquía*. Guatemala City: Museo Ixchel.

Menchú, Rigoberta. 1984. *I . . . Rigoberta Menchú: An Indian Woman in Guatemala*. Edited by Elisabeth Burgos-Debray. Translated by Ann Wright. London: Verso.

Méndez Cifuentes, Arturo. 1967. *Nociones de tejidos indígenas de Guatemala*. Guatemala City: Editorial José de Pineda Ibarra.

Miralbés de Polanco, Rosario, Eugenia Sáenz de Tejada, and Idalma Mejía de Rodas. 1990. *Zunil: Traje y economía*. Guatemala City: Museo Ixchel.

Morales Hidalgo, Italo. 1990. *U cayibal atziak / Imágenes en los tejidos Guatemaltecos / Images in Guatemalan Weavings*. Guatemala City: Ediciones Cuatro Ahau.

Munn, Nancy D. 1977. The Spatio-Temporal Transformations of Gawa Canoes. *Journal de la Société des Océanistes*. 33: 39–53.

La Nación. 1977. Turismo. 26 August, 16.

Nash, Manning. 1958. *Machine Age Maya: The Industrialization of a Guatemalan Community*. Chicago: University of Chicago Press.

Nelson, Diane M. 1991. The Reconstruction of Mayan Identity. *Report on Guatemala* 12 (2): 6–7, 14.

————. 1993. Gendering the Ethnic-National Question: Rigoberta Jokes and the Out-skirts of Fashioning Identity. Paper presented at the annual meeting of the American Anthropological Association, Washington, D.C., November 17–21.

Neuenswander, Helen L., and Shirley D. Souder. 1977. The Hot-Cold Wet-Dry Syndrome among the Quiché of Joyabaj: Two Alternative Cognitive Models. In *Cognitive Studies of Southern Mesoamerica*, edited by Helen L. Neuenswander and Dean E. Arnold, 94–125. Dallas, Tex.: Summer Institute of Linguistics Museum of Anthropology.

O'Neale, Lila M. 1945. *Textiles of Highland Guatemala*. Publication no. 567. Washington, D.C.: Carnegie Institution of Washington.

Osborne, Lilly de Jongh. 1935. *Guatemalan Textiles*. Middle American Research Series, no. 6. New Orleans: Tulane University.

————. 1965. *Indian Crafts of Guatemala and El Salvador*. Norman: University of Oklahoma Press.

Otzoy, Irma. 1992a. Identidad y trajes mayas. *Mesoamérica* 23: 95–112. (English translation: Maya Clothing and Identity. Paper delivered at the 1991 American Anthropological Association meeting, Chicago, November 20–24.)

————. 1992b. Imágenes del indio: Generación y regeneración. Paper presented at the Latin American Studies Association meeting, Los Angeles, September 24–27.

Pancake, Cherri M. 1977. Textile Traditions of the Highland Maya: Some Aspects of Development and Change. Paper presented at the International Symposium on Maya Art, Architecture, Archaeology, and Hieroglyphic Writing, Guatemala City.

Pancake, Cherri M., and Sheldon Annis. 1982. El arte de la producción: Aspectos socio-económicos del tejido a mano en San Antonio Aguas Calientes, Guatemala. *Mesoamérica* 4: 387–413.

Pansini, Joseph Jude. 1977. El Pilar: A Plantation Microcosm of Guatemalan Ethnicity. Ph.D. diss., Department of Anthropology, University of Rochester.

Paul, Lois. 1974. The Mastery of Work and the Mystery of Sex in a Guatemalan Village. In *Women, Culture, and Society*, edited by Michelle Zimbalist Rosaldo and Louise Lamphere, 281–299. Stanford: Stanford University Press.

Pettersen, Carmen L. 1976. *Maya of Guatemala: Life and Dress*. Guatemala City: Museo Ixchel; Seattle: University of Washington Press.

Photo-Studio Canche Serra. 1980. *Fácil-Easy Guatemala*. Guatemala City: Guatemala-Fácil & Co. Tourist brochure.

Polo Sifontes, Francis. 1986. *Los Cakchiqueles en la conquista de Guatemala*.

Guatemala City: CENALTEX.

Programa Nacional de Educación Bilingüe (PRONEBI). 1989. *Ri nab'ey qasolb'äl tzij: Kaqchikel-Castellano*. Guatemala City: Ministry of Education.

Rabinow, Paul. 1977. *Reflections on Fieldwork in Morocco*. Berkeley: University of California Press.

Rodríguez Guaján, José Obispo, Juan Yool Gómez, Marcos Armando Calí Semeyá, and Tomás Chacach Apén. 1988. *Gramática del idioma Kaqchikel*. Guatemala City: Proyecto Lingüístico Francisco Marroquín.

Rosales Arenales de Klose, Margarita. 1978. Mercado de textiles artesanales. Licenciatura thesis, Department of Economics, Universidad Rafael Landívar.

Rowe, Ann Pollard. 1981. *A Century of Change in Guatemalan Textiles*. New York: Center for Inter-American Relations.

Sahlins, Marshall. 1976. *Culture and Practical Reason*. Chicago: University of Chicago Press.

Saquic, Rosalio. 1948. *Tecpán: Síntesis socio-económica de una comunidad indígena guatemalteca*. Guatemala City: Instituto Indigenista Nacional and Ministerio de Educación de Guatemala.

Schele, Linda, and Mary Ellen Miller. 1986. *The Blood of Kings: Dynasty and Ritual in Maya Art*. Fort Worth, Tex.: Kimbell Art Museum.

Schevill, Margot Blum. 1985. *Evolution in Textile Design from the Highlands of Guatemala*. Occasional Papers, no. 1. Berkeley: Lowie Museum of Anthropology, University of California.

———. 1986. *Costume as Communication*. Studies in Anthropology and Material Culture, vol. 4. Bristol, R.I.: Haffenreffer Museum of Anthropology, Brown University.

Scott, James C. 1985. *Weapons of the Weak: Everyday Forms of Peasant Resistance*. New Haven: Yale University Press.

Shulman, Nicola. 1993. Undo this Button. *Times Literary Supplement*. 3 December, 32.

Simon, Jean-Marie. 1987. *Guatemala: Eternal Spring, Eternal Tyranny*. New York: W. W. Norton & Company.

Smith, Carol A., 1990a. Class Position and Class Consciousness in an Indian Community: Totonicapán in the 1970s. In *Guatemalan Indians and the State: 1540 to 1988*, edited by Carol A. Smith, 205–229. Austin: University of Texas Press.

———, ed. 1990b. *Guatemalan Indians and the State: 1540 to 1988*. Austin: University of Texas Press.

———. 1991. Maya Nationalism. *Report on the Americas* 25 (3): 29–33.

Sperlich, Norbert, and Elizabeth Katz Sperlich. 1980. *Guatemalan Backstrap Weaving*. Norman: University of Oklahoma Press.

Steiner, Wendy. 1982. *The Colors of Rhetoric: Problems in the Relation between Modern Literature and Painting*. Chicago: University of Chicago Press.

Stephens, John L. 1969 [1841]. *Incidents of Travel in Central America, Chiapas, and Yucatan*. 2 vols. New York: Dover Publications.

Stoll, David. 1982. *Fishers of Men or Founders of Empire? The Wycliffe Bible Translators in Latin America*. London: Zed Press; Cambridge, Mass.: Cultural Survival.

Tax, Sol. 1937. The Municipios of the Midwestern Highlands of Guatemala. *American Anthropologist* 39: 423–444.

———. 1971 [1953]. *Penny Capitalism: A Guatemalan Indian Economy*. New York: Octagon Books.

Tedlock, Barbara, and Dennis Tedlock. 1985. Text and Textile: Language and Technology in the Arts of the Quiché Maya. *Journal of Anthropological Research* 41 (2): 121–146.

Tedlock, Dennis, trans. 1985. *Popol Vuh: The Mayan Book of the Dawn of Life*. New York: Simon and Schuster.

Todorov, Tzvetan. 1988. Knowledge in Social Anthropology: Distancing and Universality. *Anthropology Today* 4 (2): 2–5.

Torgovnick, Marianna. 1990. *Gone Primitive: Savage Intellects, Modern Lives*. Chicago: University of Chicago Press.

Turner, Terrence. 1979. The Social Skin: Bodily Adornment, Social Meaning, and Personal Identity. Ms.

———. 1980. The Social Skin. In *Not Work Alone: A Cross-Cultural View of Activities Superfluous to Survival*, edited by Jeremy Cherfas and Roger Lewin, 112–140. Beverly Hills, Calif.: Sage Publications.

Urban, Greg, and Joel Sherzer. 1991. *Nation-States and Indians in Latin America*. Austin: University of Texas Press.

Urciuoli, Bonnie. 1983. The Cultural Construction of Linguistic Variation. Ph.D. diss., University of Chicago.

———. Forthcoming. *The Semiotics of Exclusion*. Boulder, Colo.: Westview Press.

Wagley, Charles. 1941. *Economics of a Guatemalan Village*. Memoir No. 58. Menasha, Wis.: American Anthropological Association.

Warren, Kay B. 1978. *The Symbolism of Subordination: Indian Identity in a Guatemalan Town*. Austin: University of Texas Press.

———. 1993a. Interpreting *la violencia* in Guatemala: Shapes of Mayan Silence and Resistance. In *The Violence Within: Cultural and Political Oppositions in Divided Nations*, edited by Kay B. Warren, 25–56. Boulder, Colo.: Westview Press.

————, ed. 1993b. *The Violence Within: Cultural and Political Oppositions in Divided Nations.* Boulder, Colo.: Westview Press.

Washington Office on Latin America. 1983. *Guatemala: The Roots of the Revolution.* Special Update Latin America. February. Washington, D.C.

Watanabe, John M. 1992. *Maya Saints and Souls in a Changing World.* Austin: University of Texas Press.

Willis, Michael. 1991. 500 Years of Indigenous and Popular Resistence: Report on the Second Continental Meeting. *Report on Guatemala* 12 (4): 2–5, 15.

Wood, Josephine, and Lilly de Jongh Osborne. 1966. *Indian Costumes of Guatemala.* Graz, Austria: Akademische Druck- und Verlagsanstalt.

INDEX

abandonado, 67, 71

Acatenango, 202

Acción Católica. *See* Catholic Action

acrylic fibers. *See* synthetic fibers

Adams, Marie Jeanne, 40, 216

Adams, Tani, 206, 211

advertisement, 68, 69, 71, 73–74, 84, 118, 123, 208, 210. *See also* tourism

Afro-Brazilian racial politics, 219

agribusiness, 46

agriculture, 9, 21, 23, 46–47, 92, 114, 132, 151

aire, 102

aj q'ij, 134

aldeas, 11, 18, 120

Anawalt, Patricia, 205

Anderson, Marilyn, 218

Annis, Sheldon, 15, 40

Antigua Guatemala, 28, 62, 67, 180

apron, 37, 121, 130, 173, 175, 217–218

art, 23–24, 39, 83, 144, 181, 198, 212

Asturias, Miguel Angel, 177

Asturias de Barrios, Linda, 205, 216

bag (*bolsa, morral*), 38

baptism, 103–104, 145, 176

barrios, 14, 202

bathing, 100, 101, 105, 135, 168, 175, 176, 212, 213, 217. *See also* sweatbath

bathing attire, 168, 205, 216, 217

beauty: human, 54, 55, 63, 83, 89, 93, 110, 111–112, 113, 114, 115, 116, 118, 135, 171, 213; of *traje*, 114, 116, 118–119, 146, 148, 159, 165, 198. *See also* physical attractiveness; queen contests

belt, 35, 38, 50, 51, 100–101, 103, 108, 112, 118, 121, 137, 169, 171, 176. *See also ombliguera*

Berger, John, 210

birth, 92, 98, 99–101, 212

birth control, 130

blankets, 46, 85, 102, 103, 104, 127, 181

blood, 30, 79, 113; strong, 99–100, 102

blusa, 58, 184, 187, 191. *See also huipil*

body, 98–99, 100, 101, 102, 103, 104, 116, 118, 141, 153, 170–172, 176, 213, 217, 219; desire for the, 112, 115, 170, 217; exposure of, 31, 167–168, 169, 170–171, 203–204, 213, 216; and gender differences, 103, 129, 168–169; in relation to dress, 149, 157–158, 166, 169–170, 171; socialization of, 103–104, 105–106, 152–153, 172

Bogatyrev, Petr, 40, 194–196, 205

brand names, 50, 71–72, 73–74,

146, 148, 173–174, 206;
Anchor/Ancla, 206–207
Brattleboro, Vermont, 181
Braudel, Fernand, 41–43, 205
Briggs, Charles L., 202
Brown, Robert McKenna, 210
businesses, 19–23, 96, 131, 132,
212. *See also* economy and
economic conditions

cabecera, 11–13, 18, 202
Calí Semeyá, Marcos, xiii
Cantel, 44, 48, 52, 206
Catholic Action, 15–18, 188, 218
Catholic church, 1, 13, 14, 15–18;
ceremony, 103, 120, 126, 137,
142; chasuble, 184, 187–188,
191; clergy, 1, 2, 82, 123, 126,
184, 187–188, 189, 218;
Guatemalan Church in Exile,
218; members, 15–18, 120, 138–
139, 142; and *traje*, 36–37, 50,
137, 184, 187–188, 191, 214. *See
also* baptism; *cofradías*; Catholic
Action; schools; *tradicionales*
cemetery, 131, 142
ceramics, 21, 84, 85, 203, 207,
208, 212
Chacach Apén, Tomás, xiii
Chacach Cutzal, Martín, xiii
Chenoune, Farid, 219
Chiapas, 203
Chichicastenango, 10, 21, 51, 55,
63, 82, 85, 159, 168, 180
children, 83, 101–109, 114;
clothing worn by, 55–56, 57,
58, 101–106, 107, 213; socialization of, 92, 98–99, 136. *See also*
birth; infants; schools

Chimaltenango, 10, 46, 72, 80–81,
93, 148, 202, 212
China, 44
civilizado, 67, 208
civil patrols, 190
cleanliness, 105, 147, 176–177
climate, 57–58, 127, 135
cloth. *See corte*; *huipil*; *lienzo*;
thread; *traje*; weaving
clothing. *See* dress; *traje*; *vestido*
Cobán, 52, 58, 64, 90, 92–93
cofradías, 15–18, 38, 51, 57, 134,
138–139, 165
Cojtí Cuxil, Demetrio, 203, 219
Cojtí Macario, Narciso, 219
Colombia, 44, 50, 206
Colonia Iximché, xiv, 14–15
colonial era, 13, 14, 28, 30–31, 76,
80, 83, 194, 201, 203, 219
color, 35, 37, 63, 89, 112, 146–148,
161–162, 165; black, 141–142,
147; green, 138, 147, 161;
purple, 141, 147, 181; red, 102,
147–148, 213, 214; skin, 79,
113, 148, 168; symbolism, 147–
148; white, 63, 125–126, 137,
142, 147. *See also* shine; thread
Comalapa, 10, 18, 23–24, 52, 57,
88, 93, 117, 136, 151, 159, 174,
205, 214, 215, 216
communication, 18, 59, 69
contests. *See* queen contests; *traje*
contests
Continental Campaign of 500
Years of Indigenous and
Popular Resistance, 212
corn, 9, 21, 23, 92, 109, 149, 155–
156, 160, 172, 201, 214
corte, 35, 139, 150, 170–172, 217;

cloth, 20, 62, 80, 104, 138, 150, 170–171, 181; cost of, 56, 57, 88; ritual use of, 121, 125, 126. *See also morga*; *penecita*

Cortés y Larraz, Pedro, 207

cosmetics, 82, 112

costumbre, 11, 30, 50, 60, 61, 63, 64, 87, 92, 94, 104, 115, 126, 136, 137, 141, 167, 174, 189, 197, 210, 218

costume, 27, 40, 76, 79, 84, 126, 194, 201

cotton, 44, 46–50, 149; *k'aqo'j*, 48–50, 138, 149, 165, 206, 214, 215. *See also corte*; *huipil*; threads

creativity, 43, 182–183, 191–192; instances of, in *traje*, 183–190; "stereotypical creation," 182

crochet, 57, 152

cruceta, 147, 159, 161, 163–164, 185, 188–189, 191, 216

culturalism vs. cultural politics, 219

cultural text, 67, 68

curl design, origin of, 160–161

dance and dancing, 27, 76, 79, 82, 90, 93, 127, 137, 148, 203

Danforth, Loring, 24

death, 141–143

Declaration of Iximché, xiv, 90, 91, 92

departments, 11

design motifs, 35, 39, 51, 57, 61, 63, 121, 146, 149–150, 156–165, 166, 184–185, 188–189, 191, 212, 216

diagram, 77–78

diplomas, 90, 152, 215

dirt (pollution), 89, 104–105, 106, 126, 135, 171–172, 176–177

dolls, 110, 148

domestic help, 60, 128, 130

domestic sphere, 19, 81, 87, 92, 127, 151. *See also* women

dress, 30, 43, 98–99, 201, 204–205, 219; asymmetrical rankings of, 63, 66–73, 73–5; prohibitions, 107, 112–113; sexual dimensions of, 112, 115. *See also* schools; *traje*; *vestido*

dressing, act of, 167–177

Dumont, Jean Paul, 210

Eagleton, Terry, 219

earrings, 37, 102, 112, 174–175

earthquake, 1, 6, 13, 18, 20, 25, 27, 138, 142, 178, 201, 212

economy and economic conditions, 31, 40, 46, 67, 74, 90, 91, 93, 103, 109, 115, 116, 123, 133, 206, 215, 217. *See also* businesses; *traje*

Editorial Maya Wuj, 74, 75, 208

education, 6, 10, 19, 25, 59, 94, 95, 107, 109, 129, 143, 152–153; *básico*, 111; sex, 101, 127–128, 129, 130, 172, 213–214; and weaving, 108, 109, 152. *See also* schools

Ehlers, Tracy Bachrach, 40, 206

elders, 114, 135–141, 195

embroidery. *See* needlework

ethnicity, labels for, 30–33, 203. *See also* Maya-ladino relations; non-Indian; *traje*

Europe, 32, 67–70, 72, 113, 176, 207

fair, 61, 81, 148, 211; Indian committee, 30, 61, 81–82, 86, 196–197; joint Indian-ladino committee, 81–82; ladino committee, 30, 81–82, 209–210, 211; *traje* presentation, 61, 64, 75, 114, 140–141, 160–161, 195–197. *See also* Godmother of Sports; Princess Iximché; Princess Ixmucané; queen contests; Queen of the Franciscan Fiestas

Feld, Steven, 202

fibers, 44–50. *See also* cotton; silk; synthetic fibers; wool

fieldwork, 23–30

Fischer, Edward, 214, 219

flowers, 27, 115, 116, 131, 142, 146, 147, 148, 159, 161–162, 167, 184, 189, 207

food, 21, 36, 100, 120, 123, 127, 130, 155–156. *See also* corn

fotonovelas, 4–5, 23, 25, 26, 58, 168, 170, 173, 217

France, 44, 50, 69

Friedlander, Judith, 209

Friedrich, Paul, 29–30

friends and friendship, 60, 71, 86, 111, 113, 114, 117, 213

Garlock, Jonathan, 218

games, children's, 70, 110, 207

General Archives of Central America, 27

geography, 9, 44, 74, 83, 135, 204. *See also* traje

Germany, products attributed to, 44, 206

Godmother of Sports, 209–210

godparents, 103–104, 126

Goldin, Liliana, 20

Gombrich, E. H., 78

government: Guatemalan, 11, 18–19, 25, 76, 80, 92, 94, 117, 143, 188, 190; Tecpán, 11, 18. *See also* INGUAT; mayor; military

graduation, 96–97, 115; gowns, 96–97, 117–118

Great Britain, 44, 50, 206

Guatemala City, 8, 19, 44, 71, 72, 73, 116, 117, 128, 176, 212

Guatemalan Academy of Maya Languages, xiii

Guatemalans, identity as, 32, 65, 79–81, 82, 84

"guerrilla" literature, 211–212

hair, 106, 112, 117, 118, 135, 167, 174

hair ribbons, 35, 89, 174

Hanchard, Michael, 219

hands, 108, 152–153, 172; by hand, 44, 108

hand spinning, 49

hat, 38

head covering, 100, 101–102. *See also* hat; *servilleta*

highlife, 73, 117

Hill, Robert M., 202, 207

history, 30, 41–43, 197–198. *See also* time; *traje*

hot-cold continuum, 99, 100, 102

huipil, 35, 170, 210; cost of, 35, 56, 57, 88, 138, 139, 148, 157–158, 202, 207; and municipal identity, 35, 51–55; parts of, 156–158, 216; patchwork, 105; *de Tecpán*, 162, 189; types of, 162–165; *xilon*, 2, 3, 5, 53, 54, 55, 164, 186, 189, 190,

191. *See also blusa*; body; *lienzo*; *sobre huipil*

husband-wife relationship, 58, 126–127, 129

hypoicon, 77

icons, 77–78

identity. *See corte*; ethnicity; *huipil*; politics, of identity; *traje*

image, 76–78, 97

images of Indians, 76–77, 208; as Guatemalan, 79–81; by Indians, 87–95, 95 97; negative, 84–87, 87–91, 93, 118, 152, 211; by non-Indians, 79–87; positive 79–84, 91–93, 94-95, 152; and tourism, 83–86, 88; as women, 81, 211. *See also* Maya; photographs and photography

income and wages, 20, 46–47, 56, 130, 138, 202. *See also* seasonal labor

Independence Day, 2, 53, 54, 55, 186, 190

Indian, 30, 203. *See also* images of Indians; Maya; Maya-ladino relations

indígena, 30, 203, 204. *See also* Maya

Indigenous Professional Association, 82. *See also* professionals

indio, 76, 94, 116, 177, 197, 203, 219. *See also* Maya

infants, 99–104

INGUAT (Instituto Guatemalteco de Turismo), 54, 79, 83, 90, 93, 199, 210

Instituto Indígenista Nacional, 28, 61, 64, 160–161

Ixchel: goddess, 151; Museum of Indian Dress, 40, 206

Iximché (Iximche'), xiv, 9–10, 11, 18, 90, 199, 201, 207. *See also* Declaration of Iximché; Princess Iximché

Ixmucané (Ixmukane), xiv, 155, 207, 209. *See also* Princess Ixmucané

Ixmucané Youth Circle, 82

jacket: as part of *traje*, 38, 61, 126, 140, as part of *vestido*, 75, 123, 141; sold to tourists, 172, 181; used in revitalization activities, 61–63, 65–66, 75, 218

jaspe, 35, 48, 62, 126, 138, 173

jewelry, 89, 102, 112, 174–175, 218. *See also* earrings; necklace; ring

jokes and joking, 68, 115, 127, 170, 171, 208, 210, 217

judgment, 29, 33, 63, 77, 78, 96, 115, 183, 198

Jutiapa, 23–24, 67, 217

Kaqchikel, xiii-xiv, 9, 19, 28, 33, 64, 106, 126, 131–132, 139, 162, 164, 203, 205, 209, 219. *See also* Maya

Kayapo, 40

K'iche', xiii, 79, 155, 215

knitting, 50, 57, 72; factories, 20, 73, 132

knowledge, 29, 52, 59, 77, 95, 101, 106, 130, 135–136, 147, 152-153, 160–161, 173, 193. *See also* diplomas; education; judgment; schools

lace, 50, 125
ladino, 18, 32, 76, 204. *See also* Maya-ladino relations; non-Indian, *vestido.*
latifundios, 46
lienzo, 153–154, 156–158, 159, 164, 215
looms: backstrap, 21, 35, 44–46, 107–108, 146, 151, 153–156, 206, 211, 215; treadle, 35, 44–46, 57, 108, 123, 151, 206. *See also* weaving
López, Paula, 219

mail-order catalogs, 207
mal de ojo, 102, 148, 213
market (Tecpán), 3, 10, 20–21, 51, 73, 146, 175–176, 202, 218
marriage, 127–135; courtship and, ceremony, 115, 119–127
Martínez Barrientos, Rafael Arévalo, 177
Martínez Peláez, Severo, 219
maxi skirt, 60, 88
Maxwell, Judith, 65
Maya, 30, 92, 95, 117, 129, 151, 193–197, 203, 204; languages, xiii, 19, 30, 53, 65, 92, 94, 197, 208; people, 30, 76–77, 203, 204; rituals, 53, 134, 137, 138, 139, 178; ties with past, 85, 135–136, 151, 195. *See also* Kaqchikel; *traje*
Mayab', 30, 203. *See also* Maya
Maya-ladino relations, 18, 30-31, 62–63, 74, 77, 85, 86, 87, 94, 95–97, 196, 209, 211
Maya revitalization movement, xiv, 6, 28, 31, 36, 49, 61–63, 64, 65–66, 74–75, 94–95, 126, 137,

169, 198, 203, 207, 213, 218, 219. *See also* jacket
mayor, 18, 86, 126, 202
men, 33, 88–89, 108, 111, 115, 118–119, 129, 132, 133, 151, 168–169, 210; and interethnic communication, 62–63; *traje* worn by, 31, 38, 51–52, 60–63, 65–66, 89–90, 118, 132, 137, 140, 169, 210, 213. *See also* jacket; pants; *rodillera;* shirt; *traje*
Menchú, Rigoberta, 133, 213–214, 217
menstruation, 128–129, 130
metaphor, 77–78
methodology, 25–30
Mexico, 44, 50, 71, 203, 209, 218
Miami, 69, 71, 93
military, 2, 3–5, 117, 119, 133, 190, 209
Miller, Mary Ellen, 203
Miss Universe contest, 79, 82, 83, 116
Momostenango, 46
morga, 35, 54, 61, 137–138, 218. *See also corte; penecita*
municipal hall, 2, 13, 23, 126, 202
municipio, 11, 32. *See also traje*
Munn, Nancy D., 144–145
music, 53, 195, 202, 203

Nahualá, 214
names (people's), 118, 207, 208. *See also* brand names; design motifs
Nash, Manning, 48
natural, 30, 203. *See also* Maya
Nebaj, 24, 63, 79
necklace, 37, 112, 174–175

neckline, 166
needlework, 57, 100, 109, 131, 148, 184, 187, 191, 207
Nelson, Diane, 217
New York, 68, 69, 70, 208
nightclothes, 176, 217
non-Indian, 32, 76, 91–92, 143, 204, 212, 219; European Guatemalan, 32; *Guatemalteco*, 32; "in the middle," 32–33, 204
novia/o, 57, 111, 120–123, 126, 213

ombliguera, 101
oreja, 94
Osborne, Lilly de Jongh, 177
Otzoy, Irma, 62, 205, 208, 218–219

Panajachel, 180
pants: men's, 38, 51, 61, 89, 104, 118, 126, 137, 140, 141, 169, 175–176; women's, 103, 104, 112–113, 173
parcialidades, 202
Patzicía, 10, 148, 168, 214
Patzún, 10, 51, 52, 55, 148
Paul, Lois, 128–129, 172, 215
pedida, 120
Peirce, Charles, 77–78
penecita, 35, 82, 137–138, 139. See also *corte*; *morga*
Petén, 204
photographs and photography, 26, 39, 72, 78, 83–85, 90, 107, 136, 170, 175, 186, 217, 218
physical attractiveness, 111, 113, 114, 115, 118, 135, 167, 169. See also beauty
plaza, 3, 10, 14, 18, 20, 21, 201, 202

pleats, 123, 166
politics: of identity, xiv, 31, 81, 89–92, 99, 115, 119, 137, 184, 196-197, 198, 219; international, 70, 117; local, 19, 77, 81, 86–87, 132, 133–134, 143, 184, 188, 202. *See also* government; mayor
Polo Sifontes, Francis, 201
poncho, 38, 46. *See also* blankets
Popol Wuj, xiv, 155, 209
population, 11–13, 18, 30, 31, 32–33, 201–202, 204
po't. See huipil
preconquest era, 91, 204, 205, 212
pregnancy, 100, 102
"primitive glamour," 84, 210
Princess Iximché, xiv, 64, 81, 82
Princess Ixmucané, xiv, 64, 82, 87–88, 113–114, 184, 209
professionals, 18–19, 57, 82, 87, 94, 96, 101, 109, 120, 121, 134
PRONEBI (Programa Nacional de Educación Bilíngüe), 34
Protestant churches, 15, 112–113, 120, 123, 126, 202; clothing, prohibitions of, 112–113. *See also* schools

qawinaqi', 30, 203. *See also* Maya
queen contests, 52, 54, 78, 79, 81, 82, 86, 93–94, 116, 118, 198, 212. *See also* Godmother of Sports; Miss Universe contest; Princess Iximché; Princess Ixmucané; Queen of the Franciscan Fiestas; Rabín Ajau
Queen of the Franciscan Fiestas, 81, 82, 87, 211

quetzal: currency, 206, 215; national bird, 216
Quezaltenango, 10, 57, 59, 83, 184, 207, 212
Quino, 68

Rabín Ajau, xiii, 93, 212
Rabinow, Paul, 24
race, 30, 90
refugees, 203, 218
religion, 15–18. *See also* Catholic church; Maya; Protestant churches; schools
ri'j po't. See sobre huipil
ring, 35, 37, 112, 174–175
rodillera, 35, 38, 46, 118, 126, 140, 169
Rodríguez, Guaján, José Obispo, xiii, 219
rural, 13, 18, 19, 67, 73, 74, 88, 96, 120, 133, 152, 179, 189, 201–202

Sahlins, Marshall, 40
Saint Francis of Assisi, 61
saints' blouse, 165
Salcajá, 48
Salvation Army, 14–15
San Antonio Aguas Calientes, 65, 159
San Cristóbal Totonicapán, 58, 60
sandals, 38, 54, 61, 88, 121, 126, 169, 174
San José Poaquil, 10, 18, 63, 174
San Martín Jilotepeque, 52, 53, 93, 206, 211
San Pedro la Laguna, 128, 172, 215
San Pedro Necta, 52
San Pedro Sacatepéquez, San Marcos, 206

Santa Apolonia, 10, 52, 63, 137, 207
Santa Cruz del Quiché, 64
Santa Cruz Balanyá, 10
Santiago Atitlán, 64
Santiago Chimaltenango, 212
Saquic, Rosalio, 28
Sattler, Mareike, 214, 219
Schele, Linda, 203
schools 6, 32, 34, 52, 72, 107, 110, 129, 219; Catholic, 107; Protestant, 3, 26, 107; public, 107, 110, 213; uniforms used in, 2–3, 53, 107, 211. *See also* education
science and technology, 25, 71, 80, 129, 147, 177, 208
seasonal labor, 46–47, 89, 206
servilleta, 36–37, 103, 108, 121, 126, 140, 164
sex education. *See* education
shawl, 35–36, 50, 80, 89, 102, 103, 121, 141, 173
Sherzer, Joel, 209
shine, 148–149, 150, 161, 165, 167, 174, 214. *See also* thread
shirt, 38, 61, 72, 74, 104, 118, 126, 168–169, 172, 181, 193, 207, 216
shoes, 38, 72, 73, 75, 123, 125,141, 169, 174, 175. *See also* sandals
Shulman, Nicola, 219
silk, 44, 50, 138, 150, 184
Silverstein, Michael, 40
skin. *See* color
skirts. *See corte*; maxi skirt; *vestido*
skits, 28, 79, 173, 210
Smith, Carol, 203, 209
sobre huipil, 37, 49–50, 54, 79, 82, 126, 138–141, 149, 159, 164,

165, 178, 184, 188, 191, 205, 214. *See also huipil*

Sololá, 10, 208

Spain: colonial, 9, 46, 79–80, 202; contemporary, 44, 50

Spanish (language), 28, 36, 38, 106, 164, 203, 205

Spanish Embassy massacre, 25, 90, 91

Sperlich, Elizabeth Katz, 153, 215

Sperlich, Norbert, 153, 215

sports, 132, 168, 209–210; clothes used for, 104, 113, 168, 216, 217. *See also* bathing attire

status issues, 32, 33, 63, 66, 67, 69, 74, 88, 113, 118, 160-161, 169, 189, 203, 208

Steiner, Wendy, 77–78

stereotypes, 77, 78, 97, 118, 129, 151, 177. *See also* images of Indians

stereotypical change, 42, 99

Stoll, David, 202

Sumba, Indonesia, 40, 216

Summer Institute of Linguistics, 202

survey, 27, 139, 160

sweatbath, 100, 101, 175, 212

sweaters, 75, 173, 176; production of, 20, 73, 132

symbolism, 40, 145, 147, 160

synthetic fibers, 35, 38, 49–50, 123, 139, 149–150, 214–215

Tasaday, 210

Tax, Sol, 32, 40

Tecpán, 8–23, 25, 201, 208

Tecpaneco, 10, 18–19

Tecpanidad, 87, 98, 114

Tecún Umán, xiii, 79–80, 90, 209

Tedlock, Barbara, 215

Tedlock, Dennis, 215

Téllez García, Rafael, 209

Texas, 208

textile factories, 20, 48

thread, 145–150; color, 48, 50, 146–148, 150, 165; cost, 49, 50, 146, 149–150, 202, 214, 215; dye, 20, 35, 44, 48, 50, 137, 148; fastness of, 50, 146, 148, 150, 165, 177, 214; mercerized, 20, 48, 149, 150, 214; ply, 48, 149; production of, 20, 48, 49, 50, 51; shine, 50, 139, 149, 150, 161, 165, 214; spin, 145, 214; sturdiness of, 50, 149, 150; types of, 44–51, 148–150. *See also* color; cotton; silk; synthetic fibers; wool

Tijonik Oxlajuj Aj, 28

time, 41–43, 99, 177–178, 197; *longue durée*, 41 42; social time, 42, 205; traditional history, 43, 192

típico, 33, 180, 203

Torgovnick, Marianna, 210

tortilla, 21, 36, 155–156

Totonicapán, 10, 57, 123, 207

tourism and tourists, 11, 83–84, 88, 89, 90, 91, 93, 96, 180–181, 193, 201, 208. *See also* images of Indians, INGUAT

tourist brochures, 78, 83–86, 198, 199

towels, 100, 103, 173–174

Townsend, Cameron, 202

tradicionales, 18

traditional, 33, 35, 37, 54, 85–86, 88, 120, 130, 158, 183, 191, 195, 197, 203. *See also costumbre; traje*

traje, 5–8, 33–39, 139–140, 201, 204–205, 213; abandoning, 33, 74, 75, 88–89, 96–97, 116, 117, 118, 119, 126; and awareness of world, 58–63; and climatic considerations, 50, 57–58; cultural heritage and historical roots reflected in, 54, 55, 64, 67, 75, 82, 85–86, 114, 137, 140–141, 178, 189–190, 195; economic dimensions of, 50, 54, 56–57, 81, 114, 115, 116, 119, 134, 169, 178–179; and ethnic identity, 30–31, 39, 64, 97, 119, 133, 197; fashions in, 3, 53, 54, 55, 63, 112, 137, 173, 174, 196, 206; and gender, 26, 66, 88–89, 115–119, 167; geographical dimensions of, 44–66, 73–75; historical material on, 27–28, 39–40, 136; *mero* or *tradicional*, 33, 36, 38, 112, 126, 139–140, 141, 183, 191, 195–196; and municipal identity, 38, 39, 46, 51–55, 56, 58, 63–64, 65, 66, 75, 121, 195; and national identity, 54, 79, 82, 88, 193, 194; old/used, 2–3, 53, 54, 57, 82, 115, 126, 137, 173, 177–181, 189; as "our dress," 43, 193–197, 200; and pan-Maya identity, 61, 63–66, 67, 75, 117; parts of, 33–39; used by non-Indians, 79, 118–119, 173, 193; versus *vestido*, 66–67, 73–75, 88–89, 197. *See also* beauty; Catholic church; creativity; Maya revitalization movement; men; *vestido*; weaving; women

traje contests, 52–53, 54, 63, 159–160. *See also* fair

traje presentation. *See* fair

transportation, 10, 59

travel, 59, 70–71

Turner, Terence, 40, 98

underwear, 75, 103, 121, 170, 176, 213

unified alphabet, xiii

United States, 31, 44, 67, 68–72, 74, 130, 175, 176, 218; Southwest, 207

uq. See corte

urban, 13, 18, 60, 67, 96, 117

Urban, Greg, 209

Urciuoli, Bonnie, 218

valiente, 119, 133

velvet, 35, 44, 166, 206, 207

verbal skills and pronouncements, 31, 64, 65, 74, 86, 87, 94, 119, 134, 160–161, 190. *See also* visual and verbal, relations between

vergüenza, 128

vestido, 26; economic dimensions of, 67, 71, 72, 74, 81, 103; fashions in, 66, 67, 69–70, 71, 73, 176; hierarchical ranking of, 66–75; homemade, 67, 72–73; ready-made, 72–73; tailor-made, 72, 73; used by Indians, 31, 74–75, 96, 103, 104, 113, 116–118, 119, 126, 173, 181, 193, 203–204, 207, 216. *See also* sports

violence, 2, 6, 55, 78, 81, 82, 84, 90–91, 94, 133–134, 143, 196, 217, 218

visual and verbal, relations between, 64, 77, 119, 134, 165,
190, 199, 200, 215. *See also*
verbal skills and pronouncements
wages. *See* income and wages
Warren, Kay B., 131–132, 211–212,
213, 219
washing: clothes, 58, 130, 137–138,
141, 168, 172, 176–177, 178, 213,
217. *See also* bathing
Watanabe, John, 212
weaving, 26, 39, 75, 151–167, 211;
Andean, 145; economic dimensions of, 20, 49–50, 146, 149–
150, 151, 202; and gender, 107–
109, 127, 130–132, 151–152, 206;
learning, 107–108, 144, 151–153,
214, 219; techniques, 39, 162–
165, 191. *See also lienzo*; thread
wedding. *See* marriage

women, 26, 64–65, 99–101, 115–
118, 130–135, 189, 190, 204;
and cultural maintenance, 62–
63, 131–132, 151, 152, 189, 218;
traje worn by, 35–37, 66, 88–89,
123–125, 132, 189–190. *See also*
domestic sphere; gender;
weaving
wool, 38, 44–46, 50, 51, 61
wrapping, 35, 36, 100, 101, 102,
103, 104, 127, 135, 141, 158,
159, 169, 170, 171, 172, 173,
202
Wycliffe Bible Translators, 202
Xejabí, 1, 3

Yool Gómez, Juan, xiii
youth, 33, 77, 82, 89–90, 109–119,
120, 128, 141

Zunil, 215